Accounting and Business Ethics

Despite the enormous impact of Enron on the accounting profession, the general malaise amongst the profession more broadly, and the significant legislative and institutional reforms that have taken place as a result, there are still surprisingly few textbooks on accounting ethics.

This concise introductory text takes a broad view of ethics and accounting, taking into account contemporary social trends, such as globalization and terrorism. Rather than delineating codes of professional conduct, this text pushes the reader towards an understanding of the big ethical dilemmas facing the profession and the factors that influence the ways in which accountants frame ethical questions.

The book is divided into two parts. The first part focuses on developing thinking about the different kinds of ethical questions that could be posed in relation to accounting. The second part focuses more explicitly on accounting practice, exploring the ethical function of accounting in relation to the market economy, ethics in relation to the accounting profession, and the ethics of the international accounting harmonization project.

Accounting and Business Ethics is a compact introduction aimed at both students and practitioners who want to understand more about the ethics of accounting.

Ken McPhail is Professor of Social and Ethical Accounting at the University of Glasgow, UK. He also holds an honorary professorship at Deakin University, Australia, and is co-editor of the *Journal of Business Ethics Education*.

Diane Walters is a member of the Institute of Chartered Accountants in Scotland and a part-time lecturer at Heriot-Watt University, UK.

Accounting and Business Ethics

An introduction

Ken McPhail and Diane Walters

LONDON AND NEW YORK

First published 2009
by Routledge
2 Park Square, Milton Park, Abingdon, Oxon OX14 4RN

Simultaneously published in the USA and Canada
by Routledge
711 Third Avenue, New York, NY 10017 (8th Floor)

Routledge is an imprint of the Taylor & Francis Group, an informa business

Typeset in AmasisMT-Light by
Swales & Willis Ltd, Exeter, Devon

British Library Cataloguing in Publication Data
A catalogue record for this book is available from the British Library

Library of Congress Cataloging-in-Publication Data
McPhail, Ken.
Accounting and business ethics : an introduction / Ken McPhail and Diane Walters.
p. cm.
Includes bibliographical references and index.
1. Accounts—Professional ethics. 2. Accounting—Moral and ethical aspects. 3. Business ethics. I. Walters, Diane. II. Title.
HF5625.15.M39 2009
174′.4—dc22

2008034147

ISBN10: 0–415–36235–0 (hbk)
ISBN10: 0–415–36236–9 (pbk)
ISBN10: 0–203–01262–3 (ebk)

ISBN13: 978–0–415–36235–1 (hbk)
ISBN13: 978–0–415–36236–8 (pbk)
ISBN13: 978–0–203–01262–8 (ebk)

For Mari and Bethan,
either side of my smile . . .

This is despite, because of and for you

Contents

Illustrations

FIGURES

BOXES

Preface

There is a lot of discussion about professional ethics these days and lots of developments within the accounting profession. For example, the Association of Chartered Certified Accountants has introduced a compulsory online ethics module and is attempting to reorientate the organization around the idea of professional values. The Institute of Chartered Accountants of Scotland has also added a mandatory ethics component to its professional training. IFAC will produce a revised Code of Ethics for Professional Accountants this year and continues to work on clarifying issues such as auditor independence and conflicts of interest. While these initiatives represent important developments within the profession, we wonder whether much of the discussion on the ethical challenges facing the accounting profession nevertheless remain rather narrow in their focus and limited in their impact.

In this text we have tried to take a broad view of ethics and accounting. We connect the practice of accounting into some contemporary social trends like globalization, terrorism, the knowledge society and the postmodern rejection of authority and deference towards the established professions. Another key contemporary issue, of course, is the environment. Although we mention corporate social responsibility and the environment at various points within the book we don't provide any detailed analysis as there are some excellent books that cover this material already, and we couldn't do it any better; see, for example, *Sustainability Accounting and Accountability* by Jeffrey Unerman, Jan Bebbington and Brendan O'Dwyer (London: Routledge, 2007).

Rather than attempting to delineate or analyse codes of professional conduct, we wanted to push the discussion of accounting and ethics more towards these big social trends that have defined the beginning of the twenty-first century. We wanted to help accounting practitioners and students understand the nature of ethical dilemmas and the way in which accounting encourages us to respond to these dilemmas. We wanted to stimulate some reflection on the relationship between accounting, the changing nature of professionalism, and whether accounting has any role to play in these changing times, and we also wanted to connect the practice of accounting into big ethical ideals like justice, rights and deliberative democracy.

Much of the content of the book is based on a course I teach at the University of Glasgow with the same name. The course has been running for eight years and I have attempted to distil some of my experience with the course into the text. If you are thinking about using the text as part of a course on accounting ethics then we have found it useful to intersperse the seminar material covered in each chapter with a discussion around a movie; a weekend retreat (see, for example, McPhail, 'Relocating Accounting and Business Ethics: Reflections on a Business Ethics Retreat in Scotland's National Park', *British Accounting Review*, 35(4) (2003): 367–384); a field trip to a local prison (see, for example, McPhail, 'Using Porridge to Teach Business Ethics: Reflections on a Visit to Scotland's most Notorious Prison and Some Thoughts on the Importance of Location in Teaching Business Ethics', *Journal of Teaching Business Ethics*, 6/3 (2002): 355–369); and real-life case studies. For example, the UK Thalidomide Society has led a seminar on the Thalidomide case for the past four years. You may also wish to try some of these ideas.

We spent quite a bit of time developing the resources section at the end of each of the chapters and, as you will see, have included some suggestions of films and further literature that you may wish to watch and read. This is because we are convinced that developing ethical competencies comes as much through engaging with the feelings and emotions of the other(s) as it does through grasping complex abstract ideas. For general reference purposes we recommend Stanford Encyclopaedia of Philosophy <http://plato.stanford.edu/> and Wikipedia <http://en.wikipedia.org/wiki/Main_Page>. We cite Wikipedia with the proviso that this is an open source site and some entries may be biased or unverified.

We hope you find the book interesting and challenging and we also hope that it will go some way towards helping you develop your understanding of the broader ethical questions associated with the practice of accounting.

Ken McPhail
Glasgow 2008

Acknowledgements

We would like to thank the Institute of Chartered Accountants of Scotland for granting permission to include some ideas that were originally developed during a study, which it funded, into the nature of the ethical challenges relating to individual accountants. Some of these ideas are included in Chapter 2. A copy of the report, McPhail, *Ethics and the Individual Professional Accountant: A Literature Review*, can be obtained from the Institute (see www.icas.org.uk; details available via About ICAS and Information Services links).

We would also like to thank the publishers of the journal *Critical Perspectives on Accounting* for permission to include some ideas that were originally developed in two academic articles published by the journal. Some of the material in Chapter 5 is based on ideas originally developed in a paper entitled 'The Threat of Ethical Accountants: An Application of Foucault's Concept of Ethics to Accounting Education and Some Thoughts on Ethically Educating for the Other', that appeared in volume 10 of the journal in 1999. Chapter 9 is also based on a forthcoming article in *Critical Perspectives on Accounting*, entitled, 'Where is the Ethical Knowledge in the Knowledge Economy? Power and Potential in the Emergence of Ethical Knowledge as a Component of Intellectual Capital'.

PART I

How to think ethically about accounting

1

Introduction

There aren't many textbooks on accounting ethics, at least not in comparison to business ethics textbooks. The proliferation of books on the ethics of business seems to be part of a broader ethical awareness that covers, for example, bio-ethics, medical ethics, environmental ethics, cyber-ethics, and so on. The reasons behind this burgeoning concern with ethics are undoubtedly complex and in part it relates to the pace of medical and technological progress; if you can't clone a sheep or perform a face transplant, then the ethical dilemma remains purely hypothetical. However, whatever its source, this increased public discussion of the ethical challenges posed by medical advances, bio-technology, environmental degradation and globalization does not seem to apply to the discipline of accounting, at least not to the same degree. This is despite the fact that the routine practice of financial accounting is so pervasive that it is inextricably linked to the development of bio-technology, the causes of, and solutions to environmental pollution, the allocation of scarce medical resources and, of course, it facilitates globalization. While there is considerable discussion on the role of medical staff in palliative care, for example, there is comparatively little public discussion of the role accountants should play within society.

Just as there are many reasons why particular topics seem to invite ethical investigation, so there are many reasons why accounting remains off the ethical radar. For a start, accounting is culturally maligned. Taking accounting seriously is not easy for us because we have to struggle against cultural stereotypes. Of course, post Enron, WorldCom and Parmalat, there has been quite a lot of discussion of the ethics of accountants and professional ethics more generally. However, despite the massive scale of these debacles, it is surprising how quickly they have been forgotten and how little substantive change they really engendered. This is somewhat perplexing; the lack of substantive engagement with the ethics of accounting, as opposed to the ethics of accountants, can't be because accounting is unimportant. The level of political interest in the accounting profession immediately following the Enron scandal indicates that accounting performs a hugely important function within a market-based economic system. Perhaps it is because accounting is perceived to be a technical and fairly specialized subject that it is not exposed to more public debate and discussion. Whatever the reason for accounting remaining ethically marginalized, it's wrong!

The lack of political debate and public discussion surrounding the role of accounting within contemporary society, however, does not reflect views from within the discipline. Over the past few decades a substantive body of research has given rise to a major school of critical accounting thought that challenges the conventional, technical view of accounting as a politically neutral and amoral practice. Influenced by this alternative perspective on accounting, this more critical school has begun to explore the ethics of accountants, the function and purpose of the accounting profession and the ethics of accounting. Some of the findings don't make for pleasant reading.

THE ETHICS OF ACCOUNTANTS

Accountants appear to exhibit lower levels of moral reasoning than other professional groups. Accounting students become less ethical as they progress through their accounting education. Accounting students are less ethically aware than other students. Accounting students don't recognize the broader social responsibility issues associated with professionalism. Most accounting students think that accounting is an amoral and technical activity. These are all research findings from the accounting literature!

Many academics have expressed concern over the ethical predispositions of both accounting students (see, for example, Gray *et al.* 1994) and practitioners. Some studies suggest that accountants seem to exhibit lower levels of moral reasoning than other professional groups (Eynon *et al.* 1997), and this possibility has led to a debate about the extent to which accounting education (at both the undergraduate and professional levels) either contributes towards or stultifies accountants' ethical development. Taken in its entirety, the literature presents the somewhat disturbing possibility that conventional accounting education has a more negative than positive impact on students' ethical predispositions. Fleming (1996) concludes that 'the tendency of the evidence is to suggest, if anything, that accountants either occupy the middle ground or lean towards an amoral ethical position'.

THE ETHICS OF THE ACCOUNTING PROFESSION

However, on top of this concern with accountants, there is also growing interest in the changing nature of the accounting profession, both specifically and in general. For example, some of the research points to a major socio-cultural shift in the way we relate to each other, and in particular, the way people relate to the professions and professionals. A few years ago, a study by Modic (1987) hinted at diminishing levels of trust between individuals in general and in a slightly more recent study Bruce (1996) concludes that 'the age of deference is over'. By this he means that people are not willing simply to accept what those in authority say anymore. The trend here seems to be a shift away from a reverence for and deference towards the professions, to viewing professionals in some partnership role, a shift that is also part of a broader socio-political movement for greater deliberative democracy. We will consider this issue of trust in a little more detail as we progress through the text; however, at this point we just want to connect diminishing levels of trust to a broader postmodern slippage away from authoritative anchoring points in traditional society. Undoubtedly these socio-cultural shifts have significant consequences not only for the accounting profession but for the idea of professionalism in general.

The other side to this waning deference towards professionals is an apparent shift in attitude within the professions themselves. Roberts (2001), for example, comments on the contrast between the traditional role of a professional and the accounting profession's determination to 'compete in a commercial marketplace in a wide variety of professional services'. Roberts (2001) states that the US practitioner literature is replete with evidence that commercialism is of primary importance to CPA firms and he contends that this commercial reorientation is primarily driven by declining profit margins (Fraser 1997). Indeed, Mitchell and Sikka (1993) claim that audits are now used as loss leaders in order to attract other more lucrative business and there is growing concern that the pursuit of commercial objectives has had a detrimental impact on the quality of audit services. In his 1987 study, for example, Larson refers to a number of surveys that indicated that 30–40 per cent of all audits undertaken in the US were substandard.[1]

This increasing commercialization of accounting practice reflects a broader societal shift in the expectations surrounding professional work and the way it is appraised. Craig (1994) discusses the need to provide non-audit services for partnerships to 'succeed', and concludes that 'the importance of these new services has changed the mindset of practitioners'. Boland (1982) has similarly questioned the commercialization of the accounting profession, highlighting the way growth is used as an indicator of both practice and individual success. Increased commercialization, combined with greater litigation has resulted in most of the major accounting practices converting to limited liability firms (Lee 1995). Roberts (2001) also suggests that this focus on commercial services has contributed towards the consolidation of accounting firms and the merger of accounting and law firms and he contends that this process has had a profound impact on the mentality of American CPAs. Fraser (1997), for example, quotes Ron Silberstein of an American CPA firm, who says, 'when someone sitting next to me on a plane asks me what I do, I usually tell him or her I'm a salesman. Then they ask, "What do you sell?" and I tell them, "Accounting Services".' Fraser (1997) also recounts a similar comment by Stanley Nasberg, another American CA, who says, 'we have arrived because we no longer think of ourselves as merely a profession, we are a business, we are entrepreneurs'. Both these quotes extol commercial acumen and seem very far removed from ideals of public service and altruism traditionally associated with professionalism. The implication is that the value of being seen to be a professional has somehow diminished. For these accountants at least, commercial acumen appears to be more useful than *mere* professional status. Indeed Roberts (2001) suggested that accounting, more generally, has become de-professionalized (see Zeff 1987; Briloff 1990, in Roberts 2001).

However, the majority of these studies were conducted prior to the Enron debacle. While the trend towards commercialization is still dominant today, there is a growing appreciation of the importance of the idea of professionalism for the continued legitimacy of the professions themselves. Enron and other high-profile scandals like the Alder Hey organ retention scandal and the Shipman murder inquiry have diminished levels of trust in the professions and business more generally. Against the backdrop of these scandals we are witnessing a renaissance in interest in the idea of professionalism, particularly in relation to whether it needs to be re-thought or replaced, for example by occupationalism.

While in response to this crisis, the primary agenda of professional bodies has been to try to re-establish their credibility and legitimacy. The magnitude of the scandals, combined with the other major social shifts that we alluded to above, may just have disorientated professional bodies enough to cause them to reflect on whether the task is simply a matter of *re-establishing* a relationship of trust, or more fundamentally *re-conceptualizing* it and making it work within a different cultural context.

Of course, we need to distinguish between the ideal type of role that professional bodies could play within a pluralist democracy and the kind of self-interested protectionism that is all too often the reality. But it's an important contemporary question: in terms of the broader goals that we want to achieve as a society, would we be better off if there were no professions? Note the question is not if there were no doctors or lawyers or accountants but rather if these occupational groups were not given the special status of professions, and if the fields of health, accountability and the law become more participatory and deliberative.

INCREASED IMPORTANCE AND COMPLEXITY OF ACCOUNTANCY

However, on top of the concern with the ethical predispositions of *accountants* and increased uneasiness over the (re)orientation[2] of *the accounting profession*, there is also growing critical reflection on the functioning of *accounting* within society.

Traditionally, societal expectation of business was rather uncomplicated. In the words of Milton Friedman it was simply to make money. However, the last few decades have witnessed a perceptible shift in public attitude towards business more generally. Indeed, a major body of accounting research has in part influenced the emergence of the new corporate social responsibility (CSR) reporting and sustainability discourses (Gray 2002, 2001; Gray *et al.* 1998, 1987). While there is some considerable debate as to whether this discourse is likely to produce any substantive change in business practice, the emergence of social and environmental accounting as a valid academic subject, along with the growing momentum of CSR, presents significant challenges for the scope of both the professional responsibility of accountants and accounting practice (Gray 2001). The more serious discussion within CSR recognizes that it presents a challenge to our underlying notions about the function that business and accounting should serve in society.

This growing concern over the behaviour of big business also comes at a time when the organization and nature of commerce is becoming ever more complex. Globalization, financial engineering, cross-cultural issues, the knowledge economy, information technology and cyber-ethics are just some of the characteristics of the new business context against which public concern is emerging. Intangibles, complex financial instruments and pensions are just a few of the associated ethical problems that the accounting profession is struggling to resolve. However, while this increased technical complexity has focused attention on the competence of accountants and the profession's requisite body of knowledge, these issues also problematize the profession's public interest claims. For example, while resolving the issue of how companies account for pensions requires a fairly advanced level of technical competence; the emotive and very civic nature of the issue also problematizes the profession's claim to be acting in the public interest.

However, the increasingly complex and important role that accounting plays within contemporary society extends beyond the comparatively 'developed' economies of the West. The accounting profession is also playing an increasingly important role in development policy in relation to emerging economies through the influence of the likes of the World Bank and the International Monetary Fund (Lee 1995). As we shall see in Part II of the text, the imposition of free-market ideology in relation to the World Bank's structural adjustment loans is quite fundamentally linked to the work of the International Accounting Standards Board and the broader accounting harmonization project.

So Mitchell and Sikka (1993) are right to conclude that, 'accountancy has become more pervasive at the same time as we are wondering what it means'.

MORAL CONFUSION

Yet the general increase in ethical awareness, the growing pervasiveness and complexity of multinational business, and the rising importance of accounting, all come at a time when many moral philosophers are suggesting that our traditional ethical resources have been undermined. More significantly, they suggest that as a society we seem to lack the ethical competence to engage with the burgeoning ethical issues we face. In short, we are ethically illiterate.

Historically, some of the work in defining ethical issues and working out a response to them was provided by religious institutions and belief systems. Religious systems provided the predominant source of values in the past and indeed they do continue to provide an ethical anchor point for many accountants and business people today (see, for example, Laura Nash's 1994 work). Many social commentators now suggest that culturally we are living in a post-religious era. Alasdair MacIntyre (1982), when describing the emergence of this new cultural milieu, connects it with the spread of 'moral confusion'. He is not making a normative judgement here; all he is saying is that systems of values and beliefs are sustained by socio-cultural narratives and that these narratives become embedded within social structures and institutions. When the supporting narratives are disrupted, as he suggests has happened, the values that they supported begin to lose their grounding. What MacIntyre is suggesting here is that moral obligations in traditional societies were quite straightforward. They were easy to identify and fulfil since they emerged within a cultural context marked by close-knit relationships where individuals knew both the people applying the moral code and the individuals affected by their actions. MacIntyre is arguing that these conditions do not apply within modern societies. Not only have the religious and cultural institutions that prescribed the moral code been undermined, but many of the individuals who populate the key moral dilemmas that we are struggling to articulate are unknown and often alien. In fact, some commentators have understood the current crisis in professional ethics as both emerging from and as a response to this cultural shift.

Again, we would caution against an overly simplistic view of these social trends. Religious institutions continue to be influential and, as with the idea of professionalism, it's difficult to miss the renaissance in religious thinking associated with hugely influential thinkers such as Jacques Derrida, Slavoj Žižek and Gayatri Spivak. However, MacIntyre's observations are important, particularly in relation to the way he focuses our attention on the connection between systems of values and socio-cultural narratives. From MacIntyre's analysis the question becomes: how are these new narratives going to emerge? and how are they going to be institutionally embedded? As we shall discuss in Part II of the text, some would see the discourse on human rights, for example, as being one such narrative.

The spread of 'moral confusion' obviously has significant implications for any reflection on the ethics of accounting, not only in terms of understanding how accountants may often feel when confronted with a specific ethical dilemma but also in relation to the kind of narrative and institutional work that might be associated with making accounting more just.

INTRODUCTION TO THE ETHICAL ANALYSIS OF ACCOUNTING

There does therefore seem to be an increase in the level of ethical awareness and ethical discussion at the public level more generally; however, this awareness does not seem to extend with anything like the same kind of urgency to the function of accounting within society. Business, the traditional site of accounting, is becoming increasingly more complex but there seems to be a lack of public and political engagement with the ethics of accounting. At a time when societal expectations are increasing and business is becoming more complex, the traditional resources that may have provided the grounds for addressing these problems in the past has diminished and there is growing concern that we lack the ethical capacity within the accounting profession to engage seriously with these challenges. Despite its professional claims and its hugely important current socio-political function, many accounting students and practitioners seem to lack not only the competencies in relation to understanding the principles behind a particular professional code, but more importantly they also seem to lack the ethical skills that would enable them to articulate the current set of rights and values which accounting promotes, critically evaluate this practice in the light of contemporary discourses, for example on corporate social responsibility, human rights and deliberative democracy, and generally participate in a dialogue about the function and the future of accounting.

Of course, we are not suggesting that accountants as individuals lack the capacity to recognize what is good behaviour and do it. Rather, our concern lies with the ability to analyse accounting ethically within its broader organizational and political/economic context. Our aim in this book is therefore not so much to explore the burgeoning number of ethical codes specifically directed towards accountants, whether at the professional or organizational level, but rather to get you thinking about the broader ethical issues related to the function of accounting and our claim to be professionals who have the public interest at heart.

EDUCATIONAL OBJECTIVES

With this general purpose in view, it might be helpful to outline some of the more specific educational objectives of the book. We are certainly not starting out with the assumption that we can make you more ethical! However, we do hope that we can contribute towards your competence in thinking ethically about accounting, which is quite a different thing altogether. Actually thinking about the kinds of ethical competencies that should be the objective of ethical education is quite a complicated and widely debated topic. Try to develop your own list of objectives for a professional ethics course and see how difficult it is! We have two simple objectives. First, the book aims to develop your ability to recognize the broad range of ethical issues associated with accounting in the first instance: issues associated with the way accounting frames apparently routine decisions; regular, everyday practices like producing a set of audited accounts; mundane issues like being part of a professional body; and apparently bland issues like whether or not we manage to develop a set of globally accepted accounting standards. All these issues are related to a fundamental set of values and the objective of the book is to help you articulate both what these values are and their contested nature. Second, the book aims to provide you with the concepts and language to help you frame these dilemmas ethically in order that we might helpfully talk about them. In other words it aims to provide you with the skills to be able to start articulating and discussing these challenges in ways that might help us collectively understand them better.

STRUCTURE OF THE TEXT

The book is split into two parts. In Part I we cover some of the more theoretical literature and get you thinking about the different kinds of ethical questions that could be posed in relation to accounting. For example, how do accountants behave ethically in practice? and what factors influence the way we frame ethical dilemmas as accountants? How should accountants behave? Why is it important that accountants behave ethically? and how do accountants become ethical beings? By engaging with these broad questions we hope to develop our understanding of ethics and accounting.

In the first part of the book we grapple with these questions by introducing some broad themes within the moral philosophy literature. Such is the richness of the history of the discipline, and our limited grasp of it, that it will be possible only to outline some of the main questions that have concerned the discipline and sketch out the way they have been explored. The aim is simply to identify the kinds of issues we need to consider in order to begin seriously engaging with accounting ethics.

When we started writing this book the big story in the UK press was about a little three-year-old girl. She was abducted from her house and sexually assaulted. Police charged a 26-year-old man with the assault. I guess most people would be appalled by this story. They would, quite rightly, condemn the man's actions as heinously immoral and suggest that he be locked up for a very long time. But *why* do people do such dreadful things and how do we *know* that this was a bad thing to do? This is a relatively easy example. Have a look at the Ford Pinto case in Box 1.1. Ford's decision is actually based on a very well-established ethical position within the moral philosophy literature: one that is deeply embedded in the majority of undergraduate and professional accounting education! The first section of the book introduces some literature that might help us see that accounting is far from amoral.

Exploring the ethics of accounting, in any sophisticated way, therefore unfortunately requires that we also engage with the discipline of moral philosophy. We say unfortunately because this prospect will undoubtedly seem a little daunting to most accountants. It's a feeling, however, that is quite insightful in itself. The problem is that we are not used to formally analysing issues from a moral perspective. Of course we make moral judgements all the time; however, these implicit decisions are often so deeply embedded that the goodness or badness of an action is almost assumed. Many of us may feel as though we know what is right and wrong; however, we lack the vocabulary to explain why or to critique an opposing point of view. As accountants, we rarely critically discuss ethical issues, at least not in a way that could be considered remotely philosophical. This is, of course, entirely different from having an opinion on some contemporary issue, for example global warming or suicide bombers. It is one thing to express concern about global warming, and even to allow that concern to affect our lives through purchasing decisions; it is another thing to be able to defend your concern philosophically, or more importantly to link environmental degradation and suicide bombers to the practice of accounting!

This lack of ethical competence seems to be quite pronounced among students of accounting and presents a significant barrier to the study of accounting ethics. As

Box 1.1 The Ford Pinto

The Ford Pinto began to roll off the production lines in the early 1970s. The car was rushed into production in an attempt to capture a major share of the lucrative compact market, against stiff competition from Volkswagen. Conservative estimates suggest that 500 people burned to death in the Pinto due to the design and positioning of its fuel tank. Apparently the problem was picked up in pre-production testing, however, Ford conducted a cost–benefit analysis and came to the conclusion that it was more cost-effective to pay compensation to burns victims and their families than sort the car. Some reports suggest the calculation was based on US$67,000 compensation for each burns victim and US$200,000 for a life. The cost of correcting the design fault was $11 per car.

freshers we come to the study of accounting with a relatively advanced level of understanding of Mathematics and English. We don't have to start by learning how to read or count. However, when it comes to accounting ethics, such is the paucity of formal moral and ethical education at the primary and secondary levels of our education that we possess very little working knowledge of moral philosophy.

For the sake of simplicity we are going to split our consideration of moral philosophy into four broad but distinct perspectives (Grenz 1997):

1 Empirical or descriptive perspectives on how individuals behave in practice
2 Normative perspectives on how individuals should behave
3 Political perspectives – on why in broader social and political terms it's important that individuals do behave ethically
4 Post- and new-modern perspectives – on the prospects of being ethical.

The first part of the text will draw on each of these four different perspectives in order to begin to develop a framework for thinking about accounting ethics in more detail in the second part of the text.

The descriptive moral philosophy literature explores how individuals make ethical decisions in practice. This seems like an obvious place to begin our study as the subject of accounting ethics no doubt invokes a series of quite rudimentary, empirical questions. How do accountants behave in practice, are they generally ethical or unethical? What factors influence their ethical predispositions? Do accountants respond to ethical dilemmas as professional accountants in a different way than they would if they experienced the same dilemmas in some other capacity? And what does ethical development mean, how can we say that one accountant is more or less ethically developed than another? Chapter 2 draws on the extensive empirical literature in order to provide some insights into these and other questions.

Western, secular reflection on ethics can be traced back to Socrates and his question: 'How ought I to behave?' Chapter 3 provides some brief insights into this normative debate on how people should behave. Two traditional responses to this question are briefly described, one based on deduced principles, the other on virtue theory. This brief outline provokes us to consider some more fundamental questions in relation to the ethics of accountants, not least the question: how should accountants behave? This literature will provide us with some insights into how accountants are taught, both explicitly and implicitly, what constitutes appropriate moral behaviour. However, it will also highlight that this particular modality is only one of a number of alternatives. We also provide a brief introduction to a related debate on the bases upon which individual ethical decisions should be made. Within the literature there is a significant debate between those who view reason as an appropriate basis for responding to all ethical dilemmas and others who suggest that some kind of moral empathy is required.

While Chapters 2 and 3 focus on the actions of individual accountants, Chapter 4 takes the discussion of accounting ethics to a broader socio-political level. The objective of this chapter is to introduce the literature on the basis and nature of ethics by exploring why it is important for individuals to behave in an ethical manner at all. The chapter commences by exploring the work of Jean-Jacques Rousseau. Rousseau was not so much concerned with specific individual action, as with the more fundamental question of why an individual should behave ethically. Chapter 4 will take us into the political and institutional dimensions of ethical practice. Among other things, this chapter will get you thinking about the idea of human rights in relation to accounting practice. Chapter 5 explores the ethics of accounting from a slightly different perspective. Some of the more contemporary theoretical perspectives on ethics focus on the way in which individuals become ethical subjects. Or perhaps we could also turn this around and say how individuals come to subject themselves to ethics in the sense of regulating their behaviour. We will introduce you to two perspectives in this chapter: a more postmodern perspective that attempts to think about ethics in terms of power and a second perspective that thinks of ethics in terms of processes.

The four chapters in Part II of the text focus more explicitly on accounting practice. In Chapter 6 we explore the function of accounting in relation to the market economy. Chapter 7 considers ethics in relation to the accounting profession. Chapter 8 explores the ethics of the international accounting harmonization project and Chapter 9 provides some thoughts on the ethics of accounting in relation to the knowledge economy.

QUESTIONS

1 Describe the main ethical principles that you would say govern your actions and explain where you think these values come from.
2 Develop your own list of objectives for a professional ethics course. Explain why you have chosen these objectives.
3 Describe the main ethical challenges that you think are facing the accounting profession.
4 Why do you think people generally believe that the practice of accounting does not involve any major ethical considerations?
5 Spend some time online finding out more about the Ford Pinto case. If you had been part of Ford's team, do you think you would have accepted the decision not to redesign the car?

NOTES

1 Perhaps in response to these problems, the American Accounting Association developed a new code of professional ethics in 1988. The code was accompanied by a 'practice-monitoring program'. This quality review exercise represented an attempt to address growing public concerns over substandard audit work (Huff and Kelly 1989).
2 We have put this in brackets as some commentators would suggest that the accounting profession, and the professions more generally, have always been primarily driven by economic rent.

RESOURCES

Free podcasts

Ethics Bites – Open2.net, Edmonds and Warburton, Business Ethics.

Lectures on Professional Ethics, Mark Vopat, PhD, Youngstown State University (Mark Vopat provides a series of lectures on Professional Ethics; you may wish to listen to 'Professional Ethics ch1' at this stage).

Thomas Dunfee on the Enron verdict, Knowledge@Wharton Podcasts, University of Pennsylvania.

iTunes podcasts: free channels

Berkley University of California.
Ethics Bites – Open2.net.
The Kenan Institute for Ethics, Duke University, Durham, NC.
Knowledge@Wharton.
Princeton University Podcasts.
Stanford University.

Websites

Accounting and business ethics

BBC Religion and Ethics:
<www.bbc.co.uk/radio4/religion/moralmaze.shtml>.

Centre for Accounting Ethics, University of Waterloo:
<accounting.uwaterloo.ca/ethics/index2.html>.

Centre for Applied Ethics & Legal Philosophy, University of Glasgow:
<www.gla.ac.uk/ethics>.

The Center for Business Ethics, Bentley University:
<www.bentley.edu/cbe/>.

The Center for Human Values, Princeton University:
<www.princeton.edu/~uchv/>.

The Edmond J. Safra Foundation Center for Ethics, Harvard University:
<www.ethics.harvard.edu/>.

The W. Maurice Young Centre for Applied Ethics, University of British Columbia:
<www.ethics.ubc.ca/>.

The Carol and Lawrence Zicklin Center for Business Ethics Research, the Wharton School, University of Pennsylvania:
<www.zicklincenter.org/>.

Ford Pinto case

Dowie, M. (1977) 'Pinto madness', *Mother Jones*, 2 (Sept.–Oct.): 18–32; available at: <www.motherjones.com/news/feature/1977/09/dowie.html>.

Lee, M.T. (n.d.) 'The Ford Pinto Case and the development of auto safety regulations, 1893–1978', Department of Sociology and Criminal Justice, University of Delaware; available at: <www.hnet.org/~business/bhcweb/publications/BEHprint/v027n2/p0390-p0401.pdf>.

Schwartz, G. (n.d.) 'The myth of the Ford Pinto Case', based on conference paper, Third Annual Lecture, Pfizer Distinguished Visitors' Series, Rutgers University, Newark, 14 November 1990; available at: <www.pointoflaw.com/articles/The_Myth_of_the_Ford_Pinto_Case.pdf>.

READING

Ethics: general introductory reading

MacIntyre, A. (1967) *A short history of ethics: A history of moral philosophy from the Homeric age to the twentieth century* (London: Routledge & Kegan Paul).
Singer, P. (1999) *A companion to ethics* (Oxford: Blackwell).
Singer, P. (ed.) (1994) *Ethics* (Oxford: Oxford University Press).
Warnock, M. (1992) *The uses of philosophy* (Oxford: Blackwell).

Ethics and accounting: broad introductory reading

Arrington, C. E. (1990) 'Intellectual tyranny and public interest: The quest for the Holy Grail and the quality of life', *Advances in Public Interest Accounting*, 3: 1–16.
Dillard, J.F. (1991) 'Accounting as a critical social science', *Accounting, Auditing & Accountability Journal*, 4(1): 8–28.
Duska, R.F. and Duska, B.S. (2003) *Accounting ethics* (London: Blackwell).
Everett, J.S. (2007) 'Ethics education and the role of the symbolic market', *Journal of Business Ethics*, 76: 253–267.
Fogarty, T.J. (1995) 'Accountant ethics: A brief examination of neglected sociological dimensions', *Journal of Business Ethics*, 14(2): 103–115.
Francis, J.R. (1990) 'After virtue? Accounting as a moral and discursive practice', *Accounting, Auditing & Accountability Journal*, 13(3): 5–17.
Gowthorpe, C. and Black, J. (eds) (1998) *Ethical issues in accounting* (London: Routledge).
Gray, R.H. (1990) 'Accounting and economics: The psychopathic siblings: A review essay', *British Accounting Review*, 22: 373–388.
Kjonstad, B. and H. Willmott (1995) 'Business ethics: Restrictive or empowering?', *Journal of Business Ethics*, 14(6): 445–464.
Lehman, C.R. (2005) 'Accounting and the public interest: All the world's a stage', *Accounting, Auditing & Accountability Journal*, 18(5): 675–689.
Lehman, C.R. (1988) 'Accounting ethics: Surviving survival of the fittest', in M. Neimark, T. Tinker and B. Merino (eds), *Advances in public interest accounting*, vol. 2 (Greenwich, CT: JAI Press), 71–82.

Macintosh, N.B. (2004) 'Comment on "Recovering Accounting" ', *Critical Perspectives on Accounting*, 15: 529–541.

Misiewicz, K.M. (2007) 'The normative impact of CPA firms, professional organizations, and state boards on accounting ethics education', *Journal of Business Ethics*, 70: 15–21.

Neu, D. and Green, D. (2006) *Truth or profit, the ethics of public accounting* (Halifax, Nova Scotia: Fernwood Publishing).

Williams, P.F. (2004) 'You reap what you sow: The ethical discourse of professional accounting', *Critical Perspectives on Accounting*, 19: 995–1001.

Williams, P.F. (1987) 'The legitimate concern with fairness', *Accounting, Organizations and Society*, 12(2): 169–189.

Ethics and education

Carson, R.A. (1994) 'Teaching ethics in the context of medical humanities', *Journal of Medical Ethics*, 20: 235–238.

Downie, R.S. (1991) 'Literature and medicine', *Journal of Medical Ethics*, 17: 93–96.

Downie, R.S., Hendry, R.A., MacNaughton, R.J. and Smith, B.H. (1997) 'Humanizing medicine: A special study module', *Medical Education*, 31: 276–280.

Gray, R.H., Bebbington, J. and McPhail, K. (1994) 'Teaching ethics and the ethics of teaching: Educating for immorality and a possible case for social and environmental accounting', *Accounting Education*, 3: 51–75.

Hiltebeitel, K.M. and Jones, S.K. (1992) 'An assessment of the ethics instruction in accounting education', *Journal of Business Ethics*, 11(1): 37–46.

Huss, H.F. and Patterson, D.M. (1993) 'Ethics in accounting: Values education without indoctrination', *Journal of Business Ethics*, 12(3): 235–243.

Loeb, S.E (1988) 'Teaching students accounting ethics: Some critical issues', *Issues in Accounting Education*, Fall: 316–329.

Low, M., Davey, H. and Hooper, K. (2008) 'Accounting scandals, ethical dilemmas and educational challenges', *Critical Perspectives on Accounting*, 19: 222–254.

McPhail, K.J. (2004) 'An emotional response to the state of accounting education: Developing accounting students' emotional intelligence', *Critical Perspectives on Accounting*, 15(4–5): 629–648.

McPhail, K.J. (2003) 'Relocating accounting and business ethics: Reflections on a business ethics retreat in Scotland's National Park', *British Accounting Review*, 35(4): 367–384.

McPhail, K.J. (2002) 'Using porridge to teach business ethics: Reflections on a visit to Scotland's most notorious prison and some thoughts on the importance of location in teaching business ethics', *Journal of Teaching Business Ethics*, 6(3): 355–369.

McPhail, K.J. (2001) 'The *other* objective of ethics education: Rehumanising the accounting profession: A study of ethics education in law, engineering, medicine and accountancy', *Journal of Business Ethics*, 34(3/4): 279–298.

Mahoney, J. (1993) 'Teaching business ethics', *Professional Manager*, March: 12–15.

Weisberg, M. and Duffin, J. (1995) 'Evoking the moral imagination: Using stories to teach ethics and professionalism to nursing, medical and law students', *Journal of Medical Humanities*, 16(4): 247–262.

Theoretical: advanced broad reading

Gorz, A. (1989) *Critique of economic reason* (London: Verso).

Marcuse, H. (1991) *One-dimensional man* (London: Routledge).

Power, M. (1992) 'After calculation? Reflections on critique of economic reason by Andre Gorz', *Accounting, Organizations and Society*, 17(5): 477–499.

Willmott, H.C. (1989), 'Serving the public interest? A critical analysis of a professional claim', in D.J. Cooper and T.M. Hooper (eds), *Critical accounts* (Basingstoke: Macmillan), 325–326.

REFERENCES

Boland, R.J. Jr. (1982) 'Myth and technology in the American accounting profession', *Journal of Management Studies*, 19(1): 109–127.

Briloff, A.J. (1990) 'Accounting and society: A covenant desecrated', *Critical Perspectives on Accounting*, 1: 5–30.

Bruce, R. (1996) 'Whiter than white?', *Accountancy*, May.

Craig, J.L. (1994) 'The business of public accounting', *CPA Journal*, 64(8): 18–24.

Eynon, G., Hill, N.T. and Stevens, K.T. (1997) 'Factors that influence the moral reasoning abilities of accountants: Implications for universities and the profession', *Journal of Business Ethics*, 16: 1297–1309.

Fleming, A.I.M. (1996) 'Ethics and accounting education in the UK: A professional approach?', *Accounting Education*, 5(3): 207–217.

Fraser, J.A. (1997) 'How many accountants does it take to change an industry?', *Inc.*, 19(5): 63–69.

Gray, R. (2002) 'Of messiness, systems and sustainability: Towards a more social and environmental finance and accounting', *British Accounting Review*, 34(4): 357–386.

Gray, R. (2001) '30 years of corporate social accounting, reporting and auditing: What (if anything) have we learnt?', *Business Ethics: A European Review*, 10(1): 9–15.

Gray, R.H., Bebbington, J. and McPhail, K. (1994) 'Teaching ethics and the ethics of teaching: Educating for immorality and a possible case for social and environmental accounting', *Accounting Education*, 3: 51–75.

Gray, R.H., Owen, D. and Maunders, K. (1998) 'Corporate social reporting: Emerging trends in accountability and the social contract', *Accounting, Auditing & Accountability Journal*, 1(1): 6–20.

Gray, R.H., Owen, D. and Maunders, K. (1987) *Corporate social reporting, accounting and accountability* (London: Prentice Hall).

Lee, T. (1995) 'The professionalisation of accountancy: A history of protecting public interest in a self-interested way', *Accounting, Auditing & Accountability Journal*, 8(4): 48–69.

MacIntyre, A. (1982) *After virtue: A study in moral theory* (London: Duckworth).

Mitchell, A. and Sikka, P. (1993) 'Accounting for change: The institutions of accountancy', *Critical Perspectives on Accounting*, 4: 29–52.

Modic, S.J. (1987) 'Corporate ethics : From commandments to commandment', *Industry Week*, December: 33–36.

Nash, L. (1994) *Believers in business* (Nashville, TN: Thomas Nelson).

Roberts, R.W. (2001) 'Commercialism and its impact on the integrity of professional tax services in the United States', *Critical Perspectives on Accounting*, 12: 589–605.

Zeff, S.A. (1987) 'Does the CPA belong to a profession?', *Accounting Horizons*, 1(2): 65–68.

2

Descriptive perspectives on accounting ethics

What factors influence the way accountants respond to ethical dilemmas?

Learning objectives

By the end of the chapter you should be able to

- Describe the factors that influence the way individual accountants experience ethical dilemmas in practice;
- Describe Kohlberg's model of Cognitive Moral Development and Gilligan's Ethics of Care and explain how both perspectives differ from each other;
- Describe how individual attributes like age and gender affect moral proclivity;
- Describe how national and organization culture affects moral dispositions;
- Explain how the notion of categorization helps us understand how individuals make ethical decisions;
- Explain Jones's model of moral intensity;
- Explain the idea of moral framing.

INTRODUCTION

In this chapter we introduce the extensive empirical literature that seeks to describe and understand how individuals, and specifically accountants, behave in practice.

Rather than trying to make any normative judgement about an individual's actions, the field of descriptive ethics attempts to identify and understand the factors that may influence how individuals respond to specific moral dilemmas in practice. As we shall be exploring some of the empirical literature, this chapter contains a few more references than you will find in subsequent chapters. We will look at four issues in particular:

1 The ethical behaviour of accountants and other professionals;
2 The personal characteristics of the individual faced with the dilemma;
3 The contextual characteristics within which the dilemma is experienced;
4 The characteristics of the dilemma itself.

After discussing some research studies of the ethical behaviour of accountants in comparison to other professional groups we will explore the ethics of individual accountants in three specific ways. First, we will look at the personal characteristics that may influence an individual's ethical predisposition. Second, we discuss the interrelationship between social and organizational structures and an individual's ethical predisposition. Finally, we explore the ethical characteristics of individual ethical dilemmas.

THE ETHICS OF ACCOUNTANTS AND OTHER PROFESSIONALS

Post Enron, the accounting profession has been going through something of a crisis (see, for example, Low *et al.* 2008). However, the accounting profession is no stranger to scandal. There are many historical examples of individual accountants who have acted unethically. For example, following extensive lobbying, the Bankruptcy Act of 1831 was amended to allow accountants to be appointed as official assignees in bankruptcy cases. One of the most prominent assignees appointed by the Lord Chancellor was a man called Peter Abbott, 'the leading public accountant of the day'. Unfortunately Abbott turned out to be a crook and perpetrated one of the profession's earliest recorded frauds. Ten years after his appointment he absconded to Brussels with £80,000 of fraudulently acquired funds. That was quite a lot in those days! (Edwards 2001).

There are many other examples of individual accountants who have behaved in quite obviously unethical ways. They are sometimes referred to as 'bad apples' in an otherwise healthy barrel. However, these historical and empirical cases present us with a series of quite fundamental ethical questions. Why do people do bad things? Why did Peter Abbott defraud his clients and colleagues? Are some accountants inherently bad? Or are there mediating circumstances that contribute towards individual behaviour? And perhaps more fundamentally, why does the idea that there is a right and wrong make sense to us at all?

Box 2.1 The collapse of Enron

The collapse of the US corporation Enron has had far-reaching political and financial implications.

Background

In only fifteen years, Enron grew from small beginnings to become the seventh biggest company in the US. It employed more than 21,000 staff in more than 40 countries worldwide.

The collapse

The company's success turned out to have been a deception. Enron lied about its profits, and hid debt and losses behind a variety of intricate financial deals, so that they did not show up in the company's accounts. As the deception unfolded, investors and creditors forced the company into bankruptcy in 2001.

Fallout

Thousands of employees lost their jobs, and pension-holders lost their right to a pension. Investors suffered too as billions of dollars of share value were erased.

The accountants

Accountants had several roles to play in this drama:

The company finance directors and managers devised the various fraudulent schemes in the first place. Several have been found guilty of financial wrongdoing, and others are still facing criminal prosecution.

One Enron employee was so disturbed by the fraudulent accounting practices in the company that she decided to become a whistle-blower – leading investigators onto the trail of the crooked practices.

Enron's auditor, Andersen, one of the 'Big Five' firms of accountants in the world, was found guilty of deliberately destroying evidence of its relationship with Enron (it shredded the relevant files). The accounting firm collapsed, and now we are left with only the 'Big Four'.

Characteristics of the accountancy profession

Over and above these isolated examples of individual misdemeanours that are often discussed in the media, a number of academic studies have also explored the question of whether certain professional groups have more general unethical predispositions. The results of these studies are quite worrying. Many academics have expressed concern over the ethical predispositions of both accounting students (Gray *et al.* 1994; Lehman 1988) and accounting practitioners (See, for example,

Denham 1991; Stanga and Turpen 1991; Beets and Killough 1990; Schlachter 1990; Ponemon 1992, 1990).

A significant number of studies indicate that accountants, as a group, seem to exhibit lower levels of moral reasoning than other professional groups (Eynon *et al.* 1997). Studies by Armstrong (1987) and Poneman (1992), for example, suggest that accountants' moral maturity is lagging behind that of other professional groups.

Other studies investigate the contribution that accounting and business education has made to this worrying observation and in particular the extent to which accounting education inhibits accountants' ethical development (Gray *et al.* 1994). Jeffrey (1993; see also Arlow 1991) contends that the ethical development of accounting students is higher than their college peers. Some studies found that while accounting students' ethical skills developed over the course of their degree programmes, this development may be attributed to their general maturation rather than any specific ethical competencies they develop while studying (Davis and Welton 1991). By contrast, Lane (1988), Mayer (1988), McCabe and colleagues (1991) and Gray and colleagues (1994) all suggest that business and accounting education has a negative effect on students' ethical development. Mayer (1988) in particular found that business students don't recognize the broader social responsibility issues associated with professionalism. Borkowski and Ugras (1992) hint that this immaturity in ethical awareness may be related to an apparent shift in ethical orientation from a justice-based perspective towards a utilitarian viewpoint (both these perspectives are explained in the following chapter).

Loeb (1991) goes as far as to suggest that students have been indoctrinated into believing simply that 'the role of business in society is to produce goods and services at a profit' (McCabe *et al.*, quoted in Loeb 1991) and that ethics and social responsibility are unimportant considerations in corporate decision-making unless they have a direct impact on production or profits (Friedman 1970, in Jensen and Wygant 1990). Merritt (1991) implies that the propagation of these kinds of ideas has 'tainted students by making them mercenary in their approach to their craft'. He contends there is a clear indication that business degrees are associated with lower ethical standards and he concludes that 'business schools have not done an adequate job of preparing students to respond ethically to the complex issues that arise in the work environment'.

However, the profession is also to blame for not insisting that ethics forms a greater part of the broader professional curriculum. Hauptman and Hill (1991) somewhat scathingly conclude that the professions are operating as 'amoral economic pressure groups immune from ethical concerns', and as a consequence, public opinion is becoming increasingly characterized by high levels of cynicism.

Taken together these studies present the somewhat disturbing possibility that conventional accounting education has a negative impact on students' ethical predispositions (Arlow 1991). Fleming (1996; see also Bebbington and Helliar 2004), for example, concludes that 'the tendency of the evidence is to suggest, if anything, that accountants either occupy the middle ground or lean towards an amoral ethical position'.

These studies suggest first that both qualified accountants and accounting students tend to view the everyday practice of accounting as an amoral activity and

Box 2.2 The heartless wench

One American academic described her experience of teaching ethics to business students at Arizona State University:

> It is very hard to teach business ethics. Students feel as if they have already sold their souls by entering an M.B.A. program, so they are resigned to, and comfortable with, all manner of ethical mischief. In short, they condone unethical conduct not because they're Gordon Gekko-style* supercapitalists, but because they're guilty liberals.
>
> One student asked me:
>
> 'If it meant that you could get the operation your mother can't afford but needs to survive, would you embezzle $1 million?'
>
> No, I said.
>
> 'Why, you heartless wench,' he replied. 'No wonder I'm getting a "C" in this class.'
>
> Oh well, if I can't teach ethics, I can teach fear. The danger of getting caught is a good motivator. If these students enter the business world with trepidation, it will be thanks to this heartless wench. They will have learned that the law still catches and disciplines businesses and executives who don't play by the rules.

(*Note*: *Gordon Gekko is a fictional character in the movie *Wall Street* – an aggressive, power-hungry stockbroker whose favourite phrase is 'greed is good'.)

second, that accounting education may be a contributing factor in the inculcation of such predispositions.

If you have been following the supporting references closely and if you know much at all about the recent history of the accounting profession, you will probably have noticed that most of these papers relate to studies that took place prior to the Enron, WorldCom and Parmalat debacles. In fact, some researchers argue that poor-quality accounting education contributed to these scandals (Low *et al.* 2008; Amernic and Craig 2004). You might therefore think that these concerns have now been addressed. However, the worry over the nature and impact of accounting education persists (Williams 2003). Low and colleagues (2008), for example, lament the continuing inability of accounting and business education to prepare accountants for the ethical capacities they require to engage with complex ethical issues. And Beggs and Dean (2006) explain that the debate continues post Enron as to whether the best way to deal with the issues is via legislation or education.

Some of the research suggests that one of the problems might be related to the

Box 2.3 Your own experience of accounting education

If you are reading this book, the chances are you will already have some experience of accounting education – perhaps at university, or as part of a professional course.

Think about your own experience as an accounting student. Did your course encourage you to actively engage with the subject and adopt a questioning and challenging approach? Or did it tend to emphasize learning of facts, figures, formulas and formats?

Your own experience will be determined by many factors, including the structure and content of your course, the personalities and approaches of your teachers, and your own personality and approach to learning.

The experience of many accounting students is that their education does not encourage them to engage with the subject, but concentrates on the rote-learning of many facts and figures, procedures and practices. It can be argued that this approach at best does not encourage students' ability to develop moral judgement skills and at worst actively discourages this ability.

kind of people who are attracted to becoming accountants (Williams 2003)! Some studies suggest that the accounting profession may attract individuals with a particular kind of cognitive style, one that is associated with lower levels of ethical maturity. Abdolmohammadi and Barker (2006; see also Radtke 2008), for example, contend that rules-based systems may be associated with lower levels of moral reasoning.

We are certainly not going to resolve the educational deficit within the professions with a few ethics courses and in some ways the earlier studies referenced above go some way towards hinting why this is the case. The studies not only tell us something about the ethical predispositions of accountants but they also imply that different structural factors may influence the way we engage with ethical dilemmas (for example the type of educational programme undertaken). The question is what other factors have impinged, and continue to impinge, on the way we engage with ethical dilemmas? And of course they also implicitly assume that different forms of education can contribute towards different levels of ethical maturity. The questions of whether and how it might be possible to 'improve' accountants' ethical awareness and how we should conceptualize 'improvement' are actually more difficult than you may think. What does it mean to be more ethical; how might it be possible to measure morality? And should we even try to do this at all? We will explore these issues in more detail in a later section; however, in the meantime let's get back to the professions and ask how the concerns being expressed within the accounting profession compare with discussions taking place within other professional groups.

Other professions

While these studies indicate some level of concern over the ethical maturity of accountants in particular, there appears to be similar unease within other professional bodies over the level of ethical competence of their members. Studies by Koehn (1991), Herkert and Viscomi (1991) and Florman (1987) all hint towards major ethical concerns within the engineering profession[1] (Koehn 1991; Kucner 1993). Indeed, Bruneau (1994) observes that 'displays of professional dissatisfaction in the trade literature have increased with alarming frequency . . . to such an extent that the casual reader may think that the profession is terminally ill'. A review of legal education studies also reveals a considerable level of concern over the ethics of lawyers. Kronman (1993) and Webb (1996) have both expressed concern at the unethical behaviour of lawyers[2] and Smith (1990) concludes that being a lawyer, 'inevitably corrupts lawyers' characters!' The medical literature too contains many expressions of concern that doctors' education may diminish their ethical sensitivity. Miles and colleagues (1989; see also Hafferty and Franks 1994; Parker 1995), for example, blame the scientific and technical focus of the medical degree syllabus for increased cynicism among medical students and declining 'humanistic sensitivity' of doctors. Hafferty and Franks (1994) conclude that the professional culture of medics has become 'ethically compromised'.

There appears therefore to be a significant level of concern across many of the traditional professions over the ethical characteristics of their members. However, the interesting issue here is, of course, not just which profession is more or less ethical than another. Rather, the lesson is that the concern over the ethics of individual professional accountants is not an isolated case but is mirrored across other professions also. This would perhaps hint at a broader crisis in professionalism that may be related to a perceptible shift in social attitudes towards the idea of professions (we will discuss the issue of professionalism in a later chapter) (see, for example, Low *et al.* 2008).

Box 2.4 How the public rate the professions for honesty and integrity

An opinion poll carried out by Gallup in 2005 asked members of the public in the US to rate the honesty and ethical standards of members of 21 professions on a five-point scale that ranged from 'very high' to 'very low'.

Only six of the professions are considered to have high or very high ethical standards – nurses (82%), pharmacists (67%), doctors (65%), teachers (64%), policemen (61%) and clergy (54%).

Accountants came in at ninth place, with 39 per cent, beating journalists (28%) and real estate agents (20%). Bottom of the survey were car salesmen (8%) and telemarketers (7%).

Gallup noted that the accountants' ratings have almost fully recovered from the business scandals of 2002 (including Enron), when their ratings dropped from a previous 41 per cent to 32 per cent.

Moral development models

Kohlberg's model

One of the problems with the studies discussed above is how they determine whether one person or profession is more or less ethical than another. They appear to imply some objective scale of morality. A considerable number of the comparative studies like those above draw on the work of Lawrence Kohlberg and his model of Cognitive Moral Development (CMD) (see Ponemon 1990). Kohlberg's model is routinely used to gauge an individual's moral maturity based on their responses to a series of hypothetical dilemmas (see the example of the Heinz dilemma in Box 2.5). Most of the conventional studies in the accounting literature use Rest's Defining Issues Test to collect data on individual predispositions and this is subsequently analysed using Kohlberg's model (Bay 2002). The model itself consists of six discrete predispositions (see Figure 2.1).

As the earlier discussion indicates, CMD has been applied to accounting students, accounting practitioners at various stages in their careers and to students studying different disciplines and practitioners from different professions. Ponemon (1990), for example, found that accountants' moral reasoning capacity increases until they reach the stage of manager or partner, at which point it subsequently decreases! (See also Trevino 1992, in Reiter 1996.) This model has also been used in comparisons of ethics in different national cultures (Kracher *et al.* 2002) and the impact of organizational culture on individual ethical behaviour (Forte 2004).

Levels	Stages	Disposition
3. Post-conventional	6	Based on universal moral principles.
	5	Impartial with a concern for everyone's interests
2. Conventional	4	Informed by society's laws
	3	Conforming to group norms
1. Pre-conventional	2	Self-interest is the primary motivation
	1	Avoid punishment

Figure 2.1 Kohlberg's model of Cognitive Moral Development (CMD).

Box 2.5 The Heinz dilemma

A woman was near death from a unique kind of cancer. There was a drug that might save her. The drug cost £4,000 per dosage. The sick woman's husband, Heinz, went to everyone he knew to borrow the money and tried every legal means, but he could get together only about £2,000. He asked the doctor who discovered the drug for a discount or to let him pay later. But the doctor refused.

Should Heinz break into the doctor's laboratory to steal the drug for his wife? Why steal or why not steal?

Stage	*Why should Heinz steal?*	*Why should Heinz not steal?*
1	He will be in trouble if his wife dies. He will be blamed for her death.	He will be caught if he breaks into the laboratory. He will end up in jail.
2	If he's caught and does some time in jail, he will still have his wife to be there for him when he gets out.	His wife will probably die before he gets out, so it will do him no good to steal.
3	If he lets his wife die, everyone will think he is a terrible person.	If he steals the drug, everyone will think he is a terrible person.
4	It is his duty to save her. He promised to look after her when he married her.	It is against the law to steal – people cannot just break the law to suit themselves.
5	Life is more important than property.	He must respect the doctor's right not to be stolen from.
6	He would always condemn himself if he let her die, for not living up to his own standards of conscience.	He would condemn himself for stealing, even if others did not blame him.

Gilligan's model

While Kohlberg's model is quite prominent within the accounting literature, there is a growing body of work that critiques his position. To begin with, there is some debate as to whether a different level of moral reasoning necessarily results in different types of behaviour (Reiter 1996). However, at a more fundamental level, Reiter (1996) critiques the model itself. She contrasts Kohlberg's conceptualization of moral development with that of Carol Gilligan (see Figure 2.2). Reiter (1996) suggests that, while

Box 2.6 The Heinz dilemma and Taiwan

Although the Heinz dilemma is, of course, not true, there are real-world parallel situations. The BBC reported the following news story in 2005:

Taiwan to ignore flu drug patent
Taiwan has responded to bird flu fears by starting work on its own version of the antiviral drug, Tamiflu, without waiting for the manufacturer's consent.

Taiwan officials said they had applied for the right to copy the drug, but the priority was to protect the public. 'We have tried our best to negotiate with [the manufacturer]. But to protect our people is the utmost important thing.'

Box 2.7 Where do you fit in?

Look again at Kohlberg and Gilligan's models, and think again about the Heinz dilemma we discussed earlier.

- Where does your own response to the Heinz dilemma fit on each model?
- Do you end up on a higher scale on one rather than another? Or do you land at approximately the same place?
- Which of the two models do you prefer?

<table>
<tr><td>Third focus</td><td>Dynamic interrelationship between the self and others.</td></tr>
<tr><td colspan="2">Transition: questioning of logic of inequality between the needs of others and the self</td></tr>
<tr><td>Second focus</td><td>Care for dependent others, involving self-sacrifice</td></tr>
<tr><td colspan="2">Transition: focus on self seen as unacceptably selfish</td></tr>
<tr><td>First focus</td><td>Caring for self and ensuring survival</td></tr>
</table>

Figure 2.2 Gilligan's hierarchy of moral development.

Kohlberg conceptualizes progress in moral thinking in terms of increased abstraction and autonomy, Gilligan's 'ethics of care' presents a more embedded and empathic view of ethical development. Gilligan was particularly concerned that Kohlberg's model appeared to be developed primarily from studies of male volunteers.

Both Gilligan's and Kohlberg's work is quite pertinent for exploring the ethics of accounting. Two issues are relevant here. First, their work encourages us to reflect on how we might conceptualize the moral development of the individual accountant. While we might all agree that we would like to see more ethical accountants, what exactly does this mean? For example, quite often accounting scandals are followed by calls for new codes of conduct; however, Kohlberg's model would imply that simply following ethical codes would represent quite a low level of ethical maturity. Both models provide us with different ways of beginning to think about the kinds of attributes that could characterize ethical maturity, so the notion of moral development is both complex and contested.

There are also obvious educational implications depending on the type of model espoused by the profession. Reiter (1996) suggests that the majority of ethics education within accounting has been underpinned by the Kohlberg model. Developing an ethics of care, as Reiter rightly points out, would require quite a significantly different form of educational practice. How do you educate for empathy? (see McPhail 2001). We will reflect again on these issues when we consider the work of Emmanuel Levinas later, in Chapter 3.

INDIVIDUAL ATTRIBUTES AND ETHICAL BEHAVIOUR: THE EFFECT OF AGE AND GENDER

Kohlberg's model has also been used to explore the impact of personal characteristics on ethical decisions. The characteristics of gender and age in particular have been explored in some detail. While Stanga and Turpen's (1991) work does not support the existence of gender differences Arlow (1991), Meising and Preble (1985) and Borkowski and Ugras (1992) all contend that females are more ethical than males. David and colleagues (1994) also suggest that women have different kinds of attitudes towards ethics and codes of ethics in particular. In fact some people have even suggested that one way to resolve the ethical problems in large accounting firms is to employ more women (Radtke 2008).

While female accountants' experiences of professionalism may indeed differ from those of their male counterparts, other studies also employ the idea of gender in a broader sense to refer to more general masculine and feminine personality traits as opposed to biological gender. There is some evidence within this literature to suggest that accounting education may promote the development of masculine character traits within students in general and that this may in turn have an impact on the way accountants, as a group, conceptualize and respond to ethical dilemmas (Bebbington *et al.*, 1997).

Cognitive moral development research has also provided overwhelming evidence that moral reasoning is also affected by age (Trevino 1992; Rest 1983; Serwenek 1992). These studies would suggest that the way in which an individual accountant engages with a moral dilemma might be influenced by that individual's age.

It would therefore seem that individual characteristics generally tend to have quite a significant influence on ethical proclivities of accountants and the way in which ethical issues are experienced. Figure 2.3 represents an attempt to begin to model or visualize the kinds of things that may have an impact on the way individual

Box 2.8 Gender and whistle-blowing

Several recent press articles have asked whether it is significant that the prominent whistle-blowers to emerge from the three great US organizational scandals of recent years were women.

- Sherron Watkins, Enron's vice president for corporate development, testified before a House Energy and Commerce Subcommittee that her company had become 'the poster child of corporate abuse'.
- Coleen Rowley had worked for the FBI for 21 years when she appeared before the Senate Judiciary Committee to testify that the agency had ignored pre-9/11 warnings about terrorist activity in the US.
- And Cynthia Cooper, WorldCom's vice president of finance, alerted the company's board to an internal fraudulent accounting scheme that ultimately led to the largest bankruptcy filing in the nation's history.

Various theories have been put forward by way of speculative explanation:

- One theory of women as whistle-blowers is that of the insider–outsider. They are less likely to be part of the 'old boy network', so they don't risk being pushed out of the club.
- Women may not be as sensitive as men to status in the workplace. And if they are not as committed to the hierarchy, they are more able to see the ramifications of a situation.
- Women may be natural whistle-blowers, because of the way they think and how they learned to play as children. Girls choose games with far fewer rules, which change if someone gets upset. Subsequently, as adults, women may be less likely to play by the rules if they don't think the rules are right.

accountants experience ethical issues. We will try to develop this model over the next few sections as we explore more of the descriptive ethics literature.

ETHICS AND STRUCTURAL CHARACTERISTICS

While research suggests that personal characteristics influence both ethical awareness and the way in which individuals respond to ethical dilemmas, other studies suggest that the context within which the individual is embedded can also have a significant impact on ethical decision-making. Indeed Fogarty (1995) contends that the tendency to separate individual accountants from their context has been one of the limitations of accounting and business ethics research. He contends that this tendency to focus on individual ethical actions is inconsistent with the emphasis within the sociological literature on the importance of the complex socio-economic

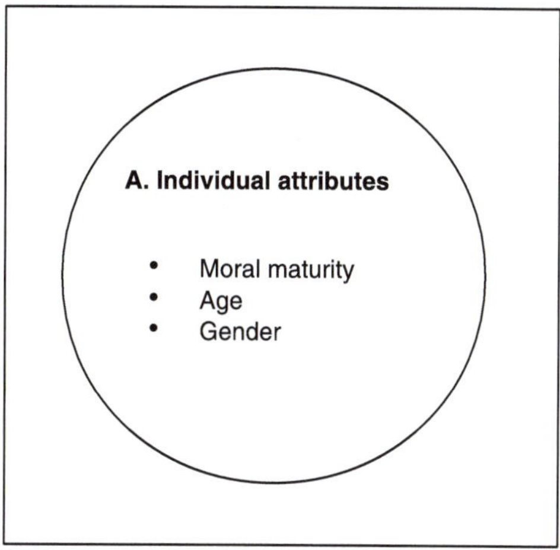

Figure 2.3 Modelling professional ethics: individual attributes.

relationships within which the individual is embedded. In this section we will focus on two issues: first, cultural issues and second, organizational factors.

Culture

There is quite a considerable discussion within the moral philosophy literature regarding the influence of culture on the ethical predispositions of individuals. The question here is whether different national value systems affect individual ethical behaviour. The evidence is mixed. Jakubowski and colleagues (2002) suggest that national differences are reflected in the ethical codes of accountants across different countries and Karnes and colleagues (1990) contend that accountants of different nationalities do have disparate perceptions of what is and is not ethical. Cohen and colleagues (1992) draw on Hofstede's cultural studies to argue that there are international differences in ethical values that could impede the effectiveness of the International Federation of Accountants (IFAC) 'Code of Ethics for Professional Accountants'. They state,

> differing cultures and levels of economic development are likely to cause professionals in many countries to find some part of international guidelines irrelevant to their needs, and even for some, antithetical to the social and economic environment in which they work.

Arnold and colleagues (2007; see also Smith and Hume 2005) also state that national culture more than corporate culture within firms seems to have a greater impact on accountants' ethical predispositions.

However, not all studies support the hypothesis that different national cultures equate to different notions of professional ethics. Lysonski and Gaidis (1991) found

Box 2.9 The IFAC Code of Ethics and cultural differences

One of the issues the Code of Ethics covers is that of gifts and hospitality. The Code states:

> A professional accountant in public practice, or an immediate or close family member, may be offered gifts and hospitality from a client. Such an offer ordinarily gives rise to threats to compliance with the fundamental principles [one of which is objectivity]. For example, self-interest threats to objectivity may be created if a gift from a client is accepted; intimidation threats to objectivity may result from the possibility of such offers being made public. The significance of such threats will depend on the nature, value and intent behind the offer.
>
> (International Federation of Accountants' Ethics Committee 2005: 30)

The issue here is that what is an acceptable level of gifts or hospitality in one culture may be very different in another culture. There is a sliding scale between gifts and hospitality – token gestures indicating friendship, which are often reciprocated, and bribes – payments to encourage people to do things they should not. In most countries, modest gifts between accountants and clients are acceptable, and in most countries bribes would be unacceptable.

But there are grey areas in between. When does a gift or hospitality cease to be 'insignificant'? Being taken out for lunch by a client may be normal and acceptable, but what about a luxury weekend in a smart hotel? The answer will be determined by cultural influences.

Similarly, in some countries 'grease' (or facilitation payments) is common – small payments to encourage people to do what their job requires them to do. Although it is a crime for UK firms to make such payments to officials overseas, in many countries such payments are normal practice.

that students' responses to ethical dilemmas were similar across cultures and Whipple and Swords (1992) similarly suggest that demographic factors have little impact on students' moral reasoning.

Organizations and groups of individuals

A second issue relates to the observation that accountants are embedded within groups within organizations. We would like to highlight two issues here that contribute towards understanding the ethical behaviour of individual accountants. These issues are *groupthink* and *organizational culture*.

Individual accountants are embedded within many different groups. Within a work-related context they are part of the accounting profession, a partnership or

Box 2.10 WorldCom – an example of 'groupthink'?

Scharff (2005) recognized aspects of groupthink as possibly having contributed to the fraud perpetrated at WorldCom.

WorldCom perpetrated the largest accounting fraud in US history. WorldCom was fined $750 million, having reported accounting irregularities of $11 billion. Several senior officials orchestrated the fraud, many of whom have been found guilty of fraud and conspiracy charges. However, WorldCom's organizational structure and culture potentially contributed not only to the fraud but also to the length of time over which it occurred.

Groupthink is a way of thinking that people engage in when they are deeply involved in a cohesive in-group. Members of the group strive for unanimity, overriding their motivation to appraise alternative courses of action realistically. It is often characterized by arrogance, and excessive levels of blind loyalty to the group.

Within WorldCom, there was a great deal of focus on teamwork and being 'team players'. Staff regularly attended 'teambuilding' exercises. Great pressure was exerted on employees to be loyal to the group. One middle-level qualified accountant was repeatedly asked to falsify accounting figures and eventually acquiesced after much persuasion that it was in the interests of the group. She was eventually sentenced to five months' jail for her part in the fraud.

Groupthink may help explain some of the issues and fraudulent activities at WorldCom as well as the pressures that were placed on employees extending over the period in which the fraud occurred.

company, a public sector organization or charity and perhaps an audit or management team. Research suggests that an individual's ethical decision-making may change when they become part of a more formal grouping (Hauptman and Hill 1991) or even a large crowd. Sims (1992) labels this phenomenon 'groupthink'. The characteristics and dynamics of the groups to which accountants belong may therefore affect the way in which individual accountants encounter and resolve ethical dilemmas. Recently, the influence of group membership on ethical behaviour has been extended through the idea of network analysis. It might be helpful to think about this development in terms of online social networking sites like Facebook and Bebo. This emerging strand of literature uses social network analysis to understand patterns of ethical behaviour (Kulik *et al.* 2008). In other words it explores whether the position that individuals employ within networks has any relationship to their ethical proclivities.

Rockness and Rockness (2005) and Kulik and colleagues (2008) imply that ethical predispositions are also affected by organizational culture in general and Douglas and colleagues (2001) found a clear link between the organizational culture within large accounting firms and ethical predispositions. Indeed, a number of studies have shown that personal values often have little impact on ethical decisions in business or within organizational contexts (Shafer *et al.* 2001; see also Akaah and Lund 1994; Finegan 1994, in Shafer *et al.* 2001). Indeed, Sims and Brinkman (2005) suggest that the corporate culture within Enron played a very influential role in the company's demise. Grey (1998) suggests the organizational settings where work takes place are generally devoid of the kind of emotion that is often associated with the identification and resolution of ethical dilemmas.

The literature also suggests that individual ethics can often change depending on the position and level (or the subgroups) an individual occupies within an organization. Ponemon (1990), for example, found that the sophistication in accountants' ethical reasoning increases as they attain supervisory levels within the firm but then decreases among managers and partners. He suggests a number of possibilities for his findings, including conflicting social influences at different hierarchical levels and the possibility of self-selection processes at work. In other words, certain types of individuals are either motivated to become managers or partners and/or certain types of individuals, with certain character traits, are selected for such positions. Tyson's (1990) work, however, would suggest that individuals generally think they are more ethical than their peers and co-workers.

These studies therefore suggest that there is a complex interrelationship between individual ethical thinking and the national and organizational contexts within which individual accountants are embedded.

Categorization: ethics and the roles accountants play

The preceding discussion of the contexts within which accountants operate highlighted different work-related groups. However, it goes without saying that accountants are also members of many different kinds of groups outside work, for example sports clubs, voluntary organizations, religious groups and, of course, family and other relational units. Drawing on these observations, some researchers have wondered whether individual accountants think about ethical issues in different ways in these different compartments of their lives and, if so, how these different categories of thinking emerge. Many of these studies are informed by theories from cognitive psychology.

Some of these studies start by thinking about the way human beings process information. The study of the way information is encoded in memory is a central issue in both learning theory and cognitive psychology (Tajfel and Fraser 1990). It has been conceptualized in both cases using the notion of *categorization* (Tajfel and Fraser 1990; Hewstone *et al.* 1993). According to prevailing learning theory, the process of categorization involves learning to ascribe specific properties to particular groups of objects (Stahlberg and Frey 1988, in Tajfel and Fraser 1990). Learning theorists suggest that the resulting connections are organized and stored in cognitive memory structures called schema[3] (Fiske and Taylor 1984; Schwarz 1985, in Hewstone *et al.* 1993; Choo 1989). These schema are assumed to direct attention to relevant information and guide its interpretation and evaluation. Categorizations are thus seen to play a primary role in developing an individual's understanding of the world and identifying appropriate ways of behaving within it (see Fogarty 1992).

Within the cognitive psychology literature the notion of *scripts* has been developed to reflect the function that sequences of actions play a part in forming the basis of different behavioural roles, for example visiting a doctor, going to the supermarket or, more pertinently, performing an audit. It is argued that *scriptal* knowledge structures[4] retain knowledge of expected sequences of behaviours, actions, and events.

If becoming an accountant is associated with the acquisition of a related 'accountant' cognitive script, then this has obvious implications for the way accountants might experience ethical issues as accountants. However, this research also hints at a more interesting possibility. It may be that accountants respond to similar ethical issues in a different way depending on the cognitive context within which they are experienced or encountered. A study by Weber (1990), for example, found that managers' moral reasoning level is lower in work-related decision situations compared to non-work-related dilemmas, and another study by Trevino (1992) similarly suggests that different values, norms and behaviours are associated with different 'life domains'.

Let's pause here and see if we can develop the model we introduced above. From this very brief introduction to some of the literature that deals with ethics, organizations and groups, it would seem our appreciation of ethical dilemmas may be influenced by a complicated mix of personal attributes and structural conditions (see Figure 2.4).

ETHICS AND THE NATURE OF THE DILEMMA: SITUATIONAL ETHICS

Thus far, this chapter has suggested that both individual attributes and broad structural or contextual characteristics influence individual ethics. However, some studies also suggest that the structure and attributes of ethical issues themselves can have a significant impact on the way individuals conceptualize and respond to specific

Box 2.11 Visiting a restaurant – a cognitive script

Most of us have visited a restaurant many times. We therefore possess a cognitive script of what such a visit involves. The cognitive script for going to a restaurant consists of entering, ordering, eating, paying and exiting. Each aspect can be further broken down. Eating, for example, becomes:

> Cook gives food to waiter; waiter gives food to customer; customer eats food.

This process is so familiar to us that we no longer need to think about it. It is only when something not normally in the script occurs that we become aware of it – for example when a waiter accidentally drops a tray.

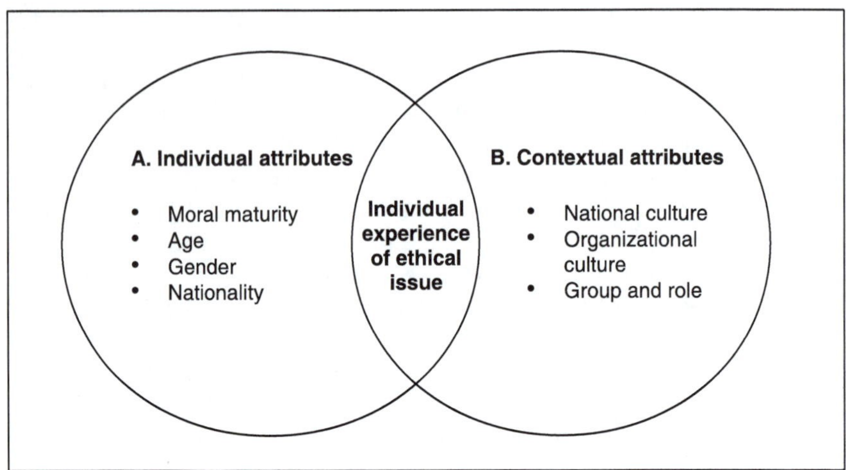

Figure 2.4 Modelling professional ethics: contextual attributes.

dilemmas. This section of the chapter introduces various attempts within the literature to model the structure of ethical issues themselves.

A significant body of work within the business ethics literature focuses on situational ethics. The main premise of this model is that both the nature of ethical issues, and an individual's response to them, will be influenced by the context within which the issue is encountered. Although not explicitly connected within the literature, there is an obvious link between situational ethics and the concept of categorization discussed above. The literature discusses two main types of situational influences: issue-related elements and context-related elements. As we discussed above, some of the context-specific issues like age, gender and organizational setting have been shown to have a significant impact on the way individuals construe their ethical obligations and respond to ethical issues. However, this body of research also recognizes that the nature of ethical issues themselves is also important in understanding an individual's ethical predisposition towards them. This section focuses specifically on two issue-related elements: first, moral intensity and second, moral framing.

Moral intensity

Jones (1991; see also Leitsch 2004) suggests that the moral intensity of an issue will be influenced by six factors.

1 The nature of the consequences
2 The social consensus
3 The possibility of effect
4 Temporal immediacy
5 Proximity
6 The concentration of effect.

The nature of the consequences relates to the magnitude of the outcome of one's actions; consider for example the consequences of stealing a few pens from an office cupboard in comparison to stealing a baby from a maternity unit. Social consensus refers to the general social attitude towards the particular issue. The possibility of effect relates to the probability that a particular set of consequences will ensue from an individual's action. Temporal immediacy relates to the speed with which the consequences are likely to come into effect, whereas proximity refers to the nearness to individuals who are likely to be affected by one's actions. The final element, concentration of effect, relates to the number of people likely to be affected by a particular action (Jones 1991). The elements of this model are quite readily applicable to accounting and business decisions in particular. Social consensus in relation to environmental pollution, for example, has changed considerably. It is also easy to see how it might be more acceptable to advocate a particular investment project if any potentially negative impacts are both uncertain and unlikely to materialize for many years.

While it may be difficult to isolate the specific impact of any one of these factors, the literature suggests that the interrelationship between them will have a significant influence on the way an individual will engage with a particular ethical issue.

Moral framing

The associated issue of moral framing suggests that individuals respond to ethical dilemmas in different ways depending on the framework within which they are experienced. Two strands of research elaborate on this premise. First, linguistic research suggests that individuals may respond to issues differently depending on the linguistic frames within which issues are discussed. The words (and numbers) used to frame the issue can quite literally affect our moral thinking about those issues.

A second strand of research explores the spatial influences in ethical thinking (Bachelard 1994). While Jones, for example, discusses the potential impact of proximity, this emerging strand of research explores the influence of location and place more generally on an individual's ethical thinking. For example, some time ago, an architect we know was involved in designing a new hospital. Through discussions with the client, the design team, of which he was a member, decided to position the management suite in the same block as the intensive care unit in the hope that this location might in some crude way remind management of the human impact of the decisions they were making!

These issue-related elements may therefore also contribute towards understanding how individual accountants may experience or respond to ethical issues in practice. The specific linguistic and spatial characteristics of accounting practice may be related to the way ethical issues are framed and subsequently experienced by professional accountants. Within the literature, there is particular concern over the sanitized, technical, algorithmic language that often frames investment decisions and other ethical issues within accounting textbooks and the accounting profession more generally. Broadbent (1998; see also DeMoss and McCann 1997), for example, implies that '*accounting logic*' reduces moral intensity because it excludes emotion

Box 2.12 Moral intensity and music piracy

One of the problems associated with stopping the widespread prevalence of music piracy, often in downloading from websites, is that the practice is generally regarded as having low moral intensity.

- The consequences are unlikely to be severe, given the extreme unlikelihood of being caught.
- Given that so many other people do it, it is perceived as being socially acceptable.
- The person copying the music may well feel that there is no real effect of their action (despite there being an undoubted financial effect on the artists and production companies, and an effect on wider society, in the form of increased music costs).
- There may appear to be no immediate or short-term effects.
- Music companies are very distant, anonymous corporations, so there is little or no proximity.

Finally, cheating an institutional entity such as a corporation is perceived as having a less concentrated effect than cheating an individual or individuals.

and McPhail (2001) suggests that managerial techniques dehumanize individuals by representing them as objects in technical and ethically neutral terms.

We have factored these issue-related elements into our model in Figure 2.5. As you can see, trying to describe the factors that may influence the way individual accountants experience ethical dilemmas is a complex issue (Buchan 2005). However, we hope it may help you begin to understand your own responses to ethical issues and also how difficult it may be to change these responses.

SUMMARY

This chapter has drawn on some of the empirical studies within the moral philosophy literature to describe the types of issues that may affect the way accountants experience ethical issues. The chapter commenced by exploring some empirical evidence that suggests that accountants and accounting students do not seem to be as morally developed as we might expect them, or at least like them, to be. However, we noted that concern over members' ethical competencies does not seem to be isolated to the accounting profession. There appears to be growing concern among the established professions in general over the ethical proclivities of doctors, lawyers and engineers as well as accountants.

However, the psychology literature suggests that the stilted ethical development of accounting students and practitioners may be specifically related to their role as

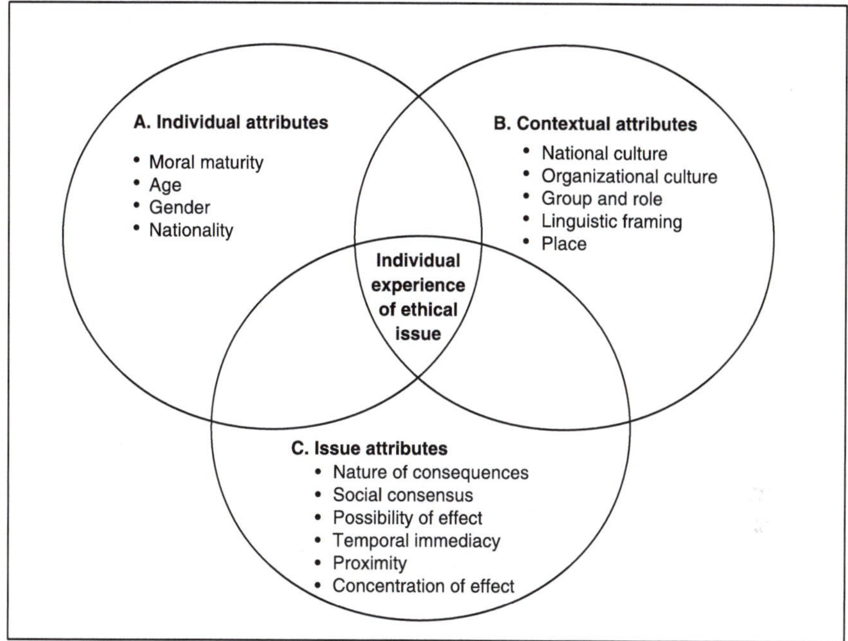

Figure 2.5 Modelling professional ethics: empirical perspectives.

accountants. These studies set up the interesting prospect that accountants may think differently about ethics in different areas of their lives. Some related literature would also suggest that any discussion of the ethics of accountants must bear in mind cultural differences and also the organizational setting within which they are situated. Finally, the chapter has suggested that accountants' experiences of ethics are likely to vary depending on their age, gender characteristics, their position within an organization and the nature and framing of the issue itself.

From this brief discussion of the descriptive/empirical ethics literature, it is possible to begin to model the complex mixture of factors that may influence how individual accountants engage with ethical dilemmas in practice, and we attempted to model these factors in Figure 2.5.

Having explored some of the issues that may influence the way accountants respond to ethical issues in practice, in the following chapter we will explore the normative question of how accountants *should* behave.

QUESTIONS

1 Describe some of the factors that may influence the way individual accountants experience ethical dilemmas in practice?
2 How does the idea of moral intensity contribute towards our understanding of accounting and ethics?

3 Explain how you might go about developing a professional ethics programme that tried to engender an ethics of care.
4 Explain the idea of categorization in relation to ethical predispositions.
5 Discuss whether you think national culture plays an important part in accountants' responses to ethical dilemmas.

NOTES

1 Tansel (1994) explains that environmental problems have had a significant impact on the increasing concern with ethics within the engineering profession.
2 This concern is being expressed both within and outside the profession (see Smith 1990, for example).
3 A schema is an abstract notion that refers to the knowledge structures which individuals may unconsciously employ in order to organize and make sense of social and organizational situations (Fiske and Kinder 1981, in Choo 1989).
4 The metaphor of the actors/actresses script may be helpful in explaining this argument. Schemas can be thought of as a script that an actor would follow in a film. The script provides the actor with an understanding of the situation and also with an idea of what she or he is expected to say and how she or he is expected to act.

RESOURCES

Films

Enron: The smartest guys in the room (2005), director Alex Gibney; from the film based on the book, B. McLean and P. Elkind (2003) *The smartest guys in the room: The amazing rise and scandalous fall of Enron* (New York: Doubleday).

The Apartment (1960); have a look at this movie in which Jack Lemmon plays an accountant in a large insurance company who allows various managers to use his flat for extra-marital liaisons in the hope that he might secure a promotion.

iTunes podcasts

Building ethical and effective companies, J. Joseph, L. Holmes and N. Pickus, Kenan Institute for Ethics, Duke University, Durham, NC.

Institutional cultures: The dynamics of ethical change in business, higher education, religion and the military, 2007, Noah Pickus, Director of the Kenan Institute for Ethics, Duke University, Durham, NC; Suzanne Shanahan, Assistant Professor of Sociology, Duke University.

Personal ethics and public decision-making, Nancy Kassebaum Baker, Alice M. Rivlin and Steve Tobocman, The Ford School's Lecture Series, The Ford School of Public Policy, University of Michigan.

Websites

BBC Radio 4, *Women's Hour*, 'Women as whistle-blowers', available online at: <www.bbc.co.uk/radio4/womanshour/2002_40_thu_01.shtml>; short radio programme extract on the role of women as whistle-blowers.

Gallup poll on honesty and ethics among professionals, available online at: <http://poll.gallup.com/poll/1654/Honesty-Ethics-Professions.aspx>.

IFAC Code of Ethics, available online at: <www.ifac.org>.

READING

Accounting ethics and gender

Bebbington, J., Thomson, I. and Wall, D. (1997) 'Accounting students and constructed gender: An exploration of gender in the context of accounting degree choices' *Journal of Accounting Education*, 15(2): 241–267.

Broadbent, J. (1998) 'The gendered nature of accounting logic: Pointers to an accounting that encompasses multiple values', *Critical Perspectives on Accounting*, 9: 267–297.

Craig Keller, C., Smith, K.T. and Smith, L.M. (2007) 'Do gender, educational level, religiosity, and work experience affect the ethical decision-making of U.S. accountants?', *Critical Perspectives on Accounting*, 18: 299–315.

Kirkham, L.M. and Loft, A. (1993) 'Gender and the construction of the professional accountant', *Accounting, Organizations and Society*, 18(6): 507–558.

Ethics culture and contexts

Boyce, G. (2008) 'The social relevance of ethics education in a global(ising) era: From individual dilemmas to systemic crises', *Critical Perspectives on Accounting*, 19: 255–290.

Cohen, J.R., Pant, L.W and Sharp, D.J. (1992) 'Cultural and socioeconomic constraints on international codes of ethics: Lessons from accounting', *Journal of Business Ethics*, 11: 687–700.

Fogarty, T.J. (1995) 'Accountant ethics: A brief examination of neglected sociological dimensions', *Journal of Business Ethics*, 14(2): 103–115.

Grey, C. (1998) 'On being a professional in a Big Six Firm', *Accounting, Organizations and Society*, 23(5/6): 569–587.

Hauptman, R. and Hill, F. (1991) 'Deride, abide or dissent: On the ethics of professional conduct', *Journal of Business Ethics*, 10: 37–44.

Ryan, J.J. (2001) 'Moral reasoning as a determinant of organizational citizenship behaviors: A study in the public accounting profession', *Journal of Business Ethics*, 33: 233–244.

Shafer, W.E. (2002) 'Ethical pressure, organizational–professional conflict, and related work outcomes among management accountants', *Journal of Business Ethics*, 38: 263–275

Yuthas, K., Dillard, F. and Rogers, R.K. (2004) 'Beyond agency and structure: Triple-loop learning', *Journal of Business Ethics*, 51: 229–243.

Ethics roles and categorization

Fogarty, T.J. (1992) 'Organisational socialisation in accounting firms: A theoretical framework and agenda for future research', *Accounting, Organizations and Society*, 17(2): 129–149.

Tajfel, H. and Fraser, C. (1990) *Introducing social psychology* (Harmondsworth: Penguin Books).

Trevino, L.K. (1992) 'Moral reasoning and business ethics: Implications for research, education and management', *Journal of Business Ethics*, 11: 445–459.

Weber, J. (1990) 'Measuring the impact of teaching ethics to future managers: A review, assessment and recommendations', *Journal of Business Ethics*, 9(3): 183–190.

Kohlberg and Gilligan

Reiter, S. (1996) 'The Kohlberg–Gilligan controversy: Lessons for accounting ethics education', *Critical Perspectives on Accounting*, 7: 33–54.

Predispositions of accountants

Bebbington, J. and Helliar, C. (2004) *Taking ethics to heart* (Edinburgh: Institute of Chartered Accountants of Scotland).

Gray, R.H., Bebbington, J. and McPhail, K. (1994) 'Teaching ethics and the ethics of teaching: Educating for immorality and a possible case for social and environmental accounting', *Accounting Education*, 3: 51–75.

Jeter, L. (2003) *Disconnected: Deceit and betrayal at WorldCom* (Hoboken, NJ: Wiley).

Loeb, S.E. (1991) 'The evaluation of outcomes of accounting ethics education', *Journal of Business Ethics*, 10(2): 77–84.

Ponemon, L.A. (1992) 'Ethical reasoning and selection: Socialization in accounting', *Accounting, Organizations and Society*, 17(3/4): 239–258.

Poneman, L.A. (1990) 'Ethical judgements in accounting: A cognitive-development perspective', *Critical Perspectives on Accounting*, 1(2):191–215.

Situational ethics and framing

Jones, T.M. (1991) 'Ethical decision making by individuals in organisations: An issue-contingent model', *Academy of Management Review*, 16(2): 366–395.

REFERENCES

Abdolmohammadi, M.J. and Barker, C.R. (2006) 'Accountants' value preferences and moral reasoning', *Journal of Business Ethics*, 69: 11–25.

Akaah, I.P. and Lund, D. (1994) 'The influence of personal and organizational values on marketing professionals' ethical behaviour', *Journal of Business Ethics*, 13: 417–430.

Amernic, J. and Craig, R. (2004) 'Reform of the accounting education in the post-Enron era: Moving accounting "Out of the Shadows" ', *Abacus*, 40(3): 342–378.

Arlow, P. (1991) 'Personal characteristics in college students' evaluations of business ethics and corporate social responsibility', *Journal of Business Ethics*, 10: 63–69.

Armstrong, M.B. (1987) 'Moral development and accounting education', *Journal of Accounting Education*, 5: 27–43.

Arnold, D.F., Bernardi, R.A., Neidermeyer, P.E. and Schmee, J. (2007) 'The effect of country and culture on perceptions of appropriate ethical actions prescribed by codes of conduct: A Western European perspective among accountants', *Journal of Business Ethics*, 70: 327–340.

Bachelard, G. (1994) *The poetics of space* (Boston, MA: Beacon Press).

Bay, D. (2002) 'A critical evaluation of the use of the audit in accounting ethics research', *Critical Perspectives on Accounting*, 13(2): 159–177.

Bebbington, J. and Helliar, C. (2004) *Taking ethics to heart* (Edinburgh: Institute of Chartered Accountants of Scotland).

Bebbington, J., Thomson, I. and Wall, D. (1997) 'Accounting students and constructed gender: An exploration of gender in the context of accounting degree choices', *Journal of Accounting Education*, 15(2): 241–267.

Beets, S.D. and Killough. L.N. (1990) 'The effectiveness of a complaint-based ethics enforcement system: Evidence from the accounting profession', *Journal Of Business Ethics*, 9: 115–126.

Beggs, J.M. and Dean, K.L. (2006) 'Legislated ethics or ethics education?: Faculty views in the post-Enron era', *Journal of Business Ethics*, 71: 15–37.

Borkowski, S.C. and Ugras, Y.F. (1992) 'The ethical attitudes of students as a function of age, sex and experience', *Journal of Business Ethics*, 11(12): 961–979.

Broadbent, J. (1998) 'The gendered nature of accounting logic: Pointers to an accounting that encompasses multiple values', *Critical Perspectives on Accounting*, 9: 267–297.

Bruneau, M. (1994) 'Strategies to enhance the well-being of the civil engineering profession', *Journal of Professional Issues in Education and Practice*, 120(4), July: 341–359.

Buchan, H.F. (2005) 'Ethical decision making in the public accounting profession: An extension of Ajzen's theory of planned behavior', *Journal of Business Ethics*, 61: 165–181.

Choo, F. (1989) 'Cognitive scripts in auditing and accounting behavior', *Accounting, Organizations and Society*, 14(5/6): 481–493.

Cohen, J.R., Pant, L.W and Sharp, D.J. (1992) 'Cultural and socioeconomic constraints on international codes of ethics: Lessons from accounting', *Journal of Business Ethics*, 11: 687–700.

David, J.M., Kantor, J. and Greenberg, I. (1994) 'Possible ethical issues and their impact on the firm: Perceptions held by public accountants', *Journal of Business Ethics*, 13: 919–937.

Davis, J.R. and Welton, R.E. (1991) 'Professional ethics : Business students' perception', *Journal of Business Ethics*, 10(6): 451–463.

DeMoss, M.A. and McCann, G.K. (1997) 'Without a care in the world: The business ethics course and its exclusion of a care perspective', *Journal of Business Ethics*, 16(4): 435–443.

Denham, R.A. (ed.) (1991) *Ethical responsibility in business and the accounting profession: Issues, opportunities and education* (Alberta, Canada: University of Alberta).

Douglas, P.C., Davidson, R.A. and Schwartz, B.N. (2001) 'The effect of organisational culture and ethical orientation on accountants' ethical judgement', *Journal of Business Ethics*, 34: 101–121.

Edwards J.R. (2001) 'Accounting regulation and the professionalisation process: An historical essay concerning the significance of P.H. Abbott', *Critical Perspectives on Accounting*, 12: 675–696.

Eynon, G., Hill, N.T. and Stevens, K.T. (1997) 'Factors that influence the moral reasoning abilities of accountants: Implications for universities and the profession', *Journal of Business Ethics*, 16: 1297–1309.

Fleming, A.I.M. (1996) 'Ethics and accounting education in the UK: A professional approach?', *Accounting Education*, 5(3): 207–217.

Finegan, J. (1994) 'The impact of personal values on judgements of ethical behaviour in the workplace', *Journal of Business Ethics*, 13: 747–755.

Fiske, S.T. and Kinder, D.R. (1981) 'Involvement, expertise and schema use: Evidence from political cognition', in N. Cantor and J.F. Kihlstrom (eds), *Personality, cognition and social interaction* (Hillsdale, N.J.: Lawrence Erlbaum), 171–190.

Fiske, S.T. and Taylor, S.E. (1984) *Social cognition* (New York: Random House).

Florman, S.C. (1987) *The civilized engineer* (New York: St Martin's Press).

Fogarty, T.J. (1995) 'Accountant ethics: A brief examination of neglected sociological dimensions', *Journal of Business Ethics*, 14(2): 103–115.

Fogarty, T.J. (1992) 'Organisational socialisation in accounting firms: A theoretical framework and agenda for future research', *Accounting, Organizations and Society*, 17(2): 129–149.

Forte, A. (2004) 'Business ethics: A study of the moral reasoning of selected business managers and the influence of organizational ethical climate', *Journal of Business Ethics*, 51(2): 167–173.

Friedman, M. (1970) 'The social responsibility of business is to increase profits', *New York Times Magazine*, 13 Sept.

Gray, R.H., Bebbington, J. and McPhail, K. (1994) 'Teaching ethics and the ethics of teaching: Educating for immorality and a possible case for social and environmental accounting', *Accounting Education*, 3: 51–75.

Grenz, S. (1997) *The moral quest: Foundations of Christian ethics* (Illinois: Inter Varsity Press).

Grey, C. (1998) 'On being a professional in a Big Six Firm', *Accounting, Organizations and Society*, 23(5/6): 569–587.

Hafferty, F.W. and Franks, F. (1994) 'The hidden curriculum, ethics teaching and the structure of medical education', *Academic Medicine*, 69(11), November.

Hauptman, R. and Hill, F. (1991) 'Deride, abide or dissent: On the ethics of professional conduct', *Journal of Business Ethics*, 10: 37–44.

Herkert, J.R. and Viscomi, V.B. (1991) 'Introducing professionalism and ethics in the engineering curriculum', *Journal of Professional Issues in Engineering Education and Practice*, 117(3), July.

Hewstone, M., Struebe, W., Codol, J. and Stephenson, G.M. (1993) *Introduction to social psychology* (Oxford: Blackwell).

Huff, B.N. and Kelly, T.P. (1989) 'Quality review and you', *Journal of Accountancy*, 34–40.

Jakubowski, S.T., Chao, P., Huh, S.K. and Maheshwari, S. (2002) 'A cross-country comparison of the codes of professional conduct of certified/chartered accountants', *Journal of Business Ethics*, 35: 111–129.

International Federation of Accountants' Ethics Committee (2005) *The Code of Ethics for Professional Accountants* (New York: International Federation of Accountants).

Jeffrey, C. (1993) 'Ethical development of accounting students, non-accounting business students and liberal arts students', *Issues in Accounting Education*, 8(1): 86–96.

Jensen L.C. and Wygant, S.A. (1990) 'The developmental self-valuing theory: A practical approach for business ethics', *Journal of Business Ethics*, 9: 215–225.

Jones, T.M. (1991) 'Ethical decision making by individuals in organisations: An issue-contingent model', *Academy of Management Review*, 16(2): 366–395.

Karnes, A., Sterner, J., Welker, R. and Wu, F. (1990) 'A bi-cultural comparison of accountants' perceptions of unethical business practices', *Accounting, Auditing & Accountability Journal*, 3(3): 45–62.

Koehn, E. (1991) 'An ethics and professionalism seminar in the civil engineering curriculum', *Journal of Professional Issues in Engineering Education and Practice*, 117(2/April): 96.

Kracher, B., Chatterjee, A. and Lundquist, A. (2002) 'Factors related to the cognitive moral development of business students and business professionals in India and the United States: Nationality, education, sex and gender', *Journal of Business Ethics*, 35: 255–268.

Kronman, A. (1993) *The last lawyer* (Cambridge, MA: Belknap Press).

Kucner, L.K. (1993) 'Professional ethics training for engineering firms', *Journal of Professional Issues in Engineering Education and Practice*, 119(2): 170–181.

Kulik, B.W., O'Fallon, M.J. and Salimath, S.M. (2008) 'Do competitive environments lead to the rise and spread of unethical behavior? Parallels from Enron', *Journal of Business Ethics*, 83(4): 703–723.

Lane, M.S. (1988) 'Pygmalion effect: An issue for business education and ethics', *Journal of Business Ethics*, 7: 223–229.

Larson, R. (1987) 'For the members by the members', *Journal of Accountancy* (October): 116–122.

Lee, T. (1972) 'Company auditing: Concepts & practices', Accountants' Publishing Co. for the Institute of Chartered Accountants of Scotland.

Lehman, C.R. (1988) 'Accounting ethics: Surviving survival of the fittest', in M. Neimark, T. Tinker and B. Merino (eds), *Advances in public interest accounting*, vol. 2 (Greenwich, CT: JAI Press), 71–82.

Leitsch, D.L. (2004) 'Differences in the perceptions of moral intensity in the moral decision process: An empirical examination of accounting students', *Journal of Business Ethics*, 53: 313–323.

Loeb, S.E. (1991) 'The evaluation of outcomes of accounting ethics education', *Journal of Business Ethics*, 10(2): 77–84.

Low, M., Davey, H. and Hooper, K. (2008) 'Accounting scandals, ethical dilemmas and educational challenges', *Critical Perspectives on Accounting*, 19: 222–254.

Lysonski, S. and Gaidis, W. (1991) 'A cross-cultural comparison of the ethics of business students', *Journal of Business Ethics*, 10: 141–150.

McCabe, D.L., Dukerich, J.M. and Duttin, J.E. (1991) 'Context, values and moral dilemmas: Comparing the choices of business students and law school students', *Journal of Business Ethics*, 10(12): 951–960.

McPhail, K.J. (2001) 'The other objective of ethics education: Re-humanising the accounting profession – A study of ethics education in law, engineering, medicine and accounting', *Journal of Business Ethics*, 34: 279–298.

Mayer, J. (1988) 'Themes of social responsibility: A survey of three professional schools', *Journal of Business Ethics*, 7(4): 313–320.

Meising, P. and Preble, J.F. (1985) 'A comparison of five business philosophies', *Journal of Business Ethics*, 4: 465–476.

Merritt, S. (1991) 'Marketing ethics and education: Some empirical findings', *Journal of Business Ethics*, 10: 623–632.

Miles, S.H., Lane, L.W., Bickle, J., Walker, R.M. and Cassel, C.K. (1989) 'Medical ethics education: Coming of age', *Academic Medicine*, 64, December: 705–714.

Parker, M. (1995) 'Autonomy, problem-based learning and the teaching of medical ethics', *Journal of Medical Ethics*, 21: 305–310.

Ponemon, L.A. (1992) 'Ethical reasoning and selection: Socialization in accounting', *Accounting, Organizations and Society*, 17(3/4): 239–258.

Poneman, L.A. (1990) 'Ethical judgements in accounting: A cognitive-development perspective', *Critical Perspectives on Accounting*, 1(2): 191–215.

Radtke, R. (2008) 'Role morality in the accounting profession: How do we compare to physicians and attorneys?', *Journal of Business Ethics*, 70: 279–297.

Reiter, S. (1996) 'The Kohlberg–Gilligan controversy: Lessons for accounting ethics education', *Critical Perspectives on Accounting*, 7: 33–54.

Rest, J. (1983) 'Morality', in P Mussen (ed.), *Manual of child psychology* (New York: Wiley), 556–629.

Rockness, H. and Rockness, J. (2005) 'Legislated ethics: From Enron to Sarbanes-Oxley, the impact on corporate America', *Journal of Business Ethics*, 57: 31–54.

Scharff, M.M. 'Understanding WorldCom's accounting fraud: Did groupthink play a role?', *Journal of Leadership & Organizational Studies*, 11(3): 109–118.

Schlachter, J. (1990) 'Organisational influences on individual ethical behaviour in public accounting', *Journal of Business Ethics*, 9: 839–853.

Serwenek, P.J. (1992) 'Demographic and related differences in ethical views among small businesses', *Journal of Business Ethics*, 11(7): 555–566.

Shafer, W.E., Morris, R.E. and Ketchland, A.A. (2001) 'Effects of personal values on auditors' ethical decisions', *Accounting, Auditing & Accountability Journal*, 254–277.

Sims, R.R. (1992) 'Linking groupthink to unethical behavior in organizations', *Journal of Business Ethics*, 11: 651–662.

Sims, R. and Brinkman, J. (2005) 'Enron ethics (or: culture matters more than codes)', *Journal of Business Ethics*, 45: 243–256.

Smith, M.B.E. (1990) 'Should lawyers listen to philosophers about legal ethics?', *Law and Philosophy*, 9: 67–93.

Smith, A. and Hume, E.C. (2005) 'Linking culture and ethics: A comparison of accountants' ethical belief systems in the individualism/collectivism and power distance contexts', *Journal of Business Ethics*, 62: 209–220.

Stahlberg, D. and Frey, D. (1988) *Angewandle Psychologie: ein Lehebuch* (Psycologi Verlags Union: Munchen).

Stanga, K.G. and Turpen, R.A. (1991) 'Ethical judgements on selected accounting issues: An empirical study', *Journal of Business Ethics*, 10: 739–747.

Tajfel, H. and Fraser, C. (1990) *Introducing social psychology* (Harmondsworth: Penguin Books).

Tansel, B. (1994) 'Outlook for environmental education in 21st century', *Journal of Professional Issues in Engineering Education and Practice*, 120(1): 129–134.

Trevino, L.K. (1992) 'Moral reasoning and business ethics: Implications for research, education and management', *Journal of Business Ethics*, 11: 445–459.

Tyson, T. (1990) 'Believing that everyone else is less ethical: Implications for work behaviour and ethics instruction', *Journal of Business Ethics*, 9: 715–721.

Webb, J. (1996) 'Inventing the good: A prospectus for clinical education and the teaching of legal ethics in England', *The Law Teacher*, 30(3): 270–294.

Weber, J. (1990) 'Measuring the impact of teaching ethics to future managers: A review, assessment and recommendations', *Journal of Business Ethics*, 9(3): 183–190.

Whipple, T.W. and Swords, D.F. (1992) 'Business ethics judgments: A cross-cultural comparison', *Journal of Business Ethics*, 11(9): 671–678.

Williams, P. (2003) 'Recovering accounting as a worthy endeavor', *Critical Perspectives on Accounting*, 15: 513–517.

3

Normative perspectives on accounting ethics

How should accountants behave?

Learning objectives

By the end of this chapter you should be able to:

- Describe and critically evaluate deontological ethics;
- Describe and evaluate the main elements of consequentialist ethics;
- Explain the distinction between rule and act utilitarianism;
- Describe the main arguments associated with virtue ethics;
- Explain the difference between rational and moral sense approaches to ethical dilemmas.

INTRODUCTION

Chapter 2 introduced the descriptive approach to the ethics of accounting, a strand of moral philosophy that addresses the way individuals engage with ethical issues in practice. This empirical literature helps us begin to understand some of the factors that may influence how accountants recognize and resolve ethical dilemmas. However, while understanding accountants' ethical behaviour represents an important advance in the ethical competencies of accountants, it is only the first step. Once we have identified how accountants behave in practice we are then left with the more tricky normative question of whether their behaviour is good or bad. In other words, how can the practice of individual accountants be ethically justified as opposed to simply ethically described? This chapter explores the ethics of accountants from this normative perspective.

Traditionally, moral philosophers have applied themselves to Socrates' proposition,

'How ought I to behave?' In this chapter we will explore the question, how *should* accountants behave? The aim of the chapter is two-fold. First, we want to explore the way accountants are implicitly taught to answer this question in practically all accounting education; second, we also want to contrast this underlying and prevailing perspective with a number of other alternative ways of establishing how one could respond to a particular ethical dilemma.

Two prominent perspectives have developed in response to this normative question. One is based on the idea of duty and is termed *deontological* ethics, the other focuses on consequences and is generally referred to as the *teleological* position. Both these perspectives, along with two other prominent theories, virtue ethics and moral sense theory, will be discussed in this chapter.

As we mentioned in the opening chapter, exploring the ethics of accounting may seem daunting not least because it involves engaging with some moral philosophy literature. As we begin to explore these theories, it might be helpful to think of the task in terms of learning a new language for discussing arguments that we often employ in practice, albeit in a fairly rudimentary fashion. It would be easy to get lost in the complexity, detail and subtle critiques of these philosophical positions so we will limit ourselves to a fairly basic analysis. We don't want you to miss the point of this chapter, which is simply to encourage you to reflect on how accountants are taught to justify their actions in particular and the other possible alternatives they could employ.

DEONTOLOGICAL ETHICS

The main proponent of the deontological position is Immanuel Kant. His position is based on two fundamental principles: *reason* and *respect*. Kant advocated that Socrates' question, how should I behave? should be answered through deductive reasoning. When reason is applied to this dilemma, Kant suggests that we will come to the conclusion that we should act in accordance with universal principles that apply, irrespective of the consequences of the actions. Knowing what to do in any situation will be determined by these universal principles, regardless of the specific context and consequences of the action. Take for example the issue of theft. If we were tempted to steal, Kant suggests that we ask ourselves whether we could accept that our children, neighbours, employees, and so on be allowed to steal at will . . . from us!? We may then conclude that stealing is always wrong, whatever the circumstances. Kant called such a principle, or rule, which must be always obeyed with no exceptions, a *categorical imperative*.

Second, however, Kant argues that we have a duty to treat other individuals as ends in themselves and to act in a way that respects their capacity to act. Kant suggests that anyone who behaves in accordance with both these principles can be described as acting out of duty and therefore acting ethically.

Let's apply Kant's position specifically to accounting. How would the actions of an individual accountant be justified from a Kantian perspective? When an accountant is faced with an ethical dilemma, they would have to consider whether they would like their proposed course of action to be a universal law. However, we also need to consider whether the normal function of the accounting profession can be justified from a Kantian perspective. Does the economic system that accounting serves, be it capitalist, command or some mixture of the two, treat individuals as means or ends?

Kant's position is generally criticized for being too general to be helpful because it ignores the specifics of individual situations. Take for example the case of a young mother in intensive care who has been involved in a bad car accident. She asks the doctor about her son who was also in the car. According to Kant a lie is wrong because of the kind of thing it is, so the doctor would be obliged to tell the woman that her son is dead, despite the possibility that the shock might send her into cardiac arrest. However, most people would accept that it is wrong to lie under oath about the circumstances of some medical negligence if the woman was administered the wrong drug and went into cardiac arrest. Some people would therefore suggest that Kant's position is too inflexible and that the goodness or badness of telling a lie, for example, depends on the circumstances. Others would criticize Kant for grounding moral decision-making exclusively in reason; however, we shall return to this point later in the chapter.

John Rawls' theory of justice represents an attempt to advance the deontological position further. Rawls suggests that while, as individuals, we might be able to see the logic of the categorical imperative and agree that it is important to treat other human beings with respect, we need some help in proceduralizing this principle. His solution comes in the form of a '*veil of ignorance*'. According to Rawls, deciding on a course of action that respects other individuals requires that I put myself in '*the original position*', behind a veil of ignorance. From an original position of equality, not knowing what or who I might become, I am therefore compelled to respond to Socrates' proposition, by placing myself in the position of everyone affected by the decision, or at least each category of individual, since I do not know whether I am likely to become one of these people.

Kant's deontological response to the question of how one ought to behave is thus based on deductive reasoning. However, Rawls' complementary position obviously requires quite a different kind of moral capacity. It takes quite a well-developed moral imagination to be able to place oneself behind the veil of ignorance or in the

Box 3.1 Broken promises

Lee is an accountant who has been looking for a new job for some time. He was eventually offered, and accepted, a post with Company A. A few days later, he was offered a much better job with a higher salary at Company B. What should Lee do?

The business world needs to operate in an atmosphere of trust. For Kant, if promise-breaking were a universal law, no one would be able to trust anyone else. To break a promise when expecting others to keep their promises is to make an exception of yourself; this is a double standard. The same rule should apply to everybody equally, and so, according to Kant, Lee should keep his promise to Company A.

circumstances of each individual who might be affected by your decisions. And, even if we were able to do this, how do we mediate between the many different perspectives? It would also seem quite difficult to translate Rawls' position into a set of institutional arrangements.

TELEOLOGICAL ETHICS

A standard distinction within the normative literature is generally drawn between deontological ethics on the one hand and teleological ethical perspectives on the other. While a deontological position focuses on the rightness or wrongness of an action in itself, a teleological position establishes the morality of a particular action by reference to the consequences of that action. Take the example of theft discussed earlier. From a deontological perspective theft may be considered morally wrong because of the kind of action it is (i.e. it contravenes the categorical imperative because we cannot will it as a universal law), regardless of whether or not the act produces good consequences, for example in the case of Robin Hood. By contrast, teleologists contend that the rightness or wrongness of an action can be established by reference to its consequences. Let's apply this type of moral thinking to an accounting dilemma. Consider the situation where a company director has deliberately manipulated the accounts but only because there is a liquidity problem that she believes will be rectified in the following one or two accounting periods. As an accountant, would you ignore the misrepresentation in an attempt to save the company and its employees? Consequentialist theory is based on an important distinction between good actions and the goal. In other words, determining whether a particular action is right or wrong is based on the consequences of that action in relation to some predetermined goal. Suppose you are the financial controller of a medium-sized clothing manufacturer. The company is trying to deciding whether to outsource part of the production process to Indonesia. If the goal is financial growth, the

Box 3.2 Rawls and accounting

A company accountant has realized that there is a material error in the company's financial statements which are just about to be published. Should the accountant demand that the accounts are restated?

According to Rawls the accountant should imagine themselves in the original position, not knowing whether they would become a shareholder, a director or a partner in the firm. Rawls' position can also be applied to the function of accounting more generally. What if the accountant were to place themselves in the original position, not knowing whether they would become an employee of a multinational working in a factory in Bangladesh, an accountant or the company director? What changes would they require in accounting practice?

common assumption underpinning virtually all financial and management accounting and market-based economics, then only a certain set of consequences are relevant. If, however, the goal is some other more obscure aspiration like fairness, then we would need to take into consideration a broader range of consequences. The questions are, how is the goal defined, who defines it and what is the goal of accounting? These are not trivial questions.

This distinction between the action and the goal highlights an important source of criticism of the consequentialist position. This criticism is based on an apparent contradiction in that it allows a course of action to be inconsistent with the goal. Suppose I am specifically concerned about the environment. Should I exemplify the kind of life that I think we need to live in order for the planet to have a sustainable future or should I spend my time travelling the world trying to persuade others of my concern, even though it is environmentally unfriendly? The consequentialist position might allow me to travel extensively by aeroplane polluting the environment in order, for example, to lobby the European Parliament against the development of regional airports.

While deontological ethics is often criticized for producing rules that are too general to be helpful in specific ethical dilemmas, the teleological position is criticized first, because identifying every possible consequence of an action is impossible, and second, more importantly, because it can be used to justify some heinous actions. Let's take a contemporary example: suppose a terrorist has planted a bomb somewhere in London. A consequentialist position could be used to justify torturing the single individual in order to save the lives of numerous others.

Box 3.3 Al Gore

Al Gore, a US politician and campaigner on environmental issues, recently won an Oscar for his movie *An Inconvenient Truth*. The movie looks at global warming, and calls for people the world over to change the way they live so that they can have less impact on the environment.

He attracted a lot of criticism of his own lifestyle – in particular, for his own personal large energy usage, and that of his family. The following is fairly typical of posts from just one of the many web-based message boards on this topic:

> Al gore best epitomizes the paradox of the environmentally sensitive 'celebrity': how do you save the environment while indulging your right to ridiculous mansions, private jets, larger and larger yachts, etc? Can a few solar panels make up for all the excesses? Gore's message seems to suggest that the 200-foot yacht might be okay so long as it's equipped with hybrid motors and all the ghetto dwellers are persuaded to switch to funny light bulbs.

Rule and act utilitarianism

We will discuss a form of consequentalist argument known as utilitarianism in Part II of the text when we consider how decisions are routinely made within accounting practice; however, at this point we would like to introduce an important distinction that is often made between the consequences of a specific individual action and the consequences of a general rule, or practice. John Rawls makes an important distinction between what is generally termed rule utilitarianism and act utilitarianism. Just think about the distinction in terms of consequences for the time being. This is an important and useful analytical distinction. For example, John Hooker (2007) draws on these different levels to explore the difference between the ethics of professions and the ethical obligations of professionals. Specifically, he explores the ethical obligations of individuals in relation to the institutions of which they are a part. Professions create expectations in lots of different ways and Professor Hooker's point is that professional obligation then involves living up to those expectations. For example, you wouldn't normally expect your bank manager to start giving you advice on the mole on your forehead when you go to enquire about re-mortgaging your house. You probably wouldn't let her examine the swelling in your left ankle either. These might seem rather silly examples, but they do highlight a number of interesting dilemmas in relation to public expectations and the boundaries of professional jurisdiction. Most would assume that the function of a profession involves more than saving us time and helping us quickly establish which experts we can trust to apply their knowledge in the way their professional status implies they would.

Professor Hooker suggests that once public expectations are established there is nothing much for professionals to do than do it and this does not involve ethics. Professional institutions serve a social function and when society has decided what that function is to be, we are obliged just to do it. The inference of this argument is that professional ethics is about performing this role well and therefore not about

Box 3.4 Dirty Harry and Jack Bauer

In *Dirty Harry*, the 1971 film by director Don Siegel, a police detective tortures a sadistic homicidal madman so he will reveal where he has buried – alive – a teenage girl before she suffocates to death. Audiences cheered, approving of the message that a girl had been saved by the torture of a vicious killer, and the actor who played the self-righteous torturer, Clint Eastwood, became an immediate superstar.

A more modern equivalent can be seen in *24* – an exciting and hugely popular television drama that in each series shows one crisis-packed day in 24 one-hour 'real time' episodes. In each series, the US government tries to foil one elaborate terrorist plot after another. The hero of each of the series is agent Jack Bauer. Bauer is fearless, courageous and honourable. He will also torture a suspected terrorist.

ethics proper. Once the rules of the game have been established, we are obliged to play by the rules. Yet for many, the action of determining whether or not to apply the expectation is not ancillary to professional practice, it is professional practice!

This is obviously a contentious area of professions and ethics. It opens up the question of individual professional judgement and where the boundaries of such judgement lie. Very often the tensions associated with these boundaries are related to conflicts between these different levels. For example, the public expectation is that pharmacists dispense medicines, but some of the most difficult professional dilemmas that individual pharmacists face relate to the point at which this expectation should no longer apply. Expressed in general terms, the dilemma is, at what point should the individual professional question the general rule that provides the institution with its legitimacy. As John Rawls (1955) says in the introduction to his famous paper, it draws out the distinction between justifying a certain practice and justifying a particular action that comes within the boundaries of that practice. Who should decide what the rules of the professional game are? And when they have been determined, how do they evolve? And when is it legitimate to question and even break those rules? The famous legal philosopher H.L.A. Hart once wrote about this dilemma in terms of proles and archangels. When can we behave like archangels, and say no, the normal rules don't apply in this particular situation?

VIRTUE-BASED APPROACHES TO INDIVIDUAL ACTION

The deontological and consequentialist positions outlined above are generally termed principle-based approaches to the problem of how one should act. However, virtue theorists provide an alternative position to these principle-based approaches. Virtue theorists contend that while it may be important to be able to articulate certain moral principles, in practice virtue is more important than abstract philosophizing (MacIntyre 1982; Collier 1995; Whetstone 2001). Hartman (1998) comments,

> virtue ethicists deny that making moral decisions is a matter of calculation as principle-based theories, particularly utilitarian ones imply . . . Even if we can describe an ethical person as one whose acts conform to certain principles, it does not follow, that the best way to teach Smith to be ethical is to give her principles to follow.

The concern of virtue theorists is that while an individual may adhere to a set of principles, this does not necessarily imply that these principles are an integral part of their character. For example, while an accountant may enact a certain principle, this may be because of routine self-interest or some other ulterior motive. It is another thing entirely to say that an accountant *is* honest. Hartman (1998) explains that the virtuous person is *inclined* to do the right thing. Virtue is therefore not about calculation, it's a matter of predisposition.

Proponents of virtue theory therefore contend that virtue is an element of character (Hartman 1998; Shaw 1997; Whetstone 2001). They also suggest that specific virtues arise from, are given meaning by, and are sustained by the broader narratives

Box 3.5 Independence and the auditor

One of the most important aspects of company auditing is that the auditor must be independent from the company being audited. We saw in Chapter 2 that the International Federation of Accountants (IFAC) has issued a 'Code of Ethics for Professional Accountants'. Much of this Code deals with practices to ensure that the auditor is independent. It can be argued that it does not matter how many guides to best practice exist, auditor independence requires an individual to be predisposed to being honest.

Tom Lee, in his classic book *Company Auditing* published in 1972, wrote:

> Independence is an elusive quality which accountants have found rather hard to define in relation to the work of the company auditor. Basically, it is an attitude of mind which does not allow the viewpoints and conclusions of its possessor to become reliant on or subordinate to the influences and pressures of conflicting interests. The auditor must maintain a continual awareness of these influences and pressures in order to maintain his objectiveness and impartiality in all aspects of his work. Thus, independence in this sense is a feature of the professional integrity of the auditor – part of the general characteristic of human honesty.

within which the individual is situated (MacIntyre 1982). Hartman (1998), for example, comments, 'a good life is an integrated life, one committed to a consistent set of values, principles, projects, people and in many cases to a community, that can give it meaning'. Francis (1990; see also Libby and Thorne 2004) brings virtue theory directly to bear on accounting practice. He says, 'I want to pose what I regard as the most important contemporary question facing accountants: Is accounting practice after virtue? That is, do accountants seek virtue and if so, how do they achieve it?' The literature on virtue theory provides a theoretical basis for beginning to explore some of the idealized characteristics often associated with accounting professionals and the broader narratives that sustain these values.

REASON AND MORAL SENSE THEORISTS

The discussion of inclination in the virtue theory literature hints at a broader debate over the way individuals should be encouraged to respond to ethical dilemmas. On the one hand some theorists suggest that reason is the only appropriate basis for ethical decision-making. However, other theorists contend that something more is required (McNaughton 1988).

Immanuel Kant, whose work we introduced above, represents one of the most celebrated proponents of the rational approach to ethics. Kant sought to ground ethics in the very nature of reason and attempted to develop universally applicable moral principles based solely on the application of reason (Mackie 1977; MacIntyre 1982). The famous English philosopher John Locke similarly contended that morality could be demonstrated like a mathematical proof (Macintyre 1998). However, the famous eighteenth-century Scottish thinker David Hume argued that reason merely furnished the individual with the facts of the matter and that the actual act of making a moral decision required something more than reason. The Earl of Shaftsbury (Macintyre 1998) and Francis Hutcheson suggested that moral distinctions depend on a moral sense rather than reason. Macintyre (1998) explains that Shaftsbury represented this sense as an *inner eye* that was able to distinguish right from wrong. He describes Shaftesbury's argument as follows,

> A moral judgement is thus the expression of a response of feeling to some property of an action . . . just as an aesthetic judgement is the expression of just such a response to the properties of shapes and figures.
>
> (Macintyre 1998)

The theorization of the importance and role of moral sense has come a long way from Shaftsbury's *inner eye*. The fundamental role of empathy towards, and the core responsibility for, others has been the subject of extensive theoretical exploration both by Zygmunt Bauman (1996; 1993) and Emmanuel Levinas (Hand 1989), whose work we shall explore in the following chapter. A more practical analysis of what this inner eye might entail has been developed through the notion of Social and Emotional Learning (SEL) (Gardiner 1983) or emotional intelligence (see McPhail 2004). Proponents of SEL suggest that there are different categories of intelligence and that the qualities associated with emotional intelligence, for example emotional self-awareness, an awareness of the emotions of others and the imaginative capability to enter into the feelings of others, can be taught in the same way that competence in deductive reasoning, or logic, can also be developed (Goleman 1995; Cohen 1999).

SUMMARY

The normative literature contributes towards our understanding of the ethics of individual accountants in a number of ways. First, it provides us with an insight into how accountants are routinely taught how to behave. Conventional models of accounting practice are based on the teleological position outlined above, and in particular, a narrow form of teleological analysis that focuses primarily on the *financial* consequences of a proposed course of action (we will explore financial utilitarianism in more detail in Chapter 6 when we explore the ethics of accounting practice).

These consequences are established through reason. For example, investment appraisal, product mix, the location of the production function, pension plan provision, the viability of a particular division, and so on, are all decisions with which accountants may be routinely involved. They are all quite complex ethical dilemmas but accountants are taught to resolve them, in part at least, by looking to the financial consequences of the proposed decision. They are not taught, for example, to put

Box 3.6 Circle time

Circle time is a group activity in which any number of people sit down together with the purpose of furthering understanding of themselves and of one another. It is used increasingly in schools, partly to help address behavioural issues such as bullying. It is a space in which children can learn the skills they need to thrive in life, such as effective communication, emotional literacy, anger management, peer mediation and conflict resolution. It's not about coercion, reprimand or correction. It is about discussion, reflection, emotional understanding, personal empowerment, personal identity and making connections.

While circle time may be encountered widely in schools, it is not a feature of the accounting or business community. Accountants facing ethical dilemmas are unlikely to have a group of peers with whom they can openly share and discuss their problems. The air of openness and understanding fostered during circle time is unlikely to be found in the workplace. As an example, the following is included in the code of ethics for a large US tyre manufacturer, which must be signed by all employees:

> I will report any suspected or known violations of this Code of Ethics to the principal compliance officer of the Company.

Box 3.7 Thalidomide

The drug Thalidomide was marketed by its producers Chemie Grunenthal as completely safe. It was used in the treatment of morning sickness. However, many of the women who took the drug gave birth to severely disabled babies. Here is a quote from one Thalidomide victim who comes to speak to our ethics class.

> After two and a half years of tests, drugs, investigative operations and various examinations, my ultimate desire – becoming a mother – was realized on November 5th 1996. Bonding with my baby commenced from the moment I gazed at my first scan picture taken eight weeks after conception. I knew that the birth of my baby would be very different to my own arrival in September 1962. Thalidomide was in the headlines and many expectant mothers were filled with dread. Despite my mother's urgent pleas to see her newborn baby, I was whisked away immediately whilst the doctors tried to decide how to break the devastating news to her. Something was not quite right with the baby. Over 24 hours later she finally had the opportunity to unwrap the blanket and study me. She touched the tiny malformed arms, shortened to elbow length, the three fingers on flipper hands and the legs

shortened at the femur, and said a silent prayer. 'Please God, if this child is going to suffer any pain, then please take her now before I grow to love her any more'. Thirty-four years later, I presented her with her first grandchild, Lois.

Of course, even those who knew me well enquired as to how I would manage. The prospect was not at all daunting. I had coped with everything else life had put my way, including finding employment, passing a driving test and living independently. As with so many other areas of my life, I tried to plan ahead of the baby's arrival for things I believed I might have difficulty with. These included the design and construction of an enormous bean bag cushion which I could place around my waist whilst seated on the floor. This provided a safe and comfortable raised surface from which to feed the baby. This cushion was well worth the valuable space it took up within the house, providing a means of cuddling her to me, and a safe sleeping environment for her during naps.

I probably experienced fewer problems than many other able-bodied first time mothers. People had enquired before Lois' arrival what I wanted. My response would be 'A good baby who sleeps a lot', and this wish appears to have been granted. I never cease to be overwhelmed at how my child continues to adapt to me. At six months she would cling to me like a limpet if I carried her. At twenty months, she could confidently climb up and down the stairs. She climbs up and down from her highchair, straps herself into her pushchair and climbs into her car seat. She seems to have inherited my strong will and independence.

Apart from family support, I receive no help with caring for my baby. Lois goes to a child minder for one and a half days a week whilst I work. I pay privately for a home help to assist me with the household chores, leaving me more time to enjoy my baby. The days are harder and longer since Lois was born. I would not want them any other way. Feeling her squeeze my shoulders when I first lift her out of her cot in the morning provides me with all the energy I need to deal with the hard day ahead.

Do some research online and see if you can find out how much an arm was worth in the compensation received by UK Thalidomide victims.

themselves behind a veil of ignorance in the original position, although from the discussion of the justification of practices, as opposed to individual actions (remember rule and act utilitarianism?), hopefully you can see that there is an argument why we may not want individual accountants to be making decisions in this way. Accountants are therefore exposed to a particular, teleological, normative ethic during their degree programmes and professional training (Gray *et al.* 1994; McPhail 1999). Financial consequentialism provides the ethical basis for everyday accounting practice and may also influence the resolution of specific ethical dilemmas.

While the normative literature allows us to label the prevailing ethical basis of accounting practice, it also highlights that there are a number of other possible alternatives that could be employed. We have only looked at two other perspectives; however, there are many others. How would accountant practice differ if it was based on a Confucian, Christian or Muslim ethic, for example? Would there be any ethical conflicts here?

Finally, an awareness of the normative moral philosophy literature encourages us to reflect on whether the teleological position is in fact the most appropriate mode of ethical thinking for accountants. There is a considerable literature that critiques the making of ethical decisions which affect other human beings, the environment and future generations solely on the basis of financial consequences (see for example Carson 1991; Daly and Cobb 1989). These critiques highlight that the ethical decisions which accountants make take place within a context. The ethical decisions that accountants make matter because they have an impact on other people. It is precisely this matter that the third strand of moral philosophy literature addresses. This literature is explored in some detail in the following chapter.

QUESTIONS

1 Describe and critically evaluate the normative ethics on which accounting practice is based.
2 Critically discuss whether you think that the profession of accounting is based on virtues.
3 If ethics is based on emotion and empathy as Shaftsbury and Hutcheson implied,

Box 3.8 Islamic accounting

Islamic accounting is an alternative accounting system which aims to provide users with information enabling them to operate businesses and organizations according to Shari'ah, or Islamic law.

Both conventional and Islamic accounting provide information and define how that information is measured, valued, recorded and communicated. Conventional accounting concentrates on identifying economic events and transactions, while Islamic accounting must identify socio-economic and religious events and transactions. These are measured in both financial and non-financial terms and the information is used to ensure Islamic organizations of all types adhere to Shari'ah law and achieve the objectives promoted by Islam. Islamic accounting is therefore not only concerned with money.

Shari'ah prohibits interest-based income and also gambling, so part of what Islamic accounting tries to do is help ensure companies do not harm others while making money and achieve an equitable allocation and distribution of wealth, not just among shareholders of a specific company but also among society in general. As with conventional accounting, this is not always achieved in practice, as can be seen from the wide variances in wealth among the populations of some Muslim countries.

then to what extent does accounting either help or hinder ethical decision-making?

4 In this chapter we have focused on quite Western justifications for individual behaviour. Conduct some research on the Internet, briefly explain one of the following ethical perspectives and explain where they are similar to or differ from the perspectives we discussed above.
   a Indian ethics
   b Buddhist ethics
   c Chinese ethics

5 Explain the difference between act and rule utilitarianism and critically discuss the circumstances in which you think it is appropriate for professional accountants to deviate from expected practice.

RESOURCES

Films

General ethical dilemmas

A Simple Plan (1998), director Sam Raimi, starring Bill Paxton, Bridget Fonda and Billy Bob Thornton. An accountant finds $4 million dollars in a crashed plane.

Global warming

An Inconvenient Truth (2006), documentary film on global warming by Al Gore and David Guggenheim; see also associated book (Gore 2006).

Torture

Dirty Harry (1971), director Don Siegal.
24 (several seasons) (2002 onwards), directors Joel Surnow and Jon Cassar.

Websites

Social and emotional learning

The Collaborative for Social and Emotional Learning:
<www.casel.org>.

Thalidomide case

BBC Inside Out, 'Thalidomide – 50 years on', available online at: <www.bbc.co.uk/insideout/content/articles/2008/04/18/london_thalidomide_s13_w8_feature.shtml>.

Thalidomide UK: <www.thalidomideuk.com/>.

The Thalidomide Trust: <www.thalidomide.org.uk/>.

iTunes podcasts

Lectures on Professional Ethics, Mark Vopat, PhD, Youngstown State University (Mark Vopat provides a series of lectures on Professional Ethics; you may wish to listen to 'Moral theories' and 'Professional ethics, ch5, Lying and lies to the sick and dying' at this stage).

READING

Accounting, business and normative perspectives

Bowie, N.E. and Dunfee, T.W. (2002) 'Confronting morality in markets', *Journal of Business Ethics*, 38: 381–393.

Drake, J.M. and Schlachter, J.T. (2007) 'A virtue-ethics analysis of supply chain collaboration', *Journal of Business Ethics*, 82: 851–864.

Lehman, G. (1995) 'A legitimate concern for environmental accounting', *Critical Perspectives on Accounting*, 6: 393–412.

Melé, D. (2005) 'Ethical education in accounting: Integrating rules, values and virtues', *Journal of Business Ethics*, 57: 97–109.

Micewski, E.R. and Troy, C. (2007) 'Business ethics: Deontologically revisited', *Journal of Business Ethics*, 72: 17–25.

Misiewicz, K.M. (2007) 'The normative impact of CPA firms, professional organizations, and state boards on accounting ethics education', *Journal of Business Ethics*, 70: 15–21.

Satava, D., Caldwell, C. and Richards, L. (2006) 'Ethics and the auditing culture: Rethinking the foundation of accounting and auditing', *Journal of Business Ethics*, 64: 271–284.

Deontology and business ethics

Bowie, N. (1999) *Business ethics: A Kantian perspective* (Oxford: Blackwell).

Bowie, N. (1998) 'A Kantian theory of meaningful work', *Journal of Business Ethics*, 17(9–10): 1083–1092.

Bowie, N. and Dunfee, T.W. (2002) 'Confronting morality in markets', *Journal of Business Ethics*, 38: 381–393.

Ladkin, D. (2006) 'When deontology and utilitarianism aren't enough: How Heidegger's notion of "dwelling" might help organizational leaders resolve ethical issues', *Journal of Business Ethics*, 65: 87–98.

Micewski, E.R. and Troy, C. (2007) 'Business ethics deontologically revisited', *Journal of Business Ethics*, 17(9–10): 17–25.

Ethics, emotion and emotional intelligence

Gardener, H. (1983) *Frames of mind: The theory of multiple intelligences* (New York: Basic Books).

Kuhn, J.W. (1998) 'Emotion as well as reason: Getting students beyond "interpersonal accountability" ', *Journal of Business Ethics*, 17: 295–308.

Lurie, Y. (2004) 'Humanizing business through emotions: On the role of emotions in ethics', *Journal of Business Ethics*, 49: 1–11.

McPhail, K.J. (2004) 'An emotional response to the state of accounting education: Developing accounting students' emotional intelligence', *Critical Perspectives on Accounting*, 15(4–5): 629–648.

Wilson, J.Q. (1993) *The moral sense* (New York: The Free Press).

Important work by Francis Hutcheson

Hutcheson, F. (1999) *Essay on the nature and conduct of passions and affections: With illustrations on the moral sense* (Manchester: Clinamen Press).

Important works by and on Immanuel Kant

Kant, I. (2003) *The moral law: Groundwork of the metaphysic of morals*, trans. H.J. Paton (London: Routledge).

—— (1996) *Critique of practical reason*, trans. W. Pluhar (Indianapolis: Hackett).

—— (1996) *Metaphysics of morals*, trans. M. Megregor (Cambridge: Cambridge University Press).

Seung, T.K. (2007) *Kant: Guide for the perplexed* (London: Continuum).

Important works by John Rawls

Rawls, J. (1999) *A theory of justice*, rev. edn (Oxford: Oxford University Press).

—— (1955) 'Two concepts of rules', *The Philosophical Review*, 3: 3–32.

Virtue theory

Francis, J.R. (1990) 'After virtue? Accounting as a moral and discursive practice', *Accounting, Auditing & Accountability Journal* 13(3): 5–17.

Hartman, E.M. (1998) 'The role of character in business ethics', *Business Ethics Quarterly*, 8(3): 547–559.

Libby, T. and Thorne, L. (2004) 'The identification and categorization of auditors' virtue', *Business Ethics Quarterly*, 14(3): 479–498.

Shaw, B. (1997) 'Sources of virtue: The market and the community', *Business Ethics Quarterly*, 7(1): 33–50.

REFERENCES

Bauman, Z. (1996) *Modernity and the Holocaust* (Oxford: Blackwell).

Bauman, Z. (1993) *Postmodern ethics* (Oxford: Blackwell).

Carson, R. (1991) *Silent spring* (London: Penguin Books).

Cohen, J. (ed.) (1999) *Educating minds and hearts, social and emotional learning and the passage into adolescence* (Teachers New York: College Press).

Collier, J. (1995) 'The virtuous organization', *Business Ethics: A European Review*, 4(3): 143–149.

Daly, H.E. and Cobb, J.B. (1989) *For the common good* (London: Merlin Press).

Francis, J.R. (1990) 'After virtue? Accounting as a moral and discursive practice', *Accounting, Auditing & Accountability Journal* 13(3): 5–17.

Gardiner, H. (1983) *Frames of mind: The theory of multiple intelligences* (New York: Basic Books).

Goleman, D. (1995) *Emotional intelligence* (New York: Bantam Books).

Gore, A. (2006) *An inconvenient truth: The planetary emergency of global warming and what we can do about it* (London: Bloomsbury).

Gray, R.H., Bebbington, J. and McPhail, K.J. (1994) 'Teaching ethics and the ethics of teaching: Educating for immorality and a possible case for social and environmental accounting', *Accounting Education*, 3: 51–75.

Hand, S. (1989) *The Levinas reader* (Oxford: Blackwell)

Hartman, E.M. (1998) 'The role of character in business ethics', *Business Ethics Quarterly*, 8(3): 547–559.

Hooker, J. (2007) 'Professional ethics: Does it matter which hat we wear?', *Journal of Business Ethics Education*, 4: 103–112.

Libby, T. and Thorne, L. (2004) 'The identification and categorization of auditors' virtue', *Business Ethics Quarterly*, 14(3): 479–498.

MacIntyre, A. (1982) *A short history of ethics: A history of moral philosophy from the Homeric age to the twentieth century* (London: Routledge and Kegan Paul).

Mackie, J.L. (1977) *Ethics: Inventing right and wrong* (Harmondsworth: Penguin).

McNaughton, D. (1988) *Moral vision: An introduction to ethics* (Oxford: Blackwell).

McPhail, K.J. (2004) 'An emotional response to the state of accounting education: Developing accounting students' emotional intelligence', *Critical Perspectives on Accounting*, 15(4–5): 629–648.

McPhail, K.J. (1999) 'The threat of ethical accountants: An application of Foucault's concept of ethics to accounting education and some thoughts on ethically educating for the other', *Critical Perspectives on Accounting*, 10: 833–866.

Rawls, J. (1955) 'Two concepts of rules', *The Philosophical Review*, 64(1): 3–32.

Schlachter, J. (1990) 'Organisational influences on individual ethical behaviour in public accounting', *Journal of Business Ethics*, 9: 839–853.

Shaw, B. (1997) 'Sources of virtue: The market and the community', *Business Ethics Quarterly*, 7(1): 33–50.

Whetstone, J.T. (2001) 'How virtue fits within business ethics', *Journal of Business Ethics*, 33: 101–114.

4

Political moral philosophy and accounting ethics

Why should accountants be good?

Learning objectives

By the end of this chapter you should be able to:

- Describe a third stream of ethical enquiry that links individual ethical behaviour to the idea of community;
- Explain Jean-Jacques Rousseau's notion of civil society and the idea of a social contract;
- Critically discuss the idea of human rights;
- Explain Emmanuel Levinas' phenomenological approach to ethics and outline how his perspective contributes towards our understanding of accounting ethics.

INTRODUCTION

In Chapters 2 and 3 we have explored two fairly fundamental questions about ethics and accounting. First, what kind of factors affect the way we, as accountants, respond to ethical issues in practice and second, when faced with an ethical dilemma, what should we as accountants do? These are both tricky questions; however, they are perhaps not quite as difficult as the third question we want to explore in this chapter. Up until now we have assumed that behaving in an ethical way is good. However, this is actually quite a big assumption and one that requires some further investigation. This kind of exploration of why it is important for individuals to behave ethically lies at the heart of a third broad strand of moral philosophy that we are going to call political moral philosophy.

We would like to start this chapter by asking you to reflect on two questions. First, spend a little time reflecting on the question: why should I behave ethically? Now spend a little time thinking about a second question: why, *as an accountant*, should I behave ethically? Were your reasons any different? As accountants, it might be possible to respond to the second question by simply stating that my professional body says that I should behave in a particular way and if I don't I run the danger of being hauled before a disciplinary committee. Or, as we explored towards the end of the previous chapter, we could respond by saying, society has a certain set of expectations of accountants and because I signed up to play the accountant's role in society then I am duty bound to behave in a way that conforms to those expectations. Or perhaps if we were being a little cynical we could respond that it is in the best long-term interests both for me as an individual accountant and the accounting profession to behave ethically. Each of these responses, however, seems just a little unsatisfactory. The material that we shall cover in this chapter pushes the debate beyond the mere self-interest of the individual accountant or the interests of the profession and focuses on the broader socio-political basis of ethical behaviour.

However, before we outline the structure of the chapter we want to say a few words about the messy distinction between some of the ideas we discussed in the previous chapter and the content of this chapter. We commented at the beginning of the book that the chapter divisions are a little artificial and that the discipline of moral philosophy, like most other subjects, and also like the ethical dilemmas with which we are faced, can't be neatly categorized. You may recollect that we discussed John Rawls' idea of the original position in the previous chapter. We discussed this idea under the heading of normative perspectives: how should I behave as an individual? However, it would be equally valid, (perhaps more so) to discuss Rawls' thesis not as an idea that I could employ in order to determine my personal behaviour, but rather as an aid to policy development, in other words as a way of thinking about how we should live together in a fair and equitable way. Perhaps we could translate this into the accounting sphere by thinking not in terms of the original position as a guiding principle for the accountant's personal code of ethics, but rather as a guiding principle for the development of the social practice of accounting. For example, try to think about how you would go about developing a standard for pensions based on substance over form, then think about how different the standard would be if it was developed along the lines of the original position, from behind a veil of ignorance. We will return to this relationship between ethics and policy later in the chapter.

This chapter briefly reviews some of the broader politically oriented moral philosophy literature in order to develop further insights into the ethics of accounting, or at least highlight the fundamental questions that a burgeoning ethical understanding of accounting should invoke. This literature can be split into two main strands.[1] A more traditional school of thought that draws on a rich vain of thinking that can be traced from Jean-Jacques Rousseau and his conceptualization of the 'social contract', through the likes of John Locke and David Hume whom we mentioned in the previous chapter. This particularly influential tradition provides the basis of the liberal democratic political system in the West. So right at the start of the chapter we want to make a connection between ethics and how we structure and organize ourselves as a society. However, a second, more post-structuralist or postmodern literature provides a counterpoint to this history of political democracy. The analytic provided in this literature focuses on the way in which power may operate through moral systems sometimes to work against liberal ideals. We will introduce the first strand of literature in this chapter and the second in the following chapter. The aim of both chapters is to broaden the kinds of ethical questions normally addressed by accountants when they consider professional ethics.

ROUSSEAU AND COMMUNITIES: OR WHO AM I?

This section begins with the work of a famous Swiss philosopher Jean-Jacques Rousseau. Rousseau, who is probably best known for his work on the social contract, was concerned not so much with specific individual action, as with the more fundamental question, 'who am I?' This may seem like a strange place to start a discussion about why individuals should behave ethically; however, try to answer this for yourself. Who are you? Here are some of the things we came up with. I am Doreen's brother; John's friend and colleague; I come from Glasgow and I am Scottish. Maybe you came up with similar types of responses. The point is that these kinds of observation locate us within a network of relationships or within communities: familial; academic; urban and national communities. This is precisely Rousseau's point. It is this fact, the fact that we are members of communities, along with the subsequent conclusion that our actions impinge on other individuals: my family, my friends, the people who live in my street or my fellow countrymen and women, that makes the question, 'how should I behave', of any relevance.

At the heart of Rousseau's perspective is a concern that people view themselves not as isolated individuals but rather as citizens, members of a group with concomitant responsibilities towards other individuals but also general civic responsibilities towards the group as a whole. He contended that, '*men* have to learn how, . . . they can act not as private individuals, as men, but rather as citizens' (Macintyre 1998). To give you a sense of how influential Rousseau's thinking has been and to bring things a little more up to date, consider the following article in the UN Declaration of Human Rights. Article 29 states, 'Everyone has duties to the community in which alone the free and full development of his personality is possible'. Sound familiar?

Let's pause at this point and try to connect Rousseau's perspective back to the ethics of accounting. Rousseau's picture of the individual embedded within a community of others, with civic responsibilities to that community, raises some challenging questions for accountants. For a start it raises the question of how accountants perceive their own professional community, and also the extent to which both the function of accounting within society and the actions of individual accountants might be construed as serving broader civic objectives, questions to which we shall return in the second part of the book when we look at the nature of professions and the practice of accounting. How would you respond to the question: how does accounting contribute towards the development of society? Try to think about this in terms of the function that professional bodies like accountants, lawyers and doctors, for example, serve within a society as well as the function of accounting within the prevailing free-market system. Believe it or not it is possible to argue both sides of the coin on this particular question. In fact much of our accounting education is based on the implicit assumption that accounting does contribute towards the development of society because it maximizes financial utility and helps to sustain a free-market liberal economic system. Adam Smith is interpreted within this kind of argument, we think somewhat erroneously, as simply saying that in fact it is the pursuit of self-interest that, through the invisible hand of the market, leads to the flourishing of society. Of course this is debatable, yet from our experience at least we would make two observations: first, both accounting students and practitioners don't seem to be terribly aware that the practice of accounting is based on some quite fundamental moral assumptions about how it contributes towards society. Second, despite all the post-Enron attempts to address the ethics education deficit within the profession, the majority of accounting degree and professional qualification programmes continue to fail miserably to furnish accountants with the capabilities of critically reflecting both on the extent to which these assumptions are valid reflections of what really goes on within the economy and also on whether they, even if they are valid, cohere with our own personal values, or what to do if we discover that there is a conflict. We will discuss these issues in more detail in the second part of the text.

Rights and duties

Rousseau's perspective is often associated with a related discussion of individual rights and duties. The connection between Rousseau and rights lies in the assumption that perhaps the best way to promote and sustain communities is to recognize that members of the community have certain rights. These concepts are often (though some would say erroneously) assumed to represent two opposite but complementary aspects of ethical relationships. The idea of a right relates to the way an individual can expect to be treated by others, including the right to be left alone! A duty refers to our obligations towards others. While we may all be familiar with the terminology of human rights, there is considerable debate as to how the idea of a right should be construed. For example, when we discuss rights are we talking about the right to do something or the right to receive something? In some instances the former might be permissive, in the sense that I may; the latter, however, is perhaps more related to entitlement. I may, as a parent, have a right to withdraw my child from state education and school them at home instead, but am I entitled to have a child, in the sense that I should have an entitlement to free fertility treatment on the NHS? The nature of individual rights and how they are to be protected is therefore quite complex.

Within financial accounting, the practice of providing a set of financial accounts is based on an entitlement right. Because shareholders are owners of the firm, their property rights entitle them to information about how their money and resources have been used. However, there is now a considerable body of literature that explores whether companies have a duty to produce information to other stakeholders based on other human rights (see, for example, Freeman, 1984; Gray 2001, 2002). The

Box 4.1 Herceptin, accounting and human rights

The issue of access to drugs on the NHS has emerged as a big issue in the UK. One notable case that has received a lot of coverage in the press relates to a drug called Herceptin. The drug, which is used in the treatment of breast cancer, has proved to be quite effective in tackling some types of treatment; however, it is very expensive.

In October 2005 Barbara Clark engaged the help of a well-known human rights lawyer to try and secure access to the drug through the NHS, arguing that withholding treatment represented a breach of her human rights. Ms Clark threatened to take her fight to the European Court of Human Rights. However, her local Primary Care Trust capitulated and ruled that she could receive the treatment.

Some doctors pointed out that the NHS has a finite pot of resources and that if Herceptin was to be made available to all patients, then the treatment of other types of illnesses, including other types of cancer, would have to be cut in order to 'balance the books'.

In one study, a team of doctors at Norwich University Hospital NHS Trust calculated that they would have to find £1.9m each year to make Herceptin available to the 75 eligible patients who presented at their hospital alone. They suggested that they could provide this treatment but only by cutting costs in relation to chemotherapy and palliative care. They could provide Herceptin to the 75 breast cancer sufferers but this would mean that 200 patients could not receive palliative chemotherapy.

In responding to another more recent case, Dr Gill Morgan of the NHS confederation said, 'PCTs have a duty to spend taxpayers' money in the most effective way possible. Every pound spent on one expensive drug or treatment is potentially at the expense of other patients.'

problem is, however, determining exactly what rights humans should have, including those that might be born a few hundred years from now! This idea is actually not as daft as it sounds. Think, for example, in relation to the environmental debate whether the current population has any duty towards future generations for the stewardship of the planet? Then, of course, why should we limit ourselves to human rights? Don't animals have rights as well?

Let's just stick with human rights for a moment and see if it helps us tease out any more issues in relation to ethics and communities. Perhaps one of the most well-known attempts to establish a comprehensive list of human rights is the Universal Declaration of Human Rights. The declaration outlines 30 articles that the General Assembly of the United Nations contended should be basic rights for all people. It was adopted by the United Nations on 10 December 1948 and provides the basis for the International Bill of Human Rights. The full declaration is provided in Appendix 1 of this chapter. We will return to this topic again in Part II when we consider the Morality of the Market and the Function of Accounting; however, for the time being, have a look at the list in Appendix 1 and consider the following questions. First, while the shareholders of the company may have certain entitlements when it comes to receiving information, to what extent do you think they have a right to the profits generated by the firm? Do the owners of an organization have a right to profits and if so, how much of the profit are they entitled to? Second, consider whether any of the rights outlined in the declaration conflict with the rights of the owners of an organization to receive a return on their investment?

Let's stay with the Declaration of Human Rights a little longer and see what else we can learn about rights and ethics. Box 4.2 contains five articles of the United Nations Declaration of Human Rights. Which of the articles would you consider to be universal human rights and which are not? We guess that you probably agreed with most of them. The fact that large swathes of the population do feel able to subscribe to many of the basic rights outlined in the declaration is actually quite informative when it comes to thinking about ethics because it suggests that in some instances, it is possible to get consensus on fundamental values and that ethics may not be entirely cultural and relativistic. Again, we shall return to this later; however, much of conventional accounting practice within the market is based on Article 3, and the right to freedom of contract, and Article 17, the right to own property. I guess that this might mean that in response to the question why should I behave in a particular way, one response might be, well because we can all agree that there are certain things that we just should do.

Box 4.2 United Nations Declaration of Human Rights

Article 3
Everyone has the right to life, liberty and security of person.

Article 4
No one shall be held in slavery or servitude; slavery and the slave trade shall be prohibited in all their forms.

Article 9
No one shall be subjected to arbitrary arrest, detention or exile.

Article 13
Everyone has the right to freedom of movement and residence within the borders of each State. Everyone has the right to leave any country, including his own, and to return to his country.

Article 17
Everyone has the right to own property alone as well as in association with others.

Box 4.3 United Nations Declaration of Human Rights: contentious rights?

Article 5
No one shall be subjected to torture or to cruel, inhuman or degrading treatment or punishment.

Article 14
Everyone has the right to seek and to enjoy in other countries asylum from persecution.

Article 16
(1) Men and women of full age, without any limitation due to race, nationality or religion, have the right to marry and to found a family. They are entitled to equal rights as to marriage, during marriage and at its dissolution.
(2) Marriage shall be entered into only with the free and full consent of the intending spouses.
(3) The family is the natural and fundamental group unit of society and is entitled to protection by society and the State.

Article 23
(1) Everyone has the right to work, to free choice of employment, to just and favourable conditions of work and to protection against unemployment.
(2) Everyone, without any discrimination, has the right to equal pay for equal work.
(3) Everyone who works has the right to just and favourable remuneration ensuring for himself and his family an existence worthy of human dignity, and supplemented, if necessary, by other means of social protection.
(4) Everyone has the right to form and to join trade unions for the protection of his interests.

Article 25
(1) Everyone has the right to a standard of living adequate for the health and well-being of himself and of his family, including food, clothing, housing and medical care and necessary social services, and the right to security in the event of unemployment, sickness, disability, widowhood, old age or other lack of livelihood in circumstances beyond his control.
(2) Motherhood and childhood are entitled to special care and assistance. All children, whether born in or out of wedlock, shall enjoy the same social protection.

Now have a look at Box 4.3. This box contains another five articles from the declaration. Would you be prepared to sign up to this list or do you think that it is permissible to treat suspected terrorists inhumanely in order to save innocent lives?

Are you happy to open the borders of your country to individuals seeking asylum? Does everyone have the right to a job and is a heterosexual family unit the natural and fundamental group unit of society? This time we are going to guess that some of you will disagree with one or two of these rights. So the question is: how do we, as a community, decide which rights will apply?

A key part of the debate is therefore how individual rights are to be determined and enforced. We are going to consider the conventional, historical response to this issue in this chapter; however, try to keep this discussion in mind when we look at the work of Jürgen Habermas in the following chapter. The work of two seventeenth-century English philosophers, Thomas Hobbes and John Locke, have had a particularly big influence on the way we think about these questions. Philosophers like Thomas Hobbes tried to address this question by starting from some basic assumptions about the natural state of human beings. We could, for example, argue that our right not to be attacked is based on the nature of our bodies, the fact that they feel pain and that life is sustained only within certain conditions; we may also argue that individuals have a right to food and water for the same reasons. Hobbes, however, in a famous work called *Leviathan*, started from a quite different position. He assumed that individuals have a natural propensity to be concerned primarily about their own interests and well-being. He famously commented that if this natural liberty was pursued by everyone then it would lead to the 'war of all against all'. Hobbes suggested that because this natural state would lead to a rather brutish and possibly short existence then we willingly forgo our natural liberty, hand over some power and authority to the state to enforce rights and create obligations upon us in the form of a social contract. In other words, Hobbes contended that people were naturally self-interested, were aware that untrammelled self-interest was not in their best interests and that, in fact, the best way to secure individual liberty is paradoxically to submit to the power of the state, with a few provisos of course. What we want to do here is introduce the link between the individual's rights and how societies are governed. The

Box 4.4 The right to die

Recently in the UK a new 'right to die' card has been launched. The card is being made available to the public in banks, libraries, GP surgeries and even pubs. The card is carried around like a donor card and allows individuals to express an Advance Decision to Refuse Treatment in the advent that they lose the ability to make a decision about treatment due to an accident or illness.

Proponents of the card argue that individuals have a right to choose whether or not they wish to receive life-sustaining treatment.

However, against this pro-choice position, pro-life campaigners argue that committing such decisions to paper in advance could place doctors in the very difficult position of having to make decisions about whether or not a full recovery from a particular illness was likely. If they thought it was, they would provide treatment, otherwise they would have to withhold treatment.

tension between the individual's right to liberty and the rights of others has been a very important aspect of this debate. In his influential work *On Liberty*, for example, the nineteenth-century philosopher John Stuart Mill explores the question of the extent to which a society can legitimately impinge on the freedom of the individual. Much of Mill's analysis centres on what is know as the harm principle, which states that an action is permissible so long as it does not harm others. As with most philosophical debates, however, an answer to one question only leads to another problem. Exactly what do we mean by harm?

The next big thinker whom we need to mention is a man called John Locke. While there is some debate as to how much Locke was influenced by Hobbes, there are certainly similarities between their views on the natural self-interested proclivity of human beings. Locke therefore articulates a similar kind of argument for why individuals would want to hand over power to some form of government; however, his *Two Treatises of Government* hints towards the legitimate function of governmental institutions and how they might continue to secure their legitimacy. There are various interpretations of what Locke is saying in this work and whether he is advocating a form of government by majority vote. However, it does seem that he focuses on the contribution of those governed to the ongoing legitimacy of the governing institutions.

According to Rousseau, Hobbes and Locke, therefore, the ethics of individuals is inextricably linked to a broader context of supporting institutions. Indeed some interpretations of Hobbes go further and suggest that in order for ethical rights and obligations to be sustained, the state must intervene to ensure equality in power. In other words, the principal objective of government is not to enforce individual rights, rather it is to sustain the types of institutional configurations that promote equality of power, the implication being that the promotion of individual rights emerges as a consequence of increased equality. Again, it is important that we pause here and make sure that we have grasped how the likes of Hobbes and Locke contribute towards our understanding of ethics and accounting. The point is that this body of literature focuses our attention on the fact that accounting is an institutional practice. Indeed in some countries, like the United States Congress for example, government technically has legal responsibility for the accounting function. The fact that this responsibility in the example is delegated to the Securities and Exchange Commission and in turn, the Financial Accounting Standards Board, does not detract from the fact that the institutions of accounting are institutions of government. There are very good reasons why we might want an independent body to be responsible for determining accounting rules, but we might want this body to be more accountable. Also, how does this tally with another fact, that what is essentially a constitutional responsibility is carried out by large, multinational limited liability partnerships that to all extents and purposes are also not accountable to the general public? We will explore the nature of the accountancy profession in more detail in the second part of the text; however, hopefully you are beginning to make the link between some of the ideas discussed within the broader political moral philosophy literature, like civil society, rights and the legitimacy of government and the institution of accounting.

We would like to look at one further issue before we leave our discussion of rights.

Box 4.5 Prem Sikka

Prem Sikka, Professor of Accounting at Essex University and regular contributor to the *Guardian*, has been an outspoken voice against the current institutional set-up of the accounting profession.

In a recent article entitled 'On with the show' (*Guardian*, 4 June 2008), Professor Sikka criticizes the relationship between the state and the big auditing firms and the relationship between the big auditing firms and their clients, arguing that neither of these relationships serves the public interest. He points out that the market for large company audits is dominated by just four big accounting firms: PricewaterhouseCoopers, Deloitte, KPMG and Ernst & Young. According to Prem, their collective global income of $80 billion dollars, which incidentally is exceeded by only 54 nation states, provides them with undue influence over the structures and rules of accounting practice. He claims that this influence can be seen in the way in which they have recently secured a liability concession.

Here is how he concludes his article:

> As a society, we continue to give auditing firms state-guaranteed markets, monopolies, lucrative fees and liability concessions. None of it has given us, or is likely to give us better audits, company accounts, corporate governance or freedom from frauds and fiddles. Without effective independent regulation, public accountability and demanding liability laws, the industry cannot provide value for money.

Read the full article at: <www.guardian.co.uk/commentisfree/2008/jun/03/onwiththeshow>

What is your immediate reaction to the articles in Box 4.6? These articles are taken from the Cairo Declaration on Human Rights in Islam, which was ratified at the Nineteenth Islamic Conference of Foreign Ministers in Cairo in 1990. In response to and in criticism of the UN Declaration, Islamic nations developed their own statement of fundamental rights. The full declaration is provided in Appendix 2. This particular alternative declaration is important for a number of reasons. First, our discussion in this chapter to date has explored one perspective on why our behaviour matters and has related this perspective to a fairly naturalist view of human rights. Yet for many people, including many practising accountants, the reason why ethical behaviour matters to them is related to religious convictions. The reason why individuals should be ethical is related to faith, and the rights of the individual are trumped by the will of God. For these people, the way conflicting ideas about rights are negotiated must also include some reference to (or in many cases must only reference) theology.

While there is no logical requirement for morality to be linked to religion (all we

Box 4.6 The Cairo Declaration of Human Rights in Islam

Article 1

(a) All human beings form one family whose members are united by submission to God and descent from Adam. All men are equal in terms of basic human dignity and basic obligations and responsibilities, without any discrimination on the grounds of race, colour, language, sex, religious belief, political affiliation, social status or other considerations. True faith is the guarantee for enhancing such dignity along the path to human perfection.

(b) All human beings are God's subjects, and the most loved by him are those who are most useful to the rest of His subjects, and no one has superiority over another except on the basis of piety and good deeds.

Article 2

(a) Life is a God-given gift and the right to life is guaranteed to every human being. It is the duty of individuals, societies and states to protect this right from any violation, and it is prohibited to take away life except for a Shari'ah-prescribed reason.

(b) It is forbidden to resort to such means as may result in the genocidal annihilation of mankind.

(c) The preservation of human life throughout the term of time willed by God is a duty prescribed by Shari'ah.

(d) Safety from bodily harm is a guaranteed right. It is the duty of the state to safeguard it, and it is prohibited to breach it without a Shari'ah-prescribed reason.

Article 6

(a) Woman is equal to man in human dignity, and has rights to enjoy as well as duties to perform; she has her own civil entity and financial independence, and the right to retain her name and lineage.

(b) The husband is responsible for the support and welfare of the family.

Article 10

Islam is the religion of unspoiled nature. It is prohibited to exercise any form of compulsion on man or to exploit his poverty or ignorance in order to convert him to another religion or to atheism.

Article 11

(a) Human beings are born free, and no one has the right to enslave, humiliate, oppress or exploit them, and there can be no subjugation but to God the Most-High.

(b) Colonialism of all types being one of the most evil forms of enslavement is totally prohibited. Peoples suffering from colonialism have the full right to freedom and self-determination. It is the duty of all States and peoples to support the struggle of colonized peoples for the liquidation of all forms of colonialism and occupation, and all States and peoples have the right to preserve their independent identity and exercise control over their wealth and natural resources.

Article 14
Everyone shall have the right to legitimate gains without monopolization, deceit or harm to oneself or to others. Usury (riba) is absolutely prohibited.

mean by this is that the idea of ethics can be logically sustained from both theistic and atheistic positions), for many accountants it is. Many practising accountants are also practising Catholics, Evangelical Christians, Muslims, Jews, Orthodox Greeks and, given that this is the case, we would like to pause and ask you to reflect on a couple of questions.

The first question is really for accountant believers, and it is this: is the practice of accounting, and in particular the function of accounting within a free-market system, compatible with the tenets of your faith? Please read through this section, even if you think you don't have a faith, as we want to make a point about value systems more generally.

A few years ago, we did some work on a theology special issue of the *Accounting, Auditing & Accountability Journal* with a theologian called Tim Gorringe. One of Tim's papers is entitled, 'Will Bankers Get into Heaven?' Of course his answer is no, a fact confirmed by the sub-prime fiasco of the early 2000s. But seriously, it may come as a surprise that some aspects of the practice of accounting may be difficult to reconcile with theological values and beliefs that we hold, particularly in relation to economic and finance theories that are generally used to ascribe the broader accounting function with meaning. Let's look at two examples from different theological traditions: one from Quakerism and Ethical Investment and the second from the emergence of Islamic Accounting.

In the first example, in an attempt to translate their faith into their finances, the Methodists and Quakers in particular played an influential role in the development of the ethical investment movement in both the UK and the US. For example, the Methodist Church in the UK established a fund in 1960 which attempted to avoid investing in sin stocks like tobacco, armaments, alcohol and gambling and in 1984, Charles Jacob translated these principles into the UK's first ethical retail fund: Stewardship.

In the second example we would like to consider Islamic Accounting. The provisions of the Cairo Declaration convey a rather different perspective on basic human rights than that implied by the UN Declaration. However, this difference in perspective also extends to the function of Islamic financial systems. As with human rights, financial practice would seem to be conditioned by Shari'ah Law. For example, interest (riba) is prohibited, charitable giving, while required, must remain undisclosed and the allocation of surplus funds is supposed to be based on whether a project is worthwhile rather than on its expected financial return. These kinds of prohibition mean that different types of contracts are required. Equity financing is therefore based on profit-sharing contracts and debt financing generally involves some kind of lease or deferred payment. For example, contracts based on *Ijarah* (lit. 'to give something on rent') permit individuals to lease required goods while *Murabahah* ('cost-plus-profit sale') contracts allow individuals to purchase raw materials and pay for them later when the finished goods are sold. Of course we could debate at length whether in substance these contracts are really different from the kinds of transactions that underpin the capitalist economy; however, if there is at least the perception that both systems are based on different sets of values then what are the prospects of reaching a consensus on a global set of accounting standards?

However, our aim here is not to trace the development of the ethical investment movement or to provide a detailed study of Islamic Accounting. Rather we want to speculate briefly on what these kinds of developments mean for the prospect of accounting and ethics more generally. The point is that these attempts to align values with investments extend well beyond religious communities, for example the Meyers Pride Value Fund (a publicly traded mutual fund with an ethical investment policy) originally screened out companies with a poor history of discrimination against gay and lesbian employees. With an increasing awareness of how our investments work to generate culture as well as returns, there is a growing trend to align all kinds of purchasing decisions with our values (one example we came across recently was an

Box 4.7 Charity ethical investment

It's not just religious organizations that invest in ethical funds, charities do so as well. In many cases this is in order to ensure a consistency with the charities' aims and objectives.

In the UK, since 1987, the Charity Commission has acknowledged that charities should not invest in companies whose activities are contrary to the purpose of the charity. Recent guidance from the Charity Commission of England and Wales (CC14) gives charities greater freedom to implement an ethical investment policy (Charity Commission 2003) and the current Statement of Recommended Practice, Accounting and Reporting by Charities (SORP) recommends that charities disclose in their annual report whether or not they have an ethical investment policy.

A recent ACCA report by Niklas Kreander, Vivien Beattie and Ken McPhail (2006) on charity ethical investment provides an example of a leading, research-based cancer charity which is 'prohibited from investing in any company perceptibly involved in the sale of tobacco or tobacco products and uses the EIRiS (Ethical Investment Research Service) definition of tobacco investments'. Although the charity still invests in retail companies such as Tesco and Sainsbury's, this is justified on the basis that selling cigarettes is a trivial, non-core part of these companies' activities.

You can access the full report at <www.accaglobal.com/publicinterest/activities/research/reports/sustainable_and_transparent/rr_097>.

online auction site called egay). The question is, how much will accounting practice have to change when perhaps, with increasing affluence, price and profit cease to be values in themselves, and instead become subordinate to values?

The point we are trying to make in relation to this problem of consensus is made much more clearly by Mary Warnock (1992: 84) when she asks, 'How is government to be carried on, if behind it, there is no consensus morality? If there is, as we are often told, no general sense of what is right and what is wrong, how are laws to be enacted?' In other words, to go back to Hobbes and Locke, in what sense would government be legitimate? While this is not a new question within moral philosophy, it's certainly not one that many accountants have grappled with. If there is no consensus on morality, how is accounting to be enacted?

The traditional political moral philosophy literature would therefore encourage us to think of the accounting profession as part of the broader political institutional structure, and it would also suggest that any consideration of accounting ethics should incorporate some reflection on the conceptualization of rights that the practice of accounting supports. In its present form, it protects the rights, and therefore serves the interests, of a group in society. However, a growing body of social and environmental literature questions whether the accounting profession could serve a broader Hobbesian function by providing a broader set of information to a greater number of stakeholders and, by doing so, protect a broader set of human rights than just property rights.

EMMANUEL LEVINAS AND THE PHENOMENOLOGY OF ETHICS, OR WHAT DOES ETHICS FEEL LIKE?

At this point we would like to change track slightly and introduce you to another, slightly more recent, influential thinker called Emmanuel Levinas. While Levinas and Rousseau present two quite different positions, there is a growing body of academic literature that focuses on the synergies between the two, particularly in relation to the relational aspects of ethics and the question, 'Who am I?'

Box 4.8 Am I my brother's keeper?

There is a well-known story in Genesis about two brothers: Cain and Abel. Cain is an arable farmer and Abel has some livestock. Both worship God, Cain by offering up some of his fruit and vegetables and Abel by killing a lamb. God says, look Cain, true worship should focus on the sacrifice that I'm going to provide for you humans. Well Cain, being the big brother, doesn't cope well with criticism and in a premeditated plot he lures Abel into the countryside and kills him. As you might imagine, God being God knows what's happened and in attempt to get Cain to own up to what he has done asks him: 'where is your brother', to which Cain famously replies: 'Am I my brother's keeper?'

Levinas' perspective seems to be significantly influenced by his Jewish history and one way to begin to access Levinas' thinking is through a particular story in the Old Testament. You might recall that in the first book of the Bible, the book of Genesis, there is a story about two brothers, Cain and Abel. Cain kills Abel and when God asks Cain about his brother he famously replies, 'Am I my brother's keeper?' Levinas' contribution to our understanding of what ethics means is to present us with the disturbing conclusion that 'yes I am my brother's keeper'. Levinas' contention is that it is in responding to the claims of others that the individual becomes an ethical subject. Levinas therefore explores the relational aspects of morality from quite a different perspective to that of the likes of Rousseau. He comes up with a fairly radical answer to the question of why it is important for people to behave in an ethical way. He says our very subjective existence depends on it. Let's try to explain Levinas' rather complicated position.

We will start by confusing you a little further! Consider this quote from Levinas:

> The absolute nakedness of a face, the absolute defenceless face, without covering, clothing or mask, is what opposes my power over it, my violence and opposes it in an absolute way, with an opposition which is opposition itself.
>
> (cited in Bauman 1993: 73)

Zygmunt Bauman paraphrases Levinas' position as follows, 'Morality begins in the face to face', and, 'morality is the encounter with the Other as face' (Bauman 1993: 48). What on earth does that mean? The face, like many other aspects of Levinas' ethics is rather obtuse, but we think that its meaning is connected to the fact that Levinas was a student of Edmund Husserl, the father of phenomenology.

Levinas approached ethics using a radically different perspective from traditional moral philosophy. He brings a phenomenological perspective to the study of ethics. For Levinas, ethics is not grounded in the questions: 'what should I do?' or 'why is it important that I behave in that way?' As he attended Husserl's classes, Levinas would have undoubtedly been told that the phenomenological method starts with the

Box 4.9 Face recognition

There is a large field of psychological research on face perception. Researchers have identified an area of the brain which seems to be particularly influential in face recognition. It's often referred to as the 'fusiform face area'.

The face seems to play a particularly important role in social interaction and research suggests that complex neurological processes are at work from birth in relation to face perception.

Other studies have found that specific types of brain injury can affect an individual's ability to recognize faces. This condition, known as prosopagnosia or face blindness, seems to relate to only the individual's appreciation of faces as they continue to be able to recognize other objects.

question: how do things presents themselves to us? So it's perhaps not surprising that Levinas came to ask, 'how does the experience of ethics present itself to us; what is the given-ness of ethics?' He concluded that it presents itself through *the Other*, through the encounter with the face; through the face to face. Levinas was therefore interested in the phenomenology of otherness and located the phenomenological given-ness of ethics in the relationship between the Self and the Other.

As the language we are using here is probably a little obscure, we will try to ground what Levinas is suggesting a little more clearly. Levinas' perspective is grounded in some quite concrete cognitive science. It is based on an understanding of consciousness and in particular is a criticism of Descartes' famous dictum *cogito ergo sum* ('I think therefore I am'). For Levinas, our consciousness is always consciousness *of something*. He says it is, 'meaningfulness, thoughts casting themselves towards something that shows itself in them' (Levinas 1993: 153). In other words we are not 'isolated egos' (Moran 2006: 328). Let's see if this quote from John Berger (1972: 1) helps clarify things. Berger says, 'Seeing comes before words. The child looks and recognises before it can speak'. So for Levinas, and many cognitive psychologists, the child's looking at faces plays a fundamental role in the development of individual subjectivity. As Moran (2006) said, it is the experience of an 'I' that is not myself that is constitutive of my self.

Levinas' grounding of ethics in the phenomenology of otherness is therefore a very different starting point from those of Rousseau, Locke, Hobbes and Hume that we discussed above. The beginning of ethics is not associated with my psychological preference for security, not my willingness to give up power to the state so that I can live in peace within a community. Rather it is the way the face of the Other makes a claim on me to restrain myself. Contrary to traditional political moral philosophy, Levinas' starting point is not what I get out of ethics, but rather the infinite claim it places upon me. He explained (in Bauman 1993: 48), 'In relation to the Face, what is affirmed is asymmetry; in the beginning, it does not matter who the other is in relation to me – that is his business'. It's as though each face calls out 'Here I am' and in doing so calls for justice. This is the point we really wanted to get to with Levinas. In our discussion above we mention rights and duties as being two sides of a symmetry that is supposed to keep society in equilibrium. As we developed this idea to talk about the institutions of government we talked about the importance of symmetry in power in establishing rights. However, it is precisely this view of ethics that Levinas challenges, and indeed in what seems like a counter-intuitive move he argues that there is a danger that all this talk of rights, apart from being logically and procedurally questionable, may actually undermine what he feels is the core of both being ethical and being human.

Zygmunt Bauman (1993: 48) explains Levinas' idea of asymmetry in ethics in the following quote: 'Face is encountered if, and only if, my relation to the other is programmatically non-symmetrical; that is, not dependent on the Other's past, present, anticipated or hoped for reciprocation'. In other words it's not based on rights and duties. Moran (2006: 321) explained that for Levinas, the phenomenology of ethics involves 'the effort to constrain one's freedom and spontaneity in order to be open to the other person, or more precisely to allow oneself to be constrained by the other'. That is its given-ness.

So Levinas uses the term 'face' in both a literal and a metaphorical sense. He uses it to refer to the literal encounter with another human being. While it's easy to be put off by Levinas' rhetoric, there is certainly evidence that the literal face-to-face encounter does play an important role in consciousness and the development of neural networks.[2] Kaulingfreks and ten Bos (2007), for example, commented:

> The idea of the face is not simply based on eye contact, Yet, by choosing the face as an idea or concept that grounds ethics, Levinas clearly relies on some sort of ocular centrism. Again and again, Levinas makes clear how important the gaze is for it is the gaze that allows us to break through the form in which the other being appears.

However, it also seems that Levinas uses the idea of the face to face as an injunction, rather than just a phenomenological description of how ethics presents itself to us. There is therefore an impassioned normative call in Levinas' work: this is the way ethics should be. Bauman (1993) interprets Levinas in this way, suggesting that the face is a moral stance that we adopt, and morality then becomes the act of acknowledging the face. The crucial point for us to notice here is the way in which Levinas' concept of ethics places the responsibility on me alone to turn the Other into a face. Again, we will turn to Bauman (1993) to help us explain how Levinas' perspective differs from the likes of Hobbes and Locke. Bauman comments,

> It will be only later, when I acknowledge the presence of the face as my responsibility, that both I and the neighbour acquire meanings: I am I who is responsible, he is he to whom I assign the right to make me responsible. It is this creation of meaning of the Other, and thus also of myself, that my freedom, my ethical freedom, comes to be.
>
> (Bauman 1993: 86)

We would like you to notice first that, from a Levinasian perspective, we become moral beings only by recognizing our responsibility to a specific Other, the individual, not the crowd of others called society that Rousseau, Hobbes and Locke use as the basis for developing their perspectives on morality. It is in this being-for-the-other, as opposed to being-with-the-other that we find morality. Bauman (1995: 60) explained some of the ramifications of this being-for-the-other when he said, 'Once identified within the realm of being-for, the realm of morality is enclosed in the frame of sympathy, of the willingness to serve, to do good. To self-sacrifice for the sake of the Other'. Again we would ask you to contrast this position with the Hobbesian assumption that individuals are basically self-interested, and that the institutions of government are legitimate only to the extent to which they create the circumstances where all individuals can legitimately pursue their own self-interests.

Second, however, contrast how Bauman employs the term 'right' with our discussion of rights above. For Levinas, a right is not something that I respect out of self-interest, because I fear the consequences of the law. It's also not something that I respect because I know that if I contravene your rights then I jeopardize the very idea of rights. Rather the idea is one of subordination, subjection and service.

Let's see if we can connect some of these ideas more firmly to accounting. Most of the models of accountability that underpin the practice of accounting assume self-interest and are predicated on power, the power to hold to account. This power is generally based on legally enforceable rights. Yet both these ideas are antithetical to an ethics of the Other. According to Levinas, these types of encounters are certainly not face-to-face encounters and therefore not ethical encounters because they provide little space for faces to emerge. Of course this defacing is not only a characteristic of economic calculation and the practice of accounting; for Levinas, it's a cultural form. The question of course is whether one might envisage any alternative forms of accounting that might create greater possibilities for the face of the Other to emerge.

SUMMARY

This chapter has introduced some of the political moral philosophy literature. We are hoping that by briefly reviewing some of the ideas within this very influential field of thinking we might be able to push the discussion of accounting ethics beyond a narrow focus on how individual accountants should behave, and begin to get you thinking about the ethics of accounting, both in terms of the practice of accounting and the broader institutions of accounting. Rousseau's work places the ethical actions of individuals within the context of society more generally and sets up a discussion of how best to sustain these kinds of communities.

QUESTIONS

1 How does accounting contribute towards the development of society?
2 What rights does the practice of accounting serve and can you think of any instances where the practice of accounting may violate human rights?
3 Discuss whether owners of a firm have a right to the profit generated by that firm and, if you think they do, how much profit they have a right to receive.
4 Discuss the extent to which the Universal Declaration of Human Rights would be a good place to start re-thinking the function of accounting within society.
5 Discuss the extent to which accounting helps us to see, 'the face of the Other'.

NOTES

1 This is quite a gross simplification; however, it is sustained for the sake of clarity.
2 Within neuroscience the brain is considered to play an important role in conveying important social information. Neuroscience would suggest that neurological processes relating to face perception can be identified even at birth. In fact, if the specific part of the brain that processes information about faces is damaged in some way, this can result in a neurological condition known as prosopagnosia which roughly translates as face blindness. Neurological science suggests that human beings have an innate predisposition to pay attention to faces (see, for example, Gauthier *et al.* 2000).

APPENDIX 1 THE UNIVERSAL DECLARATION OF HUMAN RIGHTS

Article 1

All human beings are born free and equal in dignity and rights. They are endowed with reason and conscience and should act towards one another in a spirit of brotherhood.

Article 2

(1) Everyone is entitled to all the rights and freedoms set forth in this Declaration, without distinction of any kind, such as race, colour, sex, language, religion, political or other opinion, national or social origin, property, birth or other status.

(2) Furthermore, no distinction shall be made on the basis of the political, jurisdictional or international status of the country or territory to which a person belongs, whether it be independent, trust, non-self-governing or under any other limitation of sovereignty.

Article 3

Everyone has the right to life, liberty and security of person.

Article 4

No one shall be held in slavery or servitude; slavery and the slave trade shall be prohibited in all their forms.

Article 5

No one shall be subjected to torture or to cruel, inhuman or degrading treatment or punishment.

Article 6

Everyone has the right to recognition everywhere as a person before the law.

Article 7

All are equal before the law and are entitled without any discrimination to equal protection of the law. All are entitled to equal protection against any discrimination in violation of this Declaration and against any incitement to such discrimination.

Article 8

Everyone has the right to an effective remedy by the competent national tribunals for acts violating the fundamental rights granted him by the constitution or by law.

Article 9

No one shall be subjected to arbitrary arrest, detention or exile.

Article 10

Everyone is entitled in full equality to a fair and public hearing by an independent and impartial tribunal, in the determination of his rights and obligations and of any criminal charge against him.

Article 11

(1) Everyone charged with a penal offence has the right to be presumed innocent until proved guilty according to law in a public trial at which he has had all the guarantees necessary for his defence.

(2) No one shall be held guilty of any penal offence on account of any act or omission which did not constitute a penal offence, under national or international law, at the time when it was committed. Nor shall a heavier penalty be imposed than the one that was applicable at the time the penal offence was committed.

Article 12

No one shall be subjected to arbitrary interference with his privacy, family, home or correspondence, nor to attacks upon his honour and reputation. Everyone has the right to the protection of the law against such interference or attacks.

Article 13

Everyone has the right to freedom of movement and residence within the borders of each State. Everyone has the right to leave any country, including his own, and to return to his country.

Article 14

(1) Everyone has the right to seek and to enjoy in other countries asylum from persecution.

(2) This right may not be invoked in the case of prosecutions genuinely arising from non-political crimes or from acts contrary to the purposes and principles of the United Nations.

Article 15

(1) Everyone has the right to a nationality.

(2) No one shall be arbitrarily deprived of his nationality nor denied the right to change his nationality.

Article 16

(1) Men and women of full age, without any limitation due to race, nationality or religion, have the right to marry and to found a family. They are entitled to equal rights as to marriage, during marriage and at its dissolution.

(2) Marriage shall be entered into only with the free and full consent of the intending spouses.

(3) The family is the natural and fundamental group unit of society and is entitled to protection by society and the State.

Article 17

(1) Everyone has the right to own property alone as well as in association with others.

(2) No one shall be arbitrarily deprived of his property.

Article 18

Everyone has the right to freedom of thought, conscience and religion; this right includes freedom to change his religion or belief, and freedom, either alone or in community with others and in public or private, to manifest his religion or belief in teaching, practice, worship and observance.

Article 19

Everyone has the right to freedom of opinion and expression; this right includes freedom to hold opinions without interference and to seek, receive and impart information and ideas through any media and regardless of frontiers.

Article 20

(1) Everyone has the right to freedom of peaceful assembly and association.

(2) No one may be compelled to belong to an association.

Article 21

(1) Everyone has the right to take part in the government of his country, directly or through freely chosen representatives.

(2) Everyone has the right to equal access to public service in his country.

(3) The will of the people shall be the basis of the authority of government; this will shall be expressed in periodic and genuine elections which shall be by universal and equal suffrage and shall be held by secret vote or by equivalent free voting procedures.

Article 22

Everyone, as a member of society, has the right to social security and is entitled to realization, through national effort and international co-operation and in accordance with the organization and resources of each State, of the economic, social and cultural rights indispensable for his dignity and the free development of his personality.

Article 23

(1) Everyone has the right to work, to free choice of employment, to just and favourable conditions of work and to protection against unemployment.

(2) Everyone, without any discrimination, has the right to equal pay for equal work.

(3) Everyone who works has the right to just and favourable remuneration ensuring for himself and his family an existence worthy of human dignity, and supplemented, if necessary, by other means of social protection.

(4) Everyone has the right to form and to join trade unions for the protection of his interests.

Article 24

Everyone has the right to rest and leisure, including reasonable limitation of working hours and periodic holidays with pay.

Article 25

(1) Everyone has the right to a standard of living adequate for the health and well-being of himself and of his family, including food, clothing, housing and medical care and necessary social services, and the right to security in the event of unemployment, sickness, disability, widowhood, old age or other lack of livelihood in circumstances beyond his control.

(2) Motherhood and childhood are entitled to special care and assistance. All children, whether born in or out of wedlock, shall enjoy the same social protection.

Article 26

(1) Everyone has the right to education. Education shall be free, at least in the elementary and fundamental stages. Elementary education shall be compulsory. Technical and professional education shall be made generally available and higher education shall be equally accessible to all on the basis of merit.

(2) Education shall be directed to the full development of the human personality and to the strengthening of respect for human rights and fundamental freedoms. It shall promote understanding, tolerance and friendship among all nations, racial or religious groups, and shall further the activities of the United Nations for the maintenance of peace.

(3) Parents have a prior right to choose the kind of education that shall be given to their children.

Article 27

(1) Everyone has the right freely to participate in the cultural life of the community, to enjoy the arts and to share in scientific advancement and its benefits.

(2) Everyone has the right to the protection of the moral and material interests resulting from any scientific, literary or artistic production of which he is the author.

Article 28

Everyone is entitled to a social and international order in which the rights and freedoms set forth in this Declaration can be fully realized.

Article 29

(1) Everyone has duties to the community in which alone the free and full development of his personality is possible.

(2) In the exercise of his rights and freedoms, everyone shall be subject only to such limitations as are determined by law solely for the purpose of securing due recognition and respect for the rights and freedoms of others and of meeting the just requirements of morality, public order and the general welfare in a democratic society.

(3) These rights and freedoms may in no case be exercised contrary to the purposes and principles of the United Nations.

Article 30

Nothing in this Declaration may be interpreted as implying for any State, group or person any right to engage in any activity or to perform any act aimed at the destruction of any of the rights and freedoms set forth herein.

APPENDIX 2 THE CAIRO DECLARATION ON HUMAN RIGHTS IN ISLAM

Adopted and Issued at the Nineteenth Islamic Conference of Foreign Ministers in Cairo on 5 August 1990.

The Member States of the Organization of the Islamic Conference, Reaffirming the civilizing and historical role of the Islamic Ummah which God made the best nation that has given mankind a universal and well-balanced civilization in which harmony is established between this life and the hereafter and knowledge is combined with faith; and the role that this Ummah should play to guide a humanity confused by competing trends and ideologies and to provide solutions to the chronic problems of this materialistic civilization.

Wishing to contribute to the efforts of mankind to assert human rights, to protect man from exploitation and persecution, and to affirm his freedom and right to a dignified life in accordance with the Islamic Shari'ah.

Convinced that mankind which has reached an advanced stage in materialistic science is still, and shall remain, in dire need of faith to support its civilization and of a self-motivating force to guard its rights;

Believing that fundamental rights and universal freedoms in Islam are an integral part of the Islamic religion and that no one as a matter of principle has the right to suspend them in whole or in part or violate or ignore them in as much as they are binding divine commandments, which are contained in the Revealed Books of God and were sent through the last of His Prophets to complete the preceding divine messages thereby making their observance an act of worship and their neglect or violation an abominable sin, and accordingly every person is individually responsible – and the Ummah collectively responsible – for their safeguard.

Proceeding from the above-mentioned principles,

Declare the following:

Article 1

(a) All human beings form one family whose members are united by submission to God and descent from Adam. All men are equal in terms of basic human dignity and basic obligations and responsibilities, without any discrimination on the grounds of race, colour, language, sex, religious belief, political affiliation, social status or other considerations. True faith is the guarantee for enhancing such dignity along the path to human perfection.

(b) All human beings are God's subjects, and the most loved by Him are those who are most useful to the rest of His subjects, and no one has superiority over another except on the basis of piety and good deeds.

Article 2

(a) Life is a God-given gift and the right to life is guaranteed to every human being. It is the duty of individuals, societies and states to protect this right from any violation, and it is prohibited to take away life except for a Shari'ah-prescribed reason.

(b) It is forbidden to resort to such means as may result in the genocidal annihilation of mankind.

(c) The preservation of human life throughout the term of time willed by God is a duty prescribed by Shari'ah.

(d) Safety from bodily harm is a guaranteed right. It is the duty of the state to safeguard it, and it is prohibited to breach it without a Shari'ah-prescribed reason.

Article 3

(a) In the event of the use of force and in case of armed conflict, it is not permissible to kill non-belligerents such as old men, women and children. The wounded and the sick shall have the right to medical treatment; and prisoners of war shall have the right to be fed, sheltered and clothed. It is prohibited to mutilate dead bodies.

(b) It is a duty to exchange prisoners of war and to arrange visits or reunions of the families separated by the circumstances of war.

(c) It is prohibited to fell trees, to damage crops or livestock, and to destroy the enemy's civilian buildings and installations by shelling, blasting or any other means.

Article 4

Every human being is entitled to inviolability and the protection of his good name and honour during his life and after his death. The state and society shall protect his remains and burial place.

Article 5

(a) The family is the foundation of society, and marriage is the basis of its formation. Men and women have the right to marriage, and no restrictions stemming from race, colour or nationality shall prevent them from enjoying this right.

(b) Society and the State shall remove all obstacles to marriage and shall facilitate marital procedure. They shall ensure family protection and welfare.

Article 6

(a) Woman is equal to man in human dignity, and has rights to enjoy as well as duties to perform; she has her own civil entity and financial independence, and the right to retain her name and lineage.

(b) The husband is responsible for the support and welfare of the family.

Article 7

(a) As of the moment of birth, every child has rights due from the parents, society and the state to be accorded proper nursing, education and material, hygienic and moral care. Both the fetus and the mother must be protected and accorded special care.

(b) Parents and those in such like capacity have the right to choose the type of education they desire for their children, provided they take into consideration the interest and future of the children in accordance with ethical values and the principles of the Shari'ah.

(c) Both parents are entitled to certain rights from their children, and relatives are entitled to rights from their kin, in accordance with the tenets of the Shari'ah.

Article 8

Every human being has the right to enjoy his legal capacity in terms of both obligation and commitment. Should this capacity be lost or impaired, he shall be represented by his guardian.

Article 9

(a) The quest for knowledge is an obligation, and the provision of education is a duty for society and the State. The State shall ensure the availability of ways and means to acquire education and shall guarantee educational diversity in the interest of society so as to enable man to be acquainted with the religion of Islam and the facts of the Universe for the benefit of mankind.

(b) Every human being has the right to receive both religious and worldly education from the various institutions of education and guidance, including the family, the school, the university, the media, etc., and in such an integrated and balanced manner as to develop his personality, strengthen his faith in God and promote his respect for and defence of both rights and obligations.

Article 10

Islam is the religion of unspoiled nature. It is prohibited to exercise any form of compulsion on man or to exploit his poverty or ignorance in order to convert him to another religion or to atheism.

Article 11

(a) Human beings are born free, and no one has the right to enslave, humiliate, oppress or exploit them, and there can be no subjugation but to God the Most-High.

(b) Colonialism of all types being one of the most evil forms of enslavement is totally prohibited. Peoples suffering from colonialism have the full right to freedom and self-determination. It is the duty of all States and peoples to support the struggle of colonized peoples for the liquidation of all forms of colonialism and occupation, and all States and peoples have the right to preserve their independent identity and exercise control over their wealth and natural resources.

Article 12

Every man shall have the right, within the framework of Shari'ah, to free movement and to select his place of residence whether inside or outside his country and, if persecuted, is entitled to seek asylum in another country. The country of refuge shall ensure his protection until he reaches safety, unless asylum is motivated by an act which Shari'ah regards as a crime.

Article 13

Work is a right guaranteed by the State and Society for each person able to work. Everyone shall be free to choose the work that suits him best and which serves his interests and those of society. The employee shall have the right to safety and security as well as to all other social guarantees. He may neither be assigned work beyond his capacity nor be subjected to compulsion or exploited or harmed in any way. He shall be entitled – without any discrimination between males and females – to fair wages for his work without delay, as well as to the holidays, allowances and promotions which he deserves. For his part, he shall be required to be dedicated and meticulous in his work. Should workers and employers disagree on any matter, the State shall intervene to settle the dispute and have the grievances redressed, the rights confirmed and justice enforced without bias.

Article 14

(a) Everyone shall have the right to legitimate gains without monopolization, deceit or harm to oneself or to others. Usury (riba) is absolutely prohibited.

Article 15

(a) Everyone shall have the right to own property acquired in a legitimate way, and shall be entitled to the rights of ownership, without prejudice to oneself, others or to society in general. Expropriation is not permissible except for the requirements of public interest and upon payment of immediate and fair compensation.

(b) Confiscation and seizure of property is prohibited except for a necessity dictated by law.

Article 16

Everyone shall have the right to enjoy the fruits of his scientific, literary, artistic or technical production and the right to protect the moral and material interests stemming therefrom, provided that such production is not contrary to the principles of Shari'ah.

Article 17

(a) Everyone shall have the right to live in a clean environment, away from vice and moral corruption, an environment that would foster his self-development; and it is incumbent upon the State and society in general to afford that right.

(b) Everyone shall have the right to medical and social care, and to all public amenities provided by society and the State within the limits of their available resources.

(c) The State shall ensure the right of the individual to a decent living which will enable him to meet all his requirements and those of his dependants, including food, clothing, housing, education, medical care and all other basic needs.

Article 18

(a) Everyone shall have the right to live in security for himself, his religion, his dependants, his honour and his property.

(b) Everyone shall have the right to privacy in the conduct of his private affairs, in his home, among his family, with regard to his property and his relationships. It is not permitted to spy on him, to place him under surveillance or to besmirch his good name. The State shall protect him from arbitrary interference.

(c) A private residence is inviolable in all cases. It will not be entered without permission from its inhabitants or in any unlawful manner, nor shall it be demolished or confiscated and its dwellers evicted.

Article 19

(a) All individuals are equal before the law, without distinction between the ruler and the ruled.

(b) The right to resort to justice is guaranteed to everyone.

(c) Liability is in essence personal.

(d) There shall be no crime or punishment except as provided for in the Shari'ah.

(e) A defendant is innocent until his guilt is proven in a fair trial in which he shall be given all the guarantees of defence.

Article 20

It is not permitted without legitimate reason to arrest an individual, or restrict his freedom, to exile or to punish him. It is not permitted to subject him to physical or psychological torture or to any form of humiliation, cruelty or indignity. Nor is it permitted to subject an individual to medical or scientific experimentation without his consent or at the risk of his health or of his life. Nor is it permitted to promulgate emergency laws that would provide executive authority for such actions.

Article 21

Taking hostages under any form or for any purpose is expressly forbidden.

Article 22

(a) Everyone shall have the right to express his opinion freely in such manner as would not be contrary to the principles of the Shari'ah.

(b) Everyone shall have the right to advocate what is right, and propagate what is good, and warn against what is wrong and evil according to the norms of Islamic Shari'ah.

(c) Information is a vital necessity to society. It may not be exploited or misused in such a way as may violate sanctities and the dignity of Prophets, undermine moral and ethical values or disintegrate, corrupt or harm society or weaken its faith.

(d) It is not permitted to arouse nationalistic or doctrinal hatred or to do anything that may be an incitement to any form of racial discrimination.

Article 23

(a) Authority is a trust; and abuse or malicious exploitation thereof is absolutely prohibited, so that fundamental human rights may be guaranteed.

(b) Everyone shall have the right to participate, directly or indirectly in the administration of his country's public affairs. He shall also have the right to assume public office in accordance with the provisions of Shari'ah.

Article 24

All the rights and freedoms stipulated in this Declaration are subject to the Islamic Shari'ah.

Article 25

The Islamic Shari'ah is the only source of reference for the explanation or clarification of any of the articles of this Declaration.

Cairo, 14 Muharram 1411H
5 August 1990

RESOURCES

iTunes podcasts

Business and Human Rights: Perspectives from BP and the United Nations, Christine Bader, Kenan Institute for Ethics, Duke University.

Globalization and Human Rights, Tom Cushman, Alumnae Summer Symposium, Wellesley College.

Human Rights and their Consequences, Amartya Sen, Kenan Institute for Ethics, Duke University.

Human Rights in the Post-September 11 World, The Ford School's Lecture Series, the Ford School of Public Policy.

Moral and Civic Learning, Thomas Erlich, Kenan Institute for Ethics, Duke University.

Moral Courage and Civic Responsibility, Claire Gaudiani, Kenan Institute for Ethics, Duke University.

Websites

General reference

The Global Reporting Initiative:
<www.globalreporting.org/Home>.

Herceptin

<http://news.bbc.co.uk/1/hi/england/bradford/6250877.stm>.
<http://news.bbc.co.uk/1/hi/health/4902800.stm>.
<http://news.bbc.co.uk/1/hi/health/6176008.stm>.

Human rights

Amnesty International:
<www.amnesty.org/>.

Business and Human Rights Portal:
<www.business-humanrights.org/Home>.

Cairo Declaration on Human Rights in Islam:
<www.religlaw.org/interdocs/docs/cairohrislam1990.htm>.

European Convention on Human Rights:
<www.hri.org/docs/ECHR50.html>.

Human Rights Watch:
<www.hrw.org/>.

Universal Declaration of Human Rights:
<www.unhchr.ch/udhr/>.

Emmanuel Levinas

The Institute for Levinasian Studies:
<www.levinas.eu/>.

Prem Sikka, criticisms of the audit industry

Association for Accountancy and Business Affairs, AABA Trustees, various listings under:
<http://visar.csustan.edu/aaba/PremsikkaCV.pdf>.

The Guardian (2008): 'Watching the watchdogs', 31 March, available online at:
<www.guardian.co.uk/commentisfree/2008/mar/31/watchingthewatchdogs>.

The Guardian (2008): 'On with the show', 4 June, available online at:
<www.guardian.co.uk/commentisfree/2008/jun/03/onwiththeshow>.

READING

Accounting and business papers on Levinas

Knights, D. and O'Leary, M. (2006) 'Leadership, ethics and responsibility to the other', *Journal of Business Ethics*, 67: 125–137.

Schweiker, W. (1993) 'Accounting for ourselves: Accounting practice and the discourse of ethics', *Accounting, Organizations and Society*, 18(2/3): 231–252.

Shearer, T. (2002) 'Ethics and accountability: From the for-itself to the for-the-other', *Accounting, Organizations and Society*, 27: 541–573.

Soares, C. (2007) 'Corporate legal responsibility: A Levinasian perspective', *Journal of Business Ethics*, 81(3): 545–543.

Accounting, business and social contract theory

Donaldson, T. and Dunfee, T.W. (1999) *Ties that bind: A social contracts approach to business ethics* (Cambridge, MA: Harvard Business School Press).

Donaldson, T. and Dunfee, T.W. (1994) 'Toward a unified conception of business ethics: Integrative social contract theory', *The Academy of Management Review*, 19(2): 252–284.

Dunfee, T.W. (2006) 'A critical perspective of integrative social contracts theory: Recurring criticisms and next generation research topics', *Journal of Business Ethics*, 68: 303–328.

Wempe, B. (2007) 'Four design criteria for any future contractarian theory of business ethics', *Journal of Business Ethics*, 81(3): 697–714.

Accounting, economics and religion

Booth, P. (1993) 'Accounting in churches: A research framework and agenda', *Accounting, Auditing & Accountability Journal*, 6(4): 37–67.

Faircloth, A. (1988) 'The importance of accounting to the Shakers', *Accounting Historians Journal*, 15(2): 99–129.

Gorringe, T. (2001) 'Can bankers be saved?', *Studies in Christian Ethics*, 14(1): 17–33.

Hay, D. (1989) *Economics today* (Leicester: Apollos).

Inskeep, K. (1992) 'Views on social responsibility: The investment of pension funds in the Evangelical Lutheran Church in America', *Review of Religious Research*, 33(3): 270–282.

Jacob, C. (1979) 'A Christian on the stock exchange', in R. Hopps (ed.), *Ethics in the world of finance* (London: Chester House Publications), 46–54.

Laughlin, R. (1990) 'A model of financial accountability and the Church of England', *Financial Accountability and Management*, 6(2): 93–114.

McPhail, K., Gray, R. and Gorringe, T. (2005) 'Crossing the great divide: Critiquing the sacred secular dichotomy in accounting research', *Accounting, Auditing & Accountability Journal*, 18(2): 185–188.

McPhail, K.J., Gorringe, T. and Gray, R.H. (2004) 'Accounting and theology: An introduction. Initiating a dialogue between immediacy and eternity', *Accounting, Auditing & Accountability Journal*, 17(3): 320–326.

Worden, S. (2005) 'Religion in strategic leadership: A positivistic, normative/theological, and strategic analysis', *Journal of Business Ethics*, 57: 221–239.

Accounting and ethical investment

Cowton, C. (1990) 'Where their treasure is: Anglican religious communities and ethical investment', *Crucible* (April–June): 51–58.

Harrington, J. (1992) *Investing with your conscience* (New York: John Wiley & Sons).

Kinder, P., Lydenberg, S. and Domini, A. (1993) *Investing for good* (New York: Harper Collins).

Kreander, N., McPhail, K.J. and Molyneaux, D. (2004) 'God's fund managers: A critical study of stock market investment practices of the Church of England and UK Methodists', *Accounting, Auditing & Accountability Journal*, 17(3): 408–441.

Lewis, A. and Cullis, J. (1990) 'Ethical investments: Preferences and morality', *Journal of Behavioural Economics*, 19(4): 395–411.

Lewis, A. and Mackenzie, C. (2000) 'Morals, money, ethical investing and economic psychology', *Human Relations*, 53(2): 171–191.

Mills, P. (2000) 'Investing as a Christian', in M. Schluter (ed.), *Christianity in a changing world* (London: Marshall Pickering).

Moore, G. (1988) *Towards ethical investment* (Gateshead: Traidcraft Exchange).

Shepherd, P. (2000) *A history of ethical investment* (London: UKSIF Publications).

Sparkes, R. (2001) 'Ethical investment: Whose ethics, which investment?', *Business Ethics: A European Review*, 10(3): 194–205.

Wokutch, R. (1984) 'Ethical investing: An empirical study of policies and practices of Catholic religious institutions', *Akron Business and Economic Review*, 15(4): 17–24.

Universal values

Schwartz, M.S. (2005) 'Universal moral values for corporate codes of ethics', *Journal of Business Ethics*, 59: 27–44.

Work by Thomas Hobbes

Hobbes, T. (1991) *Leviathan* (Cambridge: Cambridge University Press).

Work by David Hume

Hume, D. (1740; 2000) *A treatise of human nature: Being an attempt to introduce the experimental method of reasoning into moral subjects*, ed. D.F. Norton and M.J. Norton, Oxford Philosophical Texts (Oxford: Oxford University Press).

Works by Emmanuel Levinas

Levinas, E. (1981) *Otherwise than being, or, beyond essence*; trans. A. Lingis (The Hague: Nijhoff).

—— (*c.* 1987) *Time and the other and additional essays*, trans. R.A. Cohen (Pittsburgh, PA: Duquesne University Press).

—— (*c.* 1987) *Totality and infinity: An essay on exteriority*, trans. A. Lingis (Pittsburgh, PA: Duquesne University Press).

—— (1978) *Existence and existents*, trans. A. Lingis (The Hague: Nijhoff).

Works about and drawing on Levinas

Bauman, Z. (2005) *Liquid life* (Cambridge: Polity).
Bauman, Z. (2001) *Community: Seeking safety in an insecure world* (Cambridge: Polity Press).
Bauman, Z. (2000) *Liquid modernity* (Cambridge: Polity).
Bauman, Z. (1994) *Alone again: Ethics after certainty* (London: Demos).
Bauman, Z. (1991) *Modernity and the Holocaust* (Cambridge: Polity).
Hand, S. (ed.) (1989) *The Lévinas reader* (Cambridge, MA: Blackwell).
Moran, D. (2006) *Introduction to phenomenology* (London: Routledge).

Work by John Locke

Locke, J. (1988) *Two treatises of government*, ed. with introduction and notes, P. Laslett (Cambridge: Cambridge University Press).

Work by Jean-Jacques Rousseau

Rousseau, J.-J. (1997) *The social contract and other later political writings*, ed. V. Gourevitch (Cambridge: Cambridge University Press).

Works by John Stuart Mill

Mill, J.S. (1999) *On liberty*, ed. E. Alexander (Peterborough, Ontario: Broadview Press).
Mill, J.S. (1993 [1895]) *Utilitarianism*, 12th edn (London: Routledge).

Works on rights

Dworkin, R. (2005) *Taking rights seriously* (London: Duckworth).

REFERENCES

Bauman, Z. (1995) *Life in fragments: Essays in postmodern morality* (Oxford: Blackwell).
Bauman, Z. (1993) *Postmodern ethics* (Oxford: Blackwell).
Berger, J. (1972) *Ways of seeing* (London: Penguin).
Charity Commission (2003) *Investment of charitable funds*, CC14, Charity Commission for England and Wales (online report), <www.charity-commission.gov.uk>.
Freeman, E. (1984) *Strategic management: A stakeholder approach* (Boston: Pitman).
Gauthier, I., Tarr, M.J., Moylan, J., Skudlarski, P., Gore, J.C. and Anderson, A.W. (2000) 'The fusiform "face area" is part of a network that processes faces at the individual level', *The Journal of Cognitive Neuroscience*, 123: 495–504.
Gray, R. (2002) 'Of messiness, systems and sustainability: Towards a more social and environmental finance and accounting', *British Accounting Review*, 34(4): 357–386.

Gray, R. (2001) '30 years of corporate social accounting, reporting and auditing: What (if anything) have we learnt?', *Business Ethics: A European Review*, 10(1): 9–15.

Kaulingfreks, R. and ten Bos, R. (2007) 'On faces and defacement: the case of Kate Moss', *Business Ethics: A European Review*, 16(3): 302–312.

Levinas, E. (1993) *Outside the subject*, trans. M.B. Smith (London: Athlone Press).

Macintyre, A. (1998) *A short history of ethics: A history of moral philosophy from the Homeric age to the twentieth century* (London: Routledge & Kegan Paul).

Moran, D. (2006) *Introduction to phenomenology* (London: Routledge).

Warnock, M. (1992) *The uses of philosophy* (Cambridge, MA: Blackwell).

5

Post and new-modern perspectives on accounting ethics

How have accountants become ethical?

Learning objectives

By the end of this chapter you should be able to:

- Explain the main contribution of postmodern perspectives to our understanding of accounting ethics;
- Discuss the relationship between power and ethics;
- Explain Michel Foucault's perspective on ethics and apply it to accounting;
- Explain how the work of Jürgen Habermas contributes to our understanding of accounting ethics;
- Critically evaluate whether postmodern approaches to ethics add to or detract from the pursuit of a just form of accounting practice.

INTRODUCTION

In the previous chapter we introduced some of the more traditional political moral philosophy and also briefly mentioned a related phenomenological perspective on ethics developed by Emmanuel Levinas. While Levinas' perspective is quite different, it is also grounded in what many commentators see as the primary issue at the heart of our ethical deliberations: the problem of our existence with others. We contended that while this fact has historically provided a rationale for ethics, or a framework for helping us understand the nature of the problem that we call ethics, the work of

Emmanuel Levinas suggests that our attempts to codify, legislate and proceduralize ethics, paradoxically serves only to distance us from the face of the Other and in the process, undermines the challenge that ethics represents.

We would like to conclude this part of the book by introducing two final perspectives that will hopefully give you some further insights into the relationship between accounting and ethics and the possibility of developing a more just form of accounting practice. In this chapter we will outline a postmodern perspective and what we will call a new-modern perspective on ethics. Technically, the first theory we will introduce should be called post-structuralist. As you might imagine there is a big debate among academics about the difference between postmodernism and post-structuralism; however, given this is an introductory text, we will keep things simple. In contrast to the traditional political moral philosophy literature, postmodern perspectives develop a more critical analysis of the relationship between individual ethical identity and power (or more precisely, the way in which power may operate to construct individuals as ethical subjects). Under the heading of new-modern perspectives we will discuss the work of a famous German thinker called Jürgen Habermas. Habermas criticizes the way some postmodern perspectives appear to abandon the very possibility of rational thought, and he attempts to salvage a role for reason in addressing the challenges that we face as a society.

Box 5.1 Postmodernism

Postmodern art

Damien Hirst is probably best known for a series of works in which he preserved dead animals, including a sheep and a cow, in formaldehyde. His most recent work, a diamond-encrusted skull, is rumoured to have sold for £50 million.

Hirst is part of a group of artists known as the Young British Artists. You may have come across the work of another member of the group in the media. Tracey Emin's *My Bed* was nominated for the Turner Prize in 1999. The work consists literally of her bed, replete with stained linen.

Postmodern film

Quentin Tarantino's *Pulp Fiction* contains many postmodern characteristics and the narrative of David Lynch's 2001 film, *Mulholland Drive* is even more obviously postmodern.

Postmodern music

The avant-garde composer John Cage is probably best known for his composition *4 minutes 33 seconds*. The piece, which is possibly one of the most controversial compositions of the twentieth century, consists of 4 minutes and 33 seconds of silence!

POSTMODERN PERSPECTIVES

We will start our discussion on postmodern perspectives on ethics with another German thinker: a nineteenth-century philosopher called Friedrich Nietzsche. By essentially arguing that it was the idea of morality itself that was dangerous, rather than unethical behaviour, Nietzsche fundamentally challenged the focus of much conventional ethical analysis (MacIntyre 1998)! Postmodern analysis draws on Nietzsche's basic premise to push the study of individual ethics away from questions of how an individual should behave, towards the way in which notions of good and bad come into being, are sustained and operate. Ethics is therefore viewed not primarily in essentialist or normative terms; rather the postmodern perspective explores how the notion of ethics, in terms of what is acceptable and unacceptable, comes to be defined. Hugh Willmott (1998), for example, talks about studying what is placed inside and what is placed outside the frame of reference when the notion of ethics is invoked within a particular context or discourse. Part of the postmodern discussion of ethics therefore refers to the *work* (but not in an intentional sense) that goes on in order to sustain this frame of reference. One of the most influential applications of this kind of perspective in recent years has come through the work of a French intellectual called Michel Foucault.

Foucault's ethics

In his later work Foucault posed the question: how do individuals become ethical subjects? Or, more specifically, how does 'ethical self understanding' emerge? This kind of reflection on the underlying ethical conditions that allow moral codes to function is therefore at a level below much of the conventional moral philosophy that we have considered in earlier chapters.

Foucault thought about this underlying ethical framework in terms of four major elements (McPhail 1999):

1. **The means by which we change ourselves in order to become ethical subjects**: our self-imposed discipline;
2. **The *telos***: the type of person we aspire to be when we behave morally;
3. **Ethical substance**: that part of ourselves which is taken to be the relevant domain for ethical judgement;
4. **The mode of subjection**: the way in which individuals are incited to recognize their moral obligations. For example, some obligations may be engendered by religious invocation while others may be engendered by social conventions, and yet others by reasoned analysis.

Foucault uses the term self-discipline to refer to the disciplinary power that we often exert against ourselves in order to regulate our actions. Often when we reflect on how power works we normally think in terms of one individual or group of individuals exercising power against another less powerful individual or group. Of course this mode of power isn't always terribly effective as those against whom power is exercised can resist in lots of different ways. However, Foucault was interested in how individuals wilfully and in many ways happily exercise power against themselves. While in more overt and oppressive forms of control, individuals may only reluctantly obey, the operation of power through the construction of ethical subjectivity may have less threatening connotations. An individual may in fact feel a sense of moral goodness or uprightness through the kind of self-disciplinary power that is exercised by individuals against themselves in the name of ethics. While this kind of power might be much more effective in serving particular interests, Foucault does not suggest that there is a controlling group of individuals purposefully strategizing about how best to get us to discipline ourselves. Interests do come to be served, but the King, that central controlling metaphor, as he puts it, is long dead in Western society.

The second characteristic of Foucault's conception of ethics, the *telos*, relates to the type of individuals we aspire to be when we discipline ourselves in order to behave morally. Before we go any further with this notion let's pause and reflect for a moment. Make a mental note of the characteristics of a good accountant. Where do you think these characteristics come from and how do you think they affect your actions, if at all? How does your ideal type of accountant differ from the way accountants are presented in the media and film?

We wonder if the way accounting is taught has had any impact on your list of characteristics? Because accountancy is generally taught within the rubric of neo-classical market economics, the corporation is generally seen to be responsible to society primarily to the extent that it maximizes its own efficiency and the wealth of its shareholders. Rational economic decisions are justified purely in terms of their financial impact on profit. While the kind of person that each individual accountant

Box 5.2 The accounting telos

For many accounting students the first real experience they get of professional accounting life is the careers material gathered in preparation for the milk round.

Take time to have a look at the following student recruitment pages for the big four accounting firms:

- Deloitte: http://careers.deloitte.com/united-kingdom/students/studentgrad.aspx
- Ernst & Young: http://www.ey.com/global/content.nsf/International/Careers
- KPMG: http://www.kpmgcareers.co.uk/Graduates/default.aspx?pg=2
- PricewaterhouseCoopers: http://www.pwc.com/uk/eng/car-inexp/student/home.html

How would you describe the ideal type of good accountant portrayed in this promotional material? Do you think it is different for different firms?

aspires to be undoubtedly emerges from a complex mixture of personal histories, research suggests that notions of efficiency and wealth maximization may be firmly embedded within the accounting *telos* (McPhail 1999).

The third characteristic in Foucault's conception of ethics is *ethical substance*. This element refers to those areas of our lives that we take to be the relevant domain for ethical judgement or, to put it another way, those parts of our lives that engage our moral reasoning. Let's pause again at this point and ask you to make a mental note of all those aspects of accounting where ethics comes into play. As we noted at the start of the book, many studies indicate that accountants just don't see the practice of accounting as something that involves any ethical considerations at all.

Finally, Foucault's notion of the *mode of subjection* refers to the fundamental medium through which we come to recognize our moral obligations. For example, within accountancy, moral responsibilities are engendered primarily through rational, economic analysis; however, the mode of subjection could equally be religious maxims.

Foucault's work has therefore been used to explore how power operates in a creative sense to construct and maintain the ethical subjectivities of individual accountants. Indeed, the broader critical and post-structuralist literature would challenge the accounting profession to reflect on exactly how power operates through professional ethics in order to serve particular interests.

We have provided only a very brief and sketchy outline of some of Foucault's work on ethics as we don't want you to miss the main objective of this section. We want you only to begin to think about the way in which particular ideas of what is good and bad come to be sustained.

Box 5.3 Accountants in the movies

The Untouchables (1987)
Oscar Wallace, the accountant in *The Untouchables*, is the man behind the plan to send Al Capone down on a simple tax evasion charge. Although Elliot Ness receives all the media attention, Wallace is the real hero of the piece, championing the rule of the law and the rights of the state over rough individuals. It is Wallace who manages to secure a conviction for Capone, based on the fact that he had failed to file tax returns for many years.

Schindler's List (1993)
In *Schindler's List* it is his accountant, Itzhak Stern, who comes up with the idea that by employing Jews as forced labour in his factories, Schindler could boost profit and save them from the concentration camps.

Stern's accounting is aimed at saving his fellow Jews.

How does your own perception of the ideal accountant relate to these two examples?

NEW-MODERN PERSPECTIVES: HABERMAS AND DISCOURSE ETHICS

We will now turn to the work of Jürgen Habermas. Habermas presents quite a different perspective on ethics to that of Foucault. However, we thought the juxtaposition of both these thinkers would be helpful in illuminating quite a big debate among academics about the possibility of more ethical forms of accounting and also about what it means to do good. We will return to this debate below after explaining Habermas' contribution to the debate in a little more detail.

It might be helpful to start by trying to succinctly outline what Habermas is trying to do. Habermas is concerned with how we, as a society, can work things out together, how we can best decide as a society what to do. The focus on society's role in determining an appropriate course of action is quite important, as we shall see. Hopefully it should also ring a few bells. Remember how in the previous chapter we discussed Hobbes and Rousseau's ideas about society and the legitimacy of governing institutions? Well Habermas picks up some of their basic themes, reinvigorates them and reworks them for a public sphere that, he contends, has become colonized by instrumental rationality.

In order to begin to grasp Habermas' views on ethics (or at least the point we want to stress), once again we need to begin with quite a tricky problem: the problem of how we understand each other, or the problem of interpretation and the meaning of actions. Hopefully, if you pause and think a little about this question you will be able to guess where Habermas is going to take us. He therefore commences with quite an obvious assumption. Working things out together should be based on some form of dialogue or communicative process. However, this starting point creates a series of problems. First, how can we be sure that we understand each other? Second, how can we ensure that one contribution to the debate is not more power-laden than another? Finally, how might it be possible to reach a conclusion? To put it very simply, Habermas develops the rules of the game for this communicative process to work. Technically, a lot of the questions that Habermas engages with in relation to communication and understanding are related to a field of study called hermeneutics.

As we implied above, Habermas, like Foucault, is interested in power. In fact he comes from a tradition of famous critical thinkers associated with what is called *The Frankfurt School* in Germany. Habermas, first wants to draw our attention to the socio-economic structures and power relationships that influence the way we derive meaning and understanding from social action. Outhwaite (1994) reflects Habermas' concerns quite emphatically when he says that language is not just a means of communication but is also 'a medium of domination and social power'. Habermas conceptualizes the way in which power operates through meaning in terms of distortions in communication. So Habermas contends that we should work things out together through some form of communicative process, but he then says that this is problematic because language, or the medium of communication, is ideological and power-laden, particularly when it comes to communicating what is and is not in our particular interests.

So where do we go from here? Well, Habermas doesn't take us to an impasse and leave us there. He suggests that this is what postmodern thinkers do. Rather, he

Box 5.4 Habermas and deliberative democracy

Although Habermas' ideas on ideal speech and communication might seem a little abstract, they inform an emerging kind of deliberative democracy that is behind some websites that you may have used or heard of.

In governing, the Scottish National Party has launched a *National Dialogue* in an attempt to engage Scots in a conversation about independence and the future of Scotland. Have a look at <www.scotland.gov.uk/topics/a-national-conversation>.

The American non-profit organization *AmericaSpeaks* attempts to facilitate broader civic engagement in decisions that impact on individuals' lives. The organization has developed a number of deliberative methods in order to facilitate this objective, including the twenty-first-century Town Meeting, which can facilitate discussion for up to 5,000 individuals. You can see their website at <www.americaspeaks.org/>.

The National Issue Forums (NIF) is another US network that allows citizens the opportunite to debate important political issues like education, energy and foreign policy. By doing so it promotes the development of competencies in public deliberation. You will find their website at <www.nifi.org>.

How do you think that deliberative forms of democracy could impact on professional bodies and the way they are run?

Box 5.5 The Frankfurt School

The Frankfurt School is the name given to an influential group of thinkers associated with the Institute for Social Research at the University of Frankfurt. The group included Max Horkheimer, Walter Benjamin, Theodor Adorno, Erich Fromm and Herbert Marcuse among others. Their research, which was significantly influenced by the work of Karl Marx, was very critical of both capitalism and narrow interpretations of Marx's ideas.

Herbert Marcuse's work and his book *One-Dimensional Man* in particular, is often associated with the student protests of the 1960s and what is generally refered to as the 'Prague Spring'. He has actually been accredited with coining the phrase, 'Make love not war'.

contends that while communication is distorted by power, it can nevertheless function as an arena for critique and progressive mutual understanding. Habermas therefore suggests that it is possible to transcend distorted communication and reach a truer position of meaning and consciousness.

In contrast to the prevailing distorted communication, Habermas develops a concept of an *ideal speech* situation. Habermas' theory of communication is therefore an attempt to respond to the hermeneutic challenge raised by earlier critical theorists and by hermeneutic philosophers. Here is how Hans-Georg Gadamer, puts the question: 'how can critical theory claim to be free of the distortion it locates in others without raising itself above the role of a partner in dialogue?' (Roderick 1986). Put rather more simply, the question is: how come your communication is not distorted by ideology but everyone else's is? It's important then to appreciate that Habermas is not contending that everyone should be able to contribute to the discussion and each person's contribution is as valid as the other. No, he hangs on to the possibility that we can progressively distinguish between what we will just call more and less acceptable positions from a multiplicity of perspectives. And how are we meant to do this? Through reason. Habermas contends that the most reasonable arguments should prevail. Technically this is called 'communicative rationality'.

Now, if we were to try and join the dots between some of the ideas that we have discussed already, then we might say that Habermas is trying to translate some of Kant's deontological ethics, for example that we can work out what we should do by rationally thinking about the nature of the action we are proposing, into a process of collective communicative action. However, as you will appreciate from earlier discussions, this focus on reason is quite contentious. Wolin (1992) sums up this critique beautifully when he says that while Habermas

> recognizes men and women primarily in their capacities as 'rational animals'-[, t]heir natures as impassioned, sentient, desiring beings, who also long to satisfy a variety of eudemonistic concerns, fall[ing] out of account in this approach. In sum, the notion of ideal speech has very little to tell us about the prospects of human happiness – which, as the first generation of critical theorists realized, have long nourished the nobler utopian impulses of humankind.
>
> (Wolin 1992: 44)

The important point that we would like you to take from this discussion is Habermas' focus on action and process. For Habermas, a particular course of action cannot be justified unless it has emerged from this kind of collective communicative action, a process that he terms an *ideal speech* situation.

POSTMODERN AND NEW-MODERN PERSPECTIVES

While it may not seem like it from the outlines we have provided above, there are actually a few similarities between Foucault and Habermas. For a start, both are concerned with power and the instrumentalist way we reason, in other words the preoccupation with how efficiently and effectively we can get things done without reflecting on whether they are worth doing. Habermas talks of the way communicative action has become 'colonized' by instrumental rationality and Foucault talks about 'normalization'. However, Habermas and Foucault proffer two quite different responses and we are going to use their positions as examples of two major competing intellectual trends. One camp, including Habermas, wants to retain a belief in the

Enlightenment project and salvage a role for reason in pushing humanity forward. The second camp includes the likes of Foucault. It is less utopian in outlook and more sceptical about the role that reason might play in taking us there. For the sake of simplicity, we have called the first camp new-modern and the second postmodern, though as is the case with most good academic debates both sides object to the way in which they are labelled. Habermas calls Foucault a postmodernist 'Young Conservative, enemy of the project of modernity' (Habermas 1984), while in one interview, when he was asked about postmodernism, Foucault somewhat teasingly replied, 'What is postmodernism? I'm not up-to-date'. Seriously, however, this is quite an important debate because it dramatically impinges on the possibilities of developing a just form of accounting practice.

First, it may be helpful to provide a description of modernity as (post)modernity would appear, at least on the surface, to be related to this notion.

For simplicity's sake let's say that the key aspects of the modern attitude can be traced back to a period in history that is commonly referred to as the Enlightenment. While this term is a gross simplification of a complex of ideas and debates that emerged towards the end of the seventeenth century,[1] the famous historian of ideas, Isaiah Berlin (1993), suggests that its use can be justified because there was a core of common beliefs that distinguished the period from others before it. If it's good enough for Isaiah Berlin, then it's good enough for us. Box 5.6 outlines the types of ideas that Berlin associates with this period. Notice first the positive, optimistic tone of progress and human advancement and second the belief that science and reason were going to secure this development. To use the nomenclature of those who think and write about this topic, it presents a *grand narrative* of progress through the application of science and reason. A lot of the debate is therefore around the sense of progress and the primacy of place given to reason.

Box 5.6 Characteristics of the Enlightenment

- Nature was governed by laws that could be discovered through scientific enquiry;
- The laws that governed nature were of a similar type to those that governed human nature;
- *Man* was capable of improvement;
- Every individual pursued a number of objective human goals like happiness, knowledge and justice;
- Human poverty and depravation were due to ignorance;
- Human nature comprised a basic set of given characteristics that differentiated humanity from other species.

A strong belief that progress could be made through the application of reason.

Source: based on Berlin (1993).

Having suggested a few characteristics of the modern perspective, let's now consider what a postmodern attitude might entail. We are going to start by making a distinction between *postmodernism* and postmodernity[2] and we are going to draw on Arran Gare (1995) to define both these terms. According to Gare (1995) the term postmodernity is more of a description of the times we live in. Postmodernity is essentially a descriptive term that is not a phase that comes after modernity, but is rather the end result of modernity. As Gare says, it represents the 'crisis of modernity' (1995). It describes the society in which we live, it does not prescribe the kind of society in which we should live. It is important to note in passing that Gare implies that postmodernism is essentially about finding ways to deal with, or address, the problems of a postmodern society. As such, it appears to be a positive rather than a passive notion.

The second term, postmodernist, refers to some of the characteristics of the kinds of individuals who live within a postmodern society. Have a look at Box 5.7 for the kinds of things that Gare (1995) associates with the postmodernist view. Do you associate any of these characteristics with your own outlook? Gare describes the postmodern individual as superficial and depthless. He suggests that post-modern individuals reject the distinction between true and false consciousness and lack a sense of 'genuine praxis' (1995: 33). In other words they eschew political engagement. Gare explains:

> Postmodernists, often assuming the posture of radicals, have not only disguised the lack of opposition to the rise of the New Right and to the globalization of capitalism, but have played a major part in undermining opposition to it. Decrying the quest for political power as the problem, they have handed over responsibility for their fate and the fate of the environment to economic rationalists, to the new international bourgeoisie and the international market.
>
> (1995: 35)

Box 5.7 Characteristics of postmodernity

- The rejection of big, all-encompassing grand narratives
- The rejection of the idea of progress
- The rejection of the idea of a given human nature, often referred to as the 'decentring of the subject'
- The delegitimization of established traditions and authority
- The fragmentation of consciousness into different and often contradictory roles
- The deterioration of academia into a service industry
- Gare also suggests that the environmental crisis may be both a symptom of postmodernity and an indictment of modernity.

Source: mostly based on Gare (1995).

> [F]or postmodernists it is simply too late to oppose the momentum of industrial society. They merely resolve to stay alert and cool in its midst. Consciously complying and yet far from docile, they chronicle, amplify and augment it. They judge it as little as it judges itself. Determined to assail nothing, they are passionately impassive.
>
> (Kariel 1989, quoted in Gare 1995: 34)

Gare (1995: 34) argues that postmodern culture is the culture where 'rational critique and protest have become impossible'. From these definitions you might begin to see why the debate gets a little bit heated as to whether Foucault was describing our postmodern condition or whether he was a passionately impassive postmodernist. For what it's worth we'd go with the former interpretation of Foucault's work.

The distinction between modernism and postmodernism is therefore not that simple; however, we don't want to get bogged down in arguments that won't help with our primary objective, which is to consider what the nub of this debate adds to our understanding of ethics and accounting. So for simplicity's sake let's just say that in contrast to the hope of progress and reason normally associated with modernity, the postmodern perspective suggests that the application of technology, science and reason and many of the things we associate with progress often result in less freedom, less democracy, less justice, and so on. In other words, what are often presented as elements in the march of truth and reason are actually sites of power that come to serve particular interests.

If nothing else, the debate should make us alert to the possibility that the efforts of the accounting profession over recent years to introduce ethics courses, ethics codes and corporate social responsibility reporting may in a paradoxical way work against ethics. Although Habermas and Foucault would probably suggest that this is indeed what is happening, they would differ in their understanding of how it can be that individuals and organizations that are ostensibly intent on doing good end up achieving little substantive progress. On the one hand Habermas might suggest that this is the inevitable consequence of a colonized lifeworld whereas Foucault might put the blame on a background episteme that sets the conditions of possibility for ethical progress. But the debate also forces us to reflect on how to and indeed whether one should respond. However, we are getting ahead of ourselves and we have a little more material to cover before we will be in a position to discuss these issues in detail.

Let's explore the implications of this debate for the issue that lies at the centre of our concerns: the ethics of accounting, and how to make accounting more ethical. The real challenge of this debate is whether justice is an ethical concept that is constructed through the discourses we populate, or whether it might be possible to come to some agreement as to what we really mean when we talk about justice. As we contended, Habermas' new-modern position still has a foundation. Indeed, the perceived anti-foundationalism which, it is suggested, characterizes postmodern philosophy is challenged by Habermas who considers this position to be both dangerous and nihilistic. As we contended above, Habermas argues that we should look to the future with the hope that incorporating greater communicative rationality into society will take us towards a better society.

Yet although postmodernism is often maligned for supposedly undermining the very possibility of ethical standards, there are many who employ this genre of work in a more positive manner. Campbell Jones (2003: 241), for example, contends that postmodern approaches to ethics have 'nothing to do with a vicious relativizing of ethical standpoints'. Willmott (1998: 77) similarly commends the use of post-structuralist theory in order to 'develop an approach to ethics which accepts this contingency without embracing a nihilistic attitude of "anything goes" '. He concludes that

> Poststructuralist . . . thinking points towards a position in which the contextual embeddedness of ethical discourse is accepted without concluding that this view necessarily renders human action ethically arbitrary and/or that any ethical anchor for human conduct is impossible. But, to repeat, moving towards this position necessitates a questioning and relinquishing of established ways of thinking about ethics.
>
> (1998: 77–78)

This more positive take on postmodern ethics not only resists the tendency to present ethical behaviour in an instrumentalized way but also cautions against any comforting reassurance that ethics proper can somehow be easily identified and restored to business in some formulaic manner, and managed appropriately. These perspectives attempt to retain a commitment to broader moral, civic and democratic aspirations without slipping into crude prescriptivism.

SUMMARY

Part I has introduced the broader moral philosophy literature. In order to begin to engage with this extensive research, the discussion has focused around four main strands within the literature: descriptive, normative, political and post- and new-modern perspectives. The first part of the text has therefore attempted to tease out, from these three broad literatures, insights that might contribute towards our understanding of accounting ethics, or at least the kinds of questions that an ethical investigation of accounting needs to address. These questions will be explored in more detail as we progress through the text.

The descriptive literature suggests that the ethical dispositions of individual accountants may be understood in terms of a complex mixture of individual characteristics, contextual attributes and issue-related factors. The normative literature provides some insights into the rational, consequentialist way in which accountants are implicitly taught how to behave in practice. However, the other modalities discussed within this literature throw the prevailing accounting ethic into relief and encourage us to reflect on whether it is indeed how we want accountants to behave. Finally, the political moral philosophy literature places the practice of accounting within its broader social, political and economic context. The more traditional literature focuses on why it might be important for individuals to behave ethically and the critical and post-structuralist literature considers the way in which power might operate through individual ethical subjectivity.

The following chapters in Part II of the book build on this foundation by exploring the ethics of accounting in more specific detail.

QUESTIONS

1 Write a brief description of your image of the good accountant and
   a reflect on where your characteristics of the good accountant comes from;
   b reflect on the interests your notion of the good accountant serves.
2 Explain Michel Foucault's notion of ethics and discuss how it contributes towards our understanding of accounting ethics.
3 Discuss the extent to which you think accounting practice is consistent with Jürgen Habermas' idea of ideal speech.
4 Discuss whether postmodern approaches to ethics add to or detract from the pursuit of a just form of accounting practice.

NOTES

1 There is some debate about the exact dates that should apply to this period.
2 Gare (1995) suggests that *postmodern* has so many and varied uses that the word almost has no meaning at all. It is therefore with a recognition of their arbitrariness that these definitions are offered.

RESOURCES

Films

The Accountant (1989), made for the BBC by Geoffrey Case. Alfred Molina plays a Jewish accountant who is dumped by most of his clients because he is too honest!

See also the films *The Untouchables* and *Schindler's List* cited in Box 5.3.

ITunes podcasts

'Postmodern Imperialism', David Laitin and James Fearon, Political Science, Stanford University.

READING

Accounting: Foucault and Habermas

Armstrong, P. (1994) 'The influence of Michel Foucault on accounting research', *Critical Perspectives on Accounting*, 5: 25–55.

Broadbent, J. (1998) 'The gendered nature of "accounting logic": Pointers to an accounting that encompasses multiple values', *Critical Perspectives on Accounting*, 9(3): 267–297.

Grey, C. (1994) 'Debating Foucault: A critical reply to Neimark', *Critical Perspectives on Accounting*, 5: 5–24.

Hoskin, K.W. (1994) 'Boxing clever: For, against and beyond Foucault in the battle for accounting theory', *Critical Perspectives in Accounting*, 5: 57–85.

McPhail, K.J. (1999) 'The threat of ethical accountants: An application of Foucault's concept of ethics to accounting education and some thoughts on ethically educating for the other', *Critical Perspectives on Accounting*, 10: 833–866.

Miller, P. (1992) 'Accounting and objectivity: The intervention of calculating selves and calculable spaces', *Annals of Scholarship*, 9(1/2): 61–86.

Miller, P. and O'Leary, T. (1987) 'Accounting and the construction of the governable person', *Accounting, Organizations and Society*, 12(3): 235–265.

Neimark, M. (1990) 'The King is dead. Long live the King!', *Critical Perspectives on Accounting*, 1: 103–114.

Power, M. and Laughlin, R. (1996) 'Habermas, law and accounting', *Accounting, Organizations and Society*, 21(5): 441–465.

Books by Foucault

Foucault, M. (1977) *Discipline and punish: The birth of the prison* (London: Allen Lane).

Foucault, M. (1970) *The order of things: An archaeology of human sciences* (London: Tavistock).

Books by Habermas

Habermas, J. (1997) *Legitimation crisis*, trans. T. McCarthy (Cambridge: Polity Press).

Habermas, J. (1989) *The structural transformation of the public sphere: Inquiry into a category of bourgeois society* (Cambridge: Polity Press).

Habermas, J. (1989) *The theory of communicative action, volume 2: The critique of functional reason*, trans. T. McCarthy (Cambridge: Polity Press).

Habermas, J. (1984) *The theory of communicative action, volume 1: Reason and rationalisation of society*, trans. T. McCarthy (London: Heinemann).

Books on Habermas and Foucault

Hoy, C.D. (ed.) (1994) *Foucault: A critical reader* (Oxford: Blackwell).

Outhwaite, W. (1994) *Habermas: A critical introduction* (Oxford: Polity Press).

Outhwaite, W. (ed.) (1996) *The Habermas reader* (Oxford: Polity Press).

Poster, M. (1984) *Foucault, marxism and history: Mode of production versus mode of information* (Cambridge: Polity).

Roderick, R. (1986) *Habermas and the foundations of critical theory* (Basingstoke: Macmillan Education).

Simons, J. (1995) *Foucault and the political* (London: Routledge).

Habermas and process ethics

Hamlin, A. and Pettit, P. (1989) *The good polity, normative analysis of the state* (New York: Wiley Blackwell).

Lehman, G. (2001) 'Reclaiming the public sphere: Problems and prospects for corporate social and environmental accounting', *Critical Perspectives on Accounting*, 12: 713–733.

Richardson, A.J. (2007) 'Due process and standard-setting: An analysis of due process in three Canadian accounting and auditing standard-setting bodies', *Journal of Business Ethics*, 81(3): 679–696.

Postmodern ethics

Bauman, Z. (1997) *Postmodernity and its discontents* (Cambridge: Polity Press).

Bauman, Z. (1995) *Life in fragments: Essays in postmodern morality* (Oxford: Blackwell).

Bauman, Z. (1993) *Postmodern ethics* (Oxford: Blackwell Publishers).

Harvey, D. (1996) *The condition of postmodernity* (Cambridge, MA: Blackwell).

REFERENCES

Berlin, I. (1993) *The magus of the north: J.G. Hamann and the origins of modern irrationalism* (London: John Murray).

Gare, A.E. (1995) *Postmodernism and the environmental crisis* (London: Routledge).

Habermas, J. (1984) *The theory of communicative action, volume 1: Reason and rationalisation of society*, trans. T. McCarthy (London: Heinemann).

Jones, C. (2003) 'As if business ethics were possible, "within such limits" ', *Organization*, 10(2): 223–248.

Kariel, H.S. (1989) *The desperate politics of postmodernism* (Amherst: University of Massachusetts Press).

MacIntyre, A. (1998) *A short history of ethics: A history of moral philosophy from the Homeric age to the twentieth century* (London: Routledge & Kegan Paul).

McPhail, K.J. (1999) 'The threat of ethical accountants: An application of Foucault's concept of ethics to accounting education and some toughts on ethically educating for the other', *Critical Perspectives on Accounting*, 10: 833–866.

Outhwaite, W. (1994) *Habermas, a critical introduction* (Oxford: Polity Press).

Roderick, R. (1986) *Habermas and the foundations of critical theory* (Basingstoke: Macmillan Education).

Willmott, H. (1998) 'Towards a new ethics? The contributions of poststructuralism and posthumanism', in M. Parker (ed.), *Ethics and organization* (London: Sage), 76–121.

Wolin, R. (1992) *The politics of cultural criticism: The Frankfurt School, existentialism, postmodernism* (New York: Columbia University Press).

PART II

The ethics of accounting practice

6

The function of accounting and the morality of the market

Learning objectives

By the end of this chapter you should be able to:

- Explain how a free-market system operates;
- Describe the function that accounting performs within a free-market system;
- Explain the values that accounting supports within a free-market system;
- Explain the idea of distributive justice;
- Discuss the different ways in which unequal distributions within an economic system can be justified;
- Explain the idea of utilitarianism.

INTRODUCTION

The Enron debacle once again brought the ethics of accountants into question. Was David Duncan, Andersen's man in charge of the Enron audit, wrong to order the shredding of audit papers? If he knew it was wrong, why did he request that the evidence be destroyed? And why did his subordinates obey him? As we discussed in Chapter 2, the organizational setting within which dilemmas are experienced (or not experienced as the case may be) often influences individual ethical behaviour in quite complex ways. However, this chapter addresses a more subtle and perhaps less obvious question: are the millions of accountants, who don't break the law, who rigorously apply accounting standards and professional principles in their work and generally do their job well each day, doing something good, or something bad?

Some of the empirical literature discussed earlier would suggest that many accountants might think this is a strange question to ask as the practice of accounting is often viewed as an amoral activity. This is hardly surprising as these big questions are rarely explored within accounting education, and are often absent from professional education also. Both this chapter and the following one aim to address this particular misconception in some detail. This chapter will consider the ethics of rendering an account per se and focuses specifically on the role that accounting systems play in facilitating particular kinds of economic ideologies (Gray 1990; Gray *et al.* 1994). In other words, if accounting helps a particular system to function, we therefore need to ask whether that system is good or bad. The economic system is quite obviously not amoral. So it would seem like rather fuzzy logic to argue that a key social institution, like accounting, that helps make it work, is. If we can't provide an ethical justification for the economic ideology then there is little reason for accounting to support it.

The fragmentation of functions, particularly within bureaucratic economic systems, and the inability of different functional groups to grasp how their job serves broader ends have been a key concern for many social commentators, none more so than the celebrated sociologist Zygmunt Bauman. In his prize-winning study, *Modernity and the Holocaust* (1996), Bauman contends that one of the reasons why so many people died in the Holocaust, one reason why the killing was so efficient, was because the aim of the final solution was, by design, split into different tasks. Some people filled in forms in offices, some plumbers did the pipework in the chambers, and some people drove trains, while other organizations provided financing. Of course there were also cruel, brutal and merciless people who kicked and punished and killed. Bauman is not trying to justify what happened, nor is he attempting to diminish the responsibility of those involved; he is trying to understand it sociologically. The pertinence of Bauman's argument is therefore that sometimes, even when they are doing their job well, people might be contributing towards something that is ultimately ethically indefensible. Maybe the driver of the train drove carefully within the speed limit, maybe he was a good train driver, but he was driving Jews to Auschwitz.

Part I of this book provided some of the ethical groundwork required for us to begin to analyse accounting from an ethical perspective. With this foundation in place, we are now in a position to begin to explore the ethical principles that underpin how accounting functions within society. This chapter will focus primarily on the role that accounting plays within market-based economies. While accounting serves different roles within different types of political economic systems, we will focus on the free-market system for the obvious reason that it is the predominant global ideology (we will return to the issue of globalization later when we consider the ethics of international accounting, and harmonization in particular). The chapter will also highlight a number of more general ethical issues that characterize the function of accounting within many different types of economic systems. For example, most accounting systems are based on certain rights and consequently are related to some corresponding notion of justice and fairness.

The chapter will draw on the consequentialist position outlined in Chapter 2 and also the idea of rights introduced in Chapter 3, in order to explore the ethical values implicit within everyday accounting practice as it functions in a free-market economy. In particular, both these concepts will be used to develop an understanding of the system of *distributive justice* accounting serves and the *financial utilitarian* ethic that is used to justify this system.

The chapter is structured as follows. The first section describes the free-market capitalist economic model in some detail. It explains the role of accounting within

Box 6.1 IBM and the Holocaust

During the systematic persecution and annihilation of European Jews between 1933 and 1945 in the Holocaust, statistics and technology were key tools used by Nazi Germany in its industrialized mass murder of six million Jews.

The forerunner to the modern computer, the Hollerith machine – manufactured by International Business Machines Corporation (IBM) and its foreign subsidiaries – was used by German government statistical offices to track Jewish population centres and geographic locations of others deemed undesirable. The Hollerith machine used cards to store data which were fed into a machine that compiled the results mechanically. Each card represented a person, and each hole punched on the card was accorded a specific meaning corresponding to occupation, education, health or some other characteristic – such as Jewishness.

In his award-winning book, *IBM and the Holocaust* (2001), Edwin Black contends that IBM and its German subsidiary did not merely supply machines, but rather that they custom-designed complex solutions in order to meet the Reich's needs. They did not merely sell the machines and walk away. IBM leased these machines for high fees and became the only source of the billions of punch cards Hitler needed.

Within at least four concentration camps, Hollerith departments registered the arrival of inmates, the transfer of labourers between camps, and the deaths of prisoners.

that system and therefore the values that it consequently supports. The second section introduces the idea of *distributive justice* and explains how this notion is conceived within the capitalist model. The final section expands on the theory of *utilitarianism* because this ethical position is generally used to justify the distribution of economic returns within a capitalist system.

ACCOUNTING AND FREE-MARKET ECONOMICS

From a broad political/economic perspective, developing an ethical understanding of accounting requires an appreciation of the function of accounting within society. There is some considerable debate within the academic literature as to the specific nature of this function, and indeed whether it is helpful to view accounting through a functionalist paradigm. However, for the sake of simplicity and in order that we might begin to grapple with the ethics of accounting, this chapter will focus on the predominant information function of accounting (Gray 1990; Gray *et al.* 1994). The nature of the information and the way it is collected and presented will depend upon the particular political/economic system within which it is embedded, whether this system is a centralized economy, feudal society or a free-market system. There are therefore ethical issues associated with the function of accounting within specific economic systems. However, it is important to highlight in passing that the nature of the relationship between an accounting system and the political/economic system is complex. For example, by accounting for certain things in particular ways, the accounting system does not simply become a proceduralization of a set of values, but rather it also helps to construct reflexively certain values as being of specific importance. In other words, the accounting system does not only passively implement values; in part it actively constructs values (Hines 1988). To employ the language of the postmodern position we introduced in the previous chapter, it helps to construct ethical subjectivities.

Within the majority of Western economies, accounting is embedded within a free-market, capitalist, economic system. It helps to make that system work and it therefore implicitly promotes the values upon which that system is based. The post-Enron level of political interest in accounting, for example Gordon Brown's 2002 House of Commons Select Committee inquiry: 'The Financial Regulation of Public Limited Companies', in the UK and the Sarbanes-Oxley Act in the USA, provide some indication of at least the perceived importance of a credible accounting system for capitalist economies to work properly. In real terms, the Enron debacle had a significant effect in global markets and this in turn had a major impact on pensions and endowment mortgages, for example. It's only when we appreciate how many

Box 6.2 Accounting, sustainability and natural capital

One example of the way the accounting system constructs certain values as being of specific importance has been highlighted by environmentalists. They point out that there are two types of capital. The first is *natural* capital, such as the ozone layer, rainforests and fossil fuels. The second type is *artificial* capital, which has been created using natural capital and includes machinery, buildings, products, roads, waste materials, and so on.

Artificial capital is created and expanded at the expense of natural capital. As artificial capital expands, it is inevitable that natural capital must decline.

As accountants, we have focused exclusively on measuring the artificial capital side of this equation, and have ignored natural capital completely. Under traditional accounting, we can prudently only take as income whatever is left over after leaving our capital intact (the concept of capital maintenance). But when we include natural capital in the overall picture, it is clear that we are not leaving our capital intact, we are leaving it depleted.

By ignoring natural capital, it can be argued that the accountancy profession has not only acquiesced in allowing the environmental crisis to develop, but also has actually exacerbated the problem by fooling businesses and economies into thinking they were maintaining capital, when in fact they were doing just the opposite.

Box 6.3 The Financial Reporting Review Panel

The Financial Reporting Review Panel (FRRP) was established in 1990 as part the Financial Reporting Council. It was formed against a background of concerns about auditor independence and allegations of dubious accounting practices, especially in published financial statements carrying unqualified audit reports. The Panel states that it 'aims to support investor, market and public confidence in the financial and governance stewardship of listed and other entities by ensuring that the provision of financial information by public and large private companies complies with relevant accounting requirements'.

The Panel can ask directors to explain apparent departures from the requirements. If the Panel is not satisfied by the directors' explanations, it aims to persuade the directors to adopt a more appropriate accounting treatment. The directors may then voluntarily withdraw their accounts and replace them with revised accounts that correct the matters in error. Depending on the circumstances, the Panel may accept another form of remedial action – for example, correction of the comparative figures in the next set of annual financial statements. Failing voluntary correction, the Panel can exercise its powers to secure the necessary revision of the accounts through a court order. Also, if the case concerns accounts issued under the UK Listing Rules, the Panel may report it to the Financial Services Authority.

Critics of the FRRP argue that it is not a truly independent or transparent organization. Although it is charged with securing public confidence, it keeps the public out of its meetings. None of its files and documents relating to any investigations are made available for public scrutiny.

The FRRP's investigating teams are largely made up of representatives of the 'Big 4' accountancy firms (the four largest accountancy firms). These major accountancy firms also audit most of the published accounts that are investigated. Many of these complaints are subsequently rejected. When accounts *are* found to be 'defective' the FRRP issues a press release, briefly explaining how it has dealt with the matter. However, the auditors of the companies publishing defective audited accounts are not named.

Critics argue that under the current system, accountancy firms directly implicated in the production of 'defective' accounts do not face any sanctions. They continue to be indulged and act as both judges and juries for the FRRP.

other important social issues are tied into the performance of the market that we can begin to understand the level of political concern.

A neoclassical system of free-market economics is based on the assumption that economic growth and development, or progress, can be achieved through free unrestricted, unregulated markets. The official and somewhat abridged version of the story goes like this:

- Companies produce and sell their services/products in free competition with other companies.
- The sovereign consumer decides which product they wish to purchase.
- Companies that produce products or provide services we want, at a price we are willing to pay (in other words the efficient, innovative and effective companies), will prosper and grow.
- In order to grow and develop, companies require more capital.
- Banks and investors will provide capital to only profitable and efficient companies.
- These investors therefore require financial information about the company in order to know which companies are profitable and efficient. In other words, they require credible information in order to make investment and lending decisions.
- This information is provided by the system of financial reporting.
- The owners of the organizations have a right to continue to receive information. This entitlement is based on their property rights.

In order to understand the ethical function of accounting within this system we need to identify the defining ethical characteristics of capitalism (Bassiry and Jones 1993; Gray 1990). It is important to point out at this juncture that these characteristics are derived from a purely theoretical appreciation of capitalism. We will discuss whether these characteristics stand up to empirical scrutiny later in the chapter.

A free-market capitalist economic system has four defining characteristics. These are:

1 Private ownership of the means of production
2 Competition
3 The division between capital and labour
4 The profit motive.

Privately owned enterprises compete with each other as they strive to become more profitable. This crude representation is somewhat caricatured; however, it is a distortion that is found in the majority of accounting, finance and economic textbooks and taught either explicitly or implicitly in many accounting courses. Each of these characteristics is underpinned by, and promotes, a specific set of values. These characteristics also generate many ethical questions. For example, is there a problem of vesting the control of organizations entirely with the suppliers of capital? Is competition good or does cooperation yield greater socio-economic returns? Is the division of capital and labour equitable? And does this system distribute economic returns in a just and equitable way?

We will return to some of these questions later in the book; however, the remainder of this chapter focuses on the last question. Within moral philosophy, the way in which an economic system distributes economic returns is generally discussed under the rubric of distributional justice. In the section below we will introduce Marx's critique of the capitalist system, and in particular the division between capital and labour in order to open up the analysis.

RIGHTS AND DISTRIBUTIVE JUSTICE

Within a capitalist system, the owners of capital employ labour as a factor of production. And as a consequence this sets up a particular kind of accountability relationship between the two parties. On the one hand labour is accountable to the suppliers of capital; however, the owners of capital also have the right to benefit from labour's output. In other words, the capital providers have a right to the profits that labour helps to generate.

This relationship has been the subject of much critical analysis, most famously by Karl Marx. Marx suggested that the relationship between capital and labour was exploitative. He contended that while it is true that employees enter into an employment contract of their own free will, he nevertheless suggested that the private ownership of capital placed the owners in a position of power. This powerful position, he suggested, enabled them to extract a return from labour that exceeded the scarcity value of their capital. In other words, he suggested that the outcome of the economic system, or more specifically the profit generated by the firm, was not fairly distributed between the owners of capital and the employees. This issue relates directly to accounting practice because it is generally assumed and taught within accounting education that the business is run specifically for the benefit of the owners and not the employees. It is an assumption that is encapsulated in finance and economic theory through the maximization of shareholder return (Primeaux and Steiber 1994).

Of course accounting information can be used for wage bargaining, however, the issue here is the general orientation of the accounting profession and financial accounting information more specifically. Financial reports are not officially produced for employees; they are produced for and are addressed to investors with a view to informing their investment decisions.[1] The provision of information to existing capital providers and the requirement that managers maximize shareholder return is based on a specific right: the property rights of shareholders as the owners of the firm. As we discussed in Chapter 3, the idea of what constitutes a right is actually quite complex. For example, while many of us might construe property rights as a fairly inalienable right, it is in fact culturally specific. Within Australian Aboriginal culture, for example, the idea of private property is quite alien. Indeed property rights in themselves are often contentious and should not be accepted uncritically. An individual may own a particular piece of property, and possess legal title, however, we may decide that their ownership is somehow unethical. The ownership of Aboriginal land in Australia, for example, has generated considerable debate, as has the explosion of the housing market in the UK and Europe more generally driven by multiple home ownership.

We also noted above that we could conceive of a number of different rights, all of which are particularly relevant within our current business climate, intellectual property, animal rights, and even the rights of future generations. Of course it would be silly to suggest that the accounting profession should be responsible for enforcing all rights, even all human rights. Different rights can be protected via different institutions. For example, the rights of employees could be protected via legislation, health and safety acts and suchlike, or through the trade unions. However, it is important that we are aware that accounting practice is about rights and that within

Box 6.4 The minimum wage

The national minimum wage was introduced by the UK government in 1999. It aims to provide employees with decent minimum standards and fairness in the workplace. It applies to nearly all workers and sets hourly rates below which pay must not be allowed to fall. The government argues that it helps business by ensuring companies will be able to compete on the basis of quality of the goods and services they provide and not on low prices based predominantly on low rates of pay. The rates set are based on the recommendations of the independent Low Pay Commission.

The introduction of the minimum wage was fiercely opposed by many in the business community. The opponents of minimum wage claimed that the payment of a decent wage would increase industry's 'costs' and erode British industry's competitiveness, resulting in lower economic activity and impoverishment of low-paid employees.

Some Marxist commentators have argued that the claim that minimum wages will increase costs is underpinned by conventional accounting practices. They argue that conventional accounting is far from being neutral and unbiased, but is in fact highly political. If employees are regarded as equally legitimate stakeholders in a company, along with the shareholders, the establishment of a minimum wage would not result in any increase in costs, but would be seen as a redistribution of the wealth generated among stakeholders.

conventional free-market economics, accounting prioritizes a particularly set of rights. In other words, everyday accounting practice is about some quite fundamental ethical issues. Once we appreciate that accounting is about rights and that there are many valid rights within a business context that should be protected, then the question is whether some institutions are more powerful and effective in ensuring that certain rights are upheld in contrast to others; whether accounting practice should be based on a broader set of rights; and if so, how those rights could be constituted.

So the capitalist system is characterized in part by the relationship between capital providers and labour providers. We have begun very simply to explore whose rights the accounting system serves. Of course the reality of modern capitalism is considerably more complex than this simple caricature implies (Grant 1991). For a start we have ignored a third important group: management. However, there is a more tricky issue. In many cases the binary distinction between capital and employees does not hold. For example, employees may also be capital owners, either through incentive and bonus schemes or through pension funds or endowment mortgages (although these forms of capital ownership apply to a relatively affluent group in society).

On the one hand then there are the rights of the capital providers; however, Marx's critique is based on a second set of rights: not the property rights of the owners but the rights of the participants within the economic system to receive their fair share of

Box 6.5 Australian Aborigines

The modern notion of possessions is alien to traditional Australian Aboriginal culture. Material things were shared within groups. The idea that an individual could 'own' land was foreign to Aboriginal thinking.

When Europeans first began to colonise Australia, towards the end of the eighteenth century, they found resources and environments which were of incalculable value. Seizure of Australia by British Imperial forces was claimed to take place under British law.

Even at that time, the British legal system had developed some traditions of fair dealings with native populations inside colonies, but these constraints were not applied in Australia. Invasion and blatant land theft by settlers were justified under the astonishing legal fiction of 'Terra Nullius' – the notion that Australia was effectively unoccupied before British colonization.

The lack of indigenous systems of land ownership (in the European tradition of private land ownership) was used to give credence to the idea of Terra Nullius. The basic idea was that it was impossible to rob Aboriginal people of land, as they had previously never owned it.

Over two centuries, the continent was progressively stolen from Aboriginal people. Settlers moved in and appropriated the overwhelming majority of Australia – either for private use or in the name of the British Crown.

Box 6.6 Current population versus future population

There is a growing recognition that modern governments and businesses cannot continue to act irresponsibly in terms of their damaging effect on the environment. The Rio Earth Summit in 1992 set out a vision for the twenty-first century, calling on all governments to elaborate national strategies, plans and processes to ensure the implementation of sustainable development. This approach recognizes that profits made today at the expense of the environment are effectively a tax on future generations – those yet to be born.

This raises a conflict between intergenerational and intra-generational equity. Spending large amounts of money today on cleaner technology will hopefully improve the quality of life (in terms of reducing global warming, improving the quality of the atmosphere, reducing river pollution, and so on) for future generations. But that money could have been spent on improving the quality of life for today's poor – possibly in the form of aid to developing nations. Every pound spent on improving environmental quality and natural resources quality for future generations is a pound not spent on improving welfare today.

the output of the economic system. Marx's critique is therefore about whether the various parties in the economic system get what they deserve. This is a really fundamental question and what it boils down to is this: is capitalism just?

It may be helpful to begin our exploration of distributive justice by considering some examples of justice within different contexts. Take for example procedural justice: the idea that each individual has the right to receive a fair trial, or retributive justice: the idea that an individual should receive a punishment that is commensurate with the crime they have committed. The notion of justice can therefore be applied in different contexts, but it always involves the idea that individuals should get what they deserve, or more specifically what they have a right to receive. In a similar way, then, distributive justice relates to the way the product of the economic system is distributed. It is to do with the question of what is the most equitable way to apportion economic growth and wealth among individuals within a particular society.

The debate surrounding how equitable the neoliberal, free-market economic system is in the way it apportions wealth and property is generally justified by reference to four concepts: efficiency, liberty, entitlement and utility. Each of these ideas is briefly outlined below.

Equality and efficiency

In contrast to the notion of equality (at least in terms of distribution), the idea of efficiency is a fairly modern virtue. Free-market, neoliberal economic theory presents a tension between these two concepts (Chryssides and Kaler 1996). Efficiency is seen as a key prerequisite for economic development. If the market is to enhance our lives, through the development of new and better-quality products and services then, according to neoliberal proponents of the free market, there needs to be competition and therefore some associated disparity in financial incentives. The market, they argue, needs to reward the harder-working and more innovative employees. In other words, some inequality in the distribution of economic return is justified, that is, equality is trumped by efficiency. Indeed many would point to the apparent crippling inefficiencies in many centralized economies as empirical evidence in support of their argument for inequality.

This argument is, however, quite contentious at a number of levels. First, it is based on Hobbes' assumption that individuals are self-interested and it assumes that human beings are rational wealth maximizers. Second, it suggests that the rewards of the economic system should be distributed based on some notion of merit; however, we need to define what we mean by merit. Inequality in rewards is not just related to an individual's contribution to the economic system. The wages of employees in the UK and India are obviously not just related to the contribution or effort of individual employees, but are related to structural issues. A precondition for returns from the economic system is access to capital and there is quite obviously a huge discrepancy in an individual's ability to access capital (including capital in all its new forms, such as social capital and intellectual capital).

Equality and liberty

A second, related argument is based on the notion of liberty and more specifically freedom of contract (Chryssides and Kaler 1996). From a neoliberal perspective, individuals should be free to choose, for example, how many hours they wish to work and where. If individuals are free to enter into market transactions as they wish then this will inevitably result in an unequal distribution of economic returns. However, because it is the individual's free choice then this unequal distribution is justified. To require that the output of the economic system be distributed equally, you would either have to reward people equally for unequal effort or force everyone to contribute the same level of effort.

However, again this argument is quite contentious, primarily because it is considerably more complex than either of these scenarios suggest. The freedom to transact for a certain level of work needs to be set within the broader social realities of inequality in power and opportunity.

Liberty, for example, is not only about freedom from interference, freedom from impediments, and so on, but it is also about the ability to act. It is about having the requisite resources and also the capacity to act.

Box 6.7 Prostitution – a trade like any other or exploitation?

The liberal approach to prostitution is based on traditional liberal theory, which is committed to autonomy, individualism and minimum state interference in private choice. Prostitutes' rights groups argue that, rather than extinguishing autonomy, prostitution enables it to flourish. Prostitutes may indulge the sexual desires of others, but only for discrete periods, and under circumstances they control. They can withdraw their services at their discretion, set their hours and wages, and service only customers they choose to. Prostitutes should be allowed to organize, advertise, pay taxes and receive unemployment benefits and state pensions.

Another view is that prostitutes are exploited, and are acting in response to a lack of economic alternatives. The majority of prostitutes are women, and women the world over are poorer than men. Indeed, there is a relation between the low economic status of women and their involvement in prostitution. Unemployment, poor education, few available jobs, inadequate salaries are some of the factors which force some women into prostitution. In many countries, the absence of a social security net also contributes to the problem. For many women, prostitution is the only means available to ensure their survival and that of their families. Women who are homeless, without any help from the state, marginalized because of their race, find that prostitution is the only way out.

Equality and entitlement

Both arguments above are based on a particular notion of merit. Unequal distributions are justified because they are merited. Nozick's theory of *entitlement*, however, provides a third and quite different way of thinking about distributive justice. Writing from a neoliberal perspective, Nozick presents a *process*, as opposed to an *outcome* theory of distributive justice (Chryssides and Kaler 1996). An individual's share of the wealth should, according to Nozick, be appraised in terms of how that wealth has been accumulated. He contends that inequality in the outcome of the economic system can be justified, provided that this situation has arisen without the infringement of anyone's rights, (although he restricts rights mainly to property rights). Indeed Nozick contends that any attempt to rectify this situation and impose some form of redistribution would be unjust.

Drawing on Nozick's arguments, it might even be possible to construe the function of accounting as an attempt to ensure that the accumulation of wealth is achieved without the violation of rights. But from the discussion above, it is quite obvious that the scope of conventional accounting practice is fairly narrow when it comes to protecting rights. It is left to other organizations to ensure that the rights of others, for example employees, customers and society in general, are not contravened. It is also argued that corporations' extensive use of lobbyists ensures that certain rights do not become encoded in law.

Utilitarianism

Accounting in a free-market system does contribute towards an unequal distribution of economic outcomes. While it might be possible to justify this inequality both in terms of merit and entitlement, the main theoretical justification for this system, and the one that underpins accounting practice, is a form of consequentialist theory called utilitarianism.

From a utilitarian perspective, a particular distribution of economic resources is just, provided that it maximizes total utility (see Chryssides and Kaler 1996). You may recall, from Chapter 3, the distinction between the right and the good in teleological theory. Consequentialism is a theory of the right; however, it requires a good against which the consequences of various actions can be appraised. Utilitarianism is a theory of the good. Neoliberal, free-market economic theory is therefore based on a combination of consequentialism with a particular version of utilitarian theory.

As its name suggests, utilitarianism starts with the idea that actions can be described as ethically good only if they have some utility – if they are useful. In other words, an action is good only if it is good for something or someone. This stipulation, however, results in a second question: useful for what? Initially the answer to this question was that it must be useful for preventing pain or promoting pleasure. This, hedonistic, form of utilitarianism is similar to a slightly more sophisticated, preference satisfaction version which is generally called preference utilitarianism. From this perspective, an act is good if it satisfies an individual's preferences. To some extent

Box 6.8 Taxation – Nozick and the basketball player

Libertarians generally view taxation as theft and are against it accordingly. Many oppose all personal and corporate income taxation, including capital gains taxes and inheritance taxes, and support the eventual repeal of all taxation. Some libertarians, such as Nozick, do not envision a government that operates without taxes. However, these should be limited to providing defence against aggressors, both domestic and foreign. Any other taxes according to Nozick are theft.

Nozick illustrates his point with the tale of Wilt Chamberlain (in real life one of the greatest players in the history of American basketball). Let's say this player asks everyone who comes to see him play to pay 25 cents, and a million people come to watch during the season. The result of this is that Chamberlain will make $250,000. However, because of the taxation laws this money will not be Chamberlain's to do with as he wishes in spite of the fact that it was his skill on the basketball court that drew the crowds who willingly paid to see him demonstrate his skill. He will only get a proportion of this money as the rest will be taxed and redistributed in the way the government sees fit. If Chamberlain decides not to do his tour, everyone loses out. The fans are deprived of seeing him demonstrate his talents and he is deprived of using his skill to make money for himself, and the tax authorities get nothing. Nozick believes that taxing Chamberlain is unjust and deprived both him and his supporters from their choice to transfer their property – in this case 25 cents – which was a fair and just transaction, entered into voluntarily by those who chose to attend the game.

this attitude is implicit in the market model as the sovereign consumer decides what companies will produce. However, both hedonistic and preference models have been criticized for diminishing and demeaning the idea of morality and conflating it into consumer demand. The concern is that there may indeed be some things that are good even though no one desires them!

Utilitarianism was initially construed as a method for establishing appropriate public policies. From a utilitarian perspective, the most ethical public policy is the one that maximizes utility, after the utility of each individual involved has been summed. But this creates a problem – how do you sum different utilities? In order to do this, you need to make a number of assumptions. First, you need to assume that individuals will have similar preferences towards different products. However, the greater difficulty lies in the necessity of treating each individual's preferences as comparable. Consider the problem of allocating scarce resources in the National Health Service. How should we make the decision between a hip replacement and a cataract operation? From our perspective, we would rather be able to see than to walk. It might be easy enough for one individual to articulate their own preferences for themselves, however, how can we mediate between the preferences of different individuals? The utility that one individual might gain from a cataract operation might be less than the utility another might receive from the same operation.

This brings us to the subsequent problem of how to proceed after the utility of each individual has been ranked. We might conclude that the most appropriate course of action would result in at least one person's utility being increased while the utility of every other individual is not diminished. This approach is, however, very conservative and would certainly mitigate against any redistribution of wealth. Another approach is to suggest that while some people get more and others might get less, if, in terms of total utility, individuals are better off, then the system is just. The unequal rewards and distributions in the form of incentives are therefore justified because they maximize utility. In fact this argument is used to support the claim that some unspecified degree of inequality is required if efficiency and effectiveness are to be maximized.

Box 6.9 Resource allocation in the health service

When many people share common resources, it is rational for each individual to seek to increase their personal use of the resources. But if all individuals do this, the resources are overexploited and eventually everyone will be ruined. The National Health Service (NHS) is a common resource. A patient acts rationally in seeking an expensive treatment that produces a benefit (even if small), because the cost falls almost entirely on others. But the NHS cannot support overexploitation indefinitely. It already spends £10.3 billion a year on drugs, and costs are rising rapidly.

The NHS should not have to pay for new drugs unless they are at least as good as older ones, nor for expensive drugs whose benefits are uncertain. The National Institute for Health and Clinical Excellence (NICE) was set up in 1999 to appraise technologies that are available to the NHS and recommend whether they should be used unreservedly, with restrictions, or not at all. Part of its remit is to ensure equity, but equity is not in everyone's interests. Individuals or groups with specific interests often lobby NICE to attempt to influence its decisions.

Herceptin is a relatively new drug which can benefit some women with early stage breast cancer. In November 2005, North Stoke Primary Care Trust (PCT) decided not to fund Herceptin, which, at that time, was not licensed for the early treatment of breast cancer, for a patient with that indication, despite it having been recommended by her consultant. The patient sued the PCT, claiming the right to life under the UK Human Rights Act 1998. Following an enormous flurry of negative publicity, the PCT reversed its decision.

In April 2006, Swindon PCT's decision not to fund the drug was overturned in the Court of Appeal. In May 2006, Herceptin was licensed for use in early breast cancer and, in August, NICE issued guidance on supplying the drug. The cost of treatment is £20,000 per patient per year (by comparison, treatment for chronic heart failure is £300 per patient per year).

Needs

An alternative way to justify unequal distributions might be through the idea of need. We might envisage a society where we distribute economic return and development based on the needs of the community. These might be basic needs like health and education; however, there is a significant problem in determining legitimate needs. If the rewards of the system are based on need, then how does this impact on the effort that an individual would be willing to contribute to the economy. If my effort is used to meet the needs of others and not my own needs, then what incentive do I have to work?

Box 6.10 Two approaches to taxing income

Even John Lennon moaned about paying too much tax. The 1966 Beatles' album *Revolver* contains a song by George Harrison, called 'Taxman'. The song refers to the rates of income tax paid by high earners like the Beatles, under the Labour Government of Harold Wilson in the 1960s and 1970s, which were sometimes as high as 95 per cent of their income. This led to many top musicians and other high earners becoming tax exiles.

The UK still has a *progressive* income tax system, whereby individuals pay higher rates of tax as their income increases, although the top rates are nowhere near as high as they used to be. The rationale behind a progressive tax system is that the richer you are, the higher the amount of tax you will pay. The UK has four different marginal tax rates depending on how much you earn, with the top tax rate currently set at 40 per cent.

A *flat* tax system is one that charges a single tax rate – everyone pays the same proportion of their income regardless of how much they earn. Many countries have flat tax systems, particularly those in the former communist states of Eastern Europe. Russia has the lowest marginal tax rate of 13 per cent.

Libertarian exponents of flat tax argue that it is fairer for everybody to pay the same rate of tax. It is also argued that the lower marginal tax rates associated with flat tax systems encourage enterprise and boost growth as more people enter the labour force and work harder because less income is taken in tax. An associated benefit is that government tax revenues could potentially rise as a result. Supporters point to Russia where revenues from income taxes have risen by 50 per cent above inflation since the government introduced its 13 per cent flat tax in 2001. However, critics question how much this revenue growth is to do with the tax system and how much can be explained by high economic growth. A final benefit attributed to flat taxes is that tax evasion falls, particularly among the rich, as they no longer have to pay punitive rates of tax.

Welfare

This perspective is closely associated with a third type of utilitarianism, known as welfare utilitarianism (Chryssides and Kaler 1996). This model changes the focus from the satisfaction of preferences to the satisfaction of interests. An action is good if it serves the interests of the individual. There may often be a conflict between preferences and interests. I may prefer to smoke, for example, but it may not be in my interest. Welfare interests may be seen to precede individual preferences.

Some commentators suggest that the problem of combining preference utilities may be less of a problem from a welfare utility perspective. They assume that most people would have fairly similar ideas about basic welfare needs, for example food, clothes, shelter and education.

The idea of welfare utility is quite a powerful one. From this perspective, we might be able to argue for some quite radical redistributions of wealth, even to the extent of contravening property rights and forcefully removing what people already own. Would it be appropriate, for example, to force someone to sell their second home, in order to provide shelter for someone who has none?

Rawls

Rawls' theory of justice, and in particular his notions of the veil of ignorance and the original position that we thought about in Chapter 3, also provide us with a basis for distributing the rewards of the economic system. Commencing from behind the veil of ignorance, Rawls suggests that individuals would adopt a maxi–mini approach to the distribution of economic resources, that is, we would choose to maximize the minimum utility of each individual.

Accounting

Hopefully you have managed to stick with us through these various discussions of how we might appraise the kind of system that accounting serves and the function it serves within society. Our objective in quickly summarizing these various positions has been to show you that accounting is based on a narrow form of preference utilitarian theory known as financial utilitarianism. If investors provide capital to a firm, then they can expect that their money will be used efficiently. The investment decisions a company will make are, theoretically, based on financial utilitarianism. The investment appraisal techniques accounting students are taught are all based on this narrow form of consequentialist ethics. Try to imagine how different accounting would be if it were based on Rawls' notion of justice or a welfare model of utilitarianism!

SUMMARY

In this chapter we have begun to explore the role of accounting within a free-market economic system. We explained how a free-market system operates and discussed the values that accounting helps to promote through that system. We commenced by questioning whether the system that accounting serves is good or bad and we suggested that one way to begin to address this question is through the idea of distributive justice, that is, whether the outcome of the economy is distributed fairly. We discussed the different ways in which unequal distributions can be justified and in particular we introduced the idea of utilitarianism.

The main objective of this chapter has therefore been to get you thinking about the normal everyday function of accounting in ethical terms, as opposed to cases of individual misconduct by accountants, which much of the discussion of accounting ethics seems to focus on. The apparently mundane, everyday task of accounting is therefore about hugely important and contested ethical issues. It's about the enforcement of rights and the promotion of a particular system of distributional justice. We introduced just a few alternative models by way of contrast in order to get you thinking about the alternative kinds of function that accounting could serve.

QUESTIONS

1 Explain the values that the practice of accounting promotes within a free-market system.
2 Explain the link between distributive justice and the idea of rights.
3 Describe the idea of distributive justice and explain whether the practice of accounting contributes towards a just distribution of economic resources.
4 Discuss the different ways in which unequal distributions within an economic system can be justified.
5 Explain the idea of utilitarianism and describe the link between this theory and accounting practice.

NOTE

1 There is some interesting recent research on the new and complex ways in which accounting reports are being used by marketing and recruitment departments as calling cards and recruitment brochures. In fact a glance through any annual report will indicate that they have become more like glossy magazines than financial statements.

RESOURCES

Websites

Accounting and sustainability

CIPFA (2004) 'Advancing sustainability accounting and reporting: An agenda for public service organisations', discussion paper, available at:
<www.cipfa.org.uk/pt/sustainability/download/discussion_paper.pdf>.

The Financial Reporting Review Panel:
<www.frc.org.uk/frrp/>.

ICAEW (2004) *Sustainability: The role of accountants*, Information for Better Markets report, available at:
<www.icaew.com/index.cfm?route=117162>.

National Institute for Clinical Excellence

A guide to NICE, available at:
<www.nice.org.uk/media/EE5/AF/A_Guide_to_NICE_April2005.pdf>.

Batty, D. (2007) 'Q&A: How NICE works':
<www.guardian.co.uk/society/2007/aug/10/medicineandhealth.theissuesexplained>.

Eastham, P. (2006) 'Does NICE have to be cruel to be kind?':
<www.telegraph.co.uk/health/main.jhtml?&xml=/health/2006/10/30/hnice30.xml&page=5#scra1>.

National minimum wage

London School of Economics, Centre for Economic Performance, policy analysis, 'The national minimum wage: The evidence of its impact on jobs and inequality':
<http://cep.lse.ac.uk/pubs/download/pa006.pdf>.

Progressive taxation

Institute of Public Policy Research:
<www.ippr.org.uk/articles/index.asp?id=1701>. You will find a number of interesting articles in this archive on progressive taxation, equality and justice. You might wish to start by looking at Michael Johnson, 'At last, a tax reform to help in the fight against poverty', December 2008.

Around the world in 80 ideas, '49: One law for all':
<www.adamsmith.org/80ideas/idea/49.htm>.

Prostitution

Audet, E. (2003) 'Prostitution: Rights of women or right to women?': <http://sisyphe.org/article.php3?id_article=108>.

Otchet, A. (1998) 'Should prostitution be legal?': <www.unesco.org/courier/1998_12/uk/ethique/txt1.htm#e1>.

Rio Declaration

United Nations Environment Programme, *Rio Declaration on Environment and Development*: <www.unep.org/Documents.Multilingual/Default.asp?DocumentID=78&ArticleID=1163&l=en>.

READING

Accounting and economics

Dempsy, M. (2000) 'Ethical profit: An agenda for consolidation or radical change?', *Critical Perspectives on Accounting*, 11: 531–548.

Gray, R.H. (1990) 'Accounting and economics: The psychopathic siblings: A review essay', *British Accounting Review*, 22: 373–388.

Keller, A.C. (2007) 'Smith versus Friedman: Markets and ethics', *Critical Perspectives on Accounting*, 18: 159–188.

Macintosh, N.B. (1995) 'The ethics of profit manipulation: A dialectic of control analysis', *Critical Perspectives on Accounting*, 6: 289–315.

Accounting justice and the public interest

Baker, C.R. (2005) 'What is the meaning of "the public interest"? Examining the ideology of the American public accounting profession', *Accounting, Auditing & Accountability Journal*, 18(5): 690–703.

Lehman, C.R. (2005) 'Accounting and the public interest: All the world's a stage', *Accounting, Auditing & Accountability Journal*, 18(5): 675–689.

Accounting and marxism

Bryer, R. (2006) 'Accounting and control of the labour process', *Critical Perspectives on Accounting*, 17(5): 551–598.

Bryer, R. (1999) 'A Marxist critique of the FASB's conceptual framework', *Critical Perspectives on Accounting*, 10(5): 551–589.

Bryer, R. (1999) 'Marx and accounting', *Critical Perspectives on Accounting*, 10(5): 683–709.

Oguri, T. (2005) 'Functions of accounting and accounting regulation: Alternative perspectives based on Marxian economics', *Critical Perspectives on Accounting*, 16(2): 77–94.

Tinker, A.M. (1985) *Paper prophets: A social critique of accountancy* (Eastbourne: Holt Saunders).

Toms, S. (2006) 'Asset pricing models, the labour theory of value and their implications for accounting', *Critical Perspectives on Accounting*, 17(7): 947–965.

Australian Aborigines

Chesterman, J. and Galligan, B. (1997) *Citizens without rights: Aborigines and Australian citizenship* (Cambridge: Cambridge University Press), for an exploration of the treatment of Australian Aborigines over the last hundred years.

Distributive justice

Guidi, M.G.D., Hillier, J. and Tarbert, H. (2008) 'Maximizing the firm's value to society through ethical business decisions: Incorporating "moral debt" claims', *Critical Perspectives on Accounting*, 19: 603–619.

Jackson, K.Z. (1993) 'Global distributive justice and the corporate duty to aid', *Journal of Business Ethics*, 12: 547–551.

Shiner, R.A. (1984) 'Review essay: Deregulation and distributive justice', *Journal of Business Ethics*, 3: 235–255.

Wilhelm, P.G. (1993) 'Application of distributive justice theory to the CEO pay problem: Recommendations for reform', *Journal of Business Ethics*, 12: 469–482.

General reading on economics

Galbraith, J.K. (1972) *The new industrial state* (London: Penguin).

The Holocaust

Black, E. (2001) *IBM and the Holocaust: Strategic alliance between Nazi Germany and America's most powerful corporation* (New York: Crown Publishers); the Holocaust and the role of corporations.

Browning, C.R. (2001) *Ordinary men: Reserve police battalion 101 and the final solution in Poland* (London: Penguin); the story of a group of ordinary middle-aged policemen in provincial Germany who ended up murdering men, women and children, and the gradual steps they took along the path to atrocity.

Sustainable accounting and accountability

Unerman, J., Bebbington, J. and O'Dwyer, B. (2007) *Sustainability, accounting and accountability* (London: Routledge).

REFERENCES

Applbaum, A. (1999) *Ethics for adversaries: The reality of roles in public and professional life* (Princeton: Princeton University Press).

Bassiry, G.R. and Jones, M. (1993) 'Adam Smith and the ethics of contemporary capitalism', *Journal of Business Ethics*, 12: 621–627.

Bauman, Z. (1996) *Modernity and the Holocaust* (Oxford: Blackwell).

Chryssides, G. and Kaler, J.H. (1996) *Essentials of business ethics* (Maidenhead: McGraw-Hill).

Grant, C. (1991) 'Friedman fallacies', *Journal of Business Ethics*, 11: 907–914.

Gray, R.H. (1990) 'Accounting and economics: The psychopathic siblings: A review essay', *British Accounting Review*, 22: 373–388.

Gray, R.H., Bebbington, J. and McPhail, K. (1994) 'Teaching ethics and the ethics of teaching: Educating for immorality and a possible case for social and environmental accounting', *Accounting Education*, 3: 51–75.

Hines, R.D. (1988) 'Financial accounting: In communicating reality we construct reality', *Accounting, Organizations and Society*, 13(3): 251–261.

Nozick, R. (1974) *Anarchy, state, and utopia* (New York: Basic Books).

Primeaux, P. and Steiber, J. (1994) 'Profit maximization: The ethical mandate of business', *Journal of Business Ethics*, 13: 287–294.

Puxty, A.G., Willmott, H.C., Cooper, D.J. and Lowe, E.A. (1987) 'Modes of regulation in advanced capitalism: Locating accountancy in four countries', *Accounting, Organizations and Society*, 12(3): 273–291.

7

The ethics of being a professional accountant

Learning objectives

By the end of this chapter you should be able to:

- Outline a number of different theoretical perspectives on the nature of professional bodies;
- Describe the political function that professional bodies theoretically play within a pluralist democratic political system;
- Explain and critically evaluate a number of different attempts to define professionalism;
- Explain and critically evaluate the idea of the public interest;
- Explain and critically evaluate the idea of professional independence;
- Critically discuss the accounting professions attempts to develop a code of conduct.

INTRODUCTION

'When someone sitting next to me on a plane asks me what I do, I usually tell him or her I'm a salesman. Then they ask, "What do you sell?" and I tell them, "Accounting Services".' This is how one American CPA described his work (Fraser 1997). The culture of targets and the pressure to sell services is now quite pervasive in business, including the business of accounting. However, I guess most accountants would see themselves as more than merely salesmen or women for the Institute of Chartered Accountants for Scotland or KPMG. Accountants have, historically at least, presented themselves as professionals. The status and influence of the various accounting institutes, and the economic benefits they have been able to accrue for their members, has been built, in part, on the claim that accounting is a profession and accountants are professionals.

But what is a profession and what kind of ethical responsibilities go with being a professional? This chapter explores these and other questions relating to the ethics of being a professional accountant. The first section outlines some of the different theoretical perspectives on the professions and professionalism. The second section explains the ethical issues associated with the professions more generally, and the third section explores some of the ethical characteristics of a profession and discusses the extent to which these attributes are apparent in accounting. The final section presents some concluding remarks.

THEORETICAL ORIENTATIONS

Professions and professionals, like profits and losses, are socially constructed notions. There is nothing predetermined about them. Indeed, different types of studies have viewed the professions from quite different perspectives. There is a considerable amount of literature on the formation and practice of professional bodies, along with the spread of professionalization in general.

The *functionalist perspective* has traditionally provided the main lens through which professions are viewed (Walker 1991; Carr-Saunders and Wilson 1933 and Parsons

Box 7.1 Marketing and business development

Most large accountancy firms have codes of conduct for their staff (in addition to the ethical rules issued by the professional accountancy bodies). Here, for example, is an extract from the Professional Code of Conduct of one of the 'Big Four' in relation to clients and the marketplace:

> You should engage only in marketing, advertising, and business development efforts that promote the firm's services fairly, candidly, honestly, and in a manner that complies with all applicable laws and regulations. Newly developed services or tools must be reviewed and approved prior to marketing them. You should not issue proposals or provide services that you are not qualified to perform or that the firm is prohibited from performing by law or contractual agreement.
>
> The firm's partners and employees should not misrepresent the firm's services to current or potential clients or the public at large. They should also avoid the use of terminology or statements that might be misleading, or lead a reasonable person to have unjustified expectations of favourable results.
>
> You should not disparage the firm's competitors or make any false or inappropriate statements about their products or services. You may, however, with care and prudence, make fair and fact-based comparisons on attributes, such as industry experience and client satisfaction data.
>
> (KPMG Code of Conduct 2006, <https://secure.ethicspoint.com/domain/media/en/gui/11093/KPMG_Code_of_Conduct_5_06.pdf>)

1954, both cited in Edwards 2001). This perspective assumes that professions have emerged because they provide an important social function. From this view, a profession's social status and economic rewards are directly linked to the importance of the function it performs in society (see Hooks 1991). The *interactionist perspective* views professions as groups vying with each other for political status and economic gains (Power 1992; Sikka and Willmott 1995) and *critical perspectives* relate the function of a profession to political and structural expediencies (see Roberts 2001; Willmott 1986; Johnson 1982, in Grey 1998). For example, while a functionalist orientation might highlight the role of accountants in providing useful and credible financial information, a critical perspective would attempt to locate this function within underlying political and economic ideology and as a consequence a whole gamut of associated assumptions, ethical critique and political allegations.

The assumptions embedded within these different theoretical perspectives add a degree of complexity to the idea of professionalism and different ethical issues arise, depending on which perspective you adopt. At a guess, we imagine that most accounts might have a vague, functionalist view of both their profession and what it means to be a professional. And, as the interactionist perspective implies, this experience may also be tinted with an element of rivalry when it comes to other professions (Power 1992). Yet many studies suggest that accountants and accounting students have a very poor theoretical awareness of the broader structural or political function of the professions more generally that is the focus of the critical viewpoint.

THE POLITICAL FUNCTION OF PROFESSIONS

In the previous chapter, we thought about the specific function the accounting profession performs within a free-market capitalist system. While the function of accounting will differ depending on the nature of the economic system within which it is embedded, it will, in all cases, be predicated upon and promote certain ethical principles. However, over and above the ethical issues associated with the specific function of accounting, there are also ethical issues associated with the broader political function of the professions more generally. Preston and colleagues (1995), for example, suggest that the excesses of laissez-faire economic policy led to calls for an independent accounting profession in the US. As such, they imply that the formation of the US professional accounting bodies was driven by economic expediency.

Figure 7.1 (Puxty 1997) helps to illustrate the political function of the professions. The model classifies types of international accounting systems based on how they are regulated: by the market (where each company chooses its own rules based on the requirements of the capital markets), by the state or by the community. The four modes form a continuum, with liberalism at one end, legalism at the other and corporatism and associationism somewhere in between. Whereas state legalism forces companies to disclose, in the liberal model regulation is provided exclusively by the market. In the associationist model regulation is achieved through the development of organizations which represent and advance the interests of their members, and in the corporatist model the state develops the organization of interest

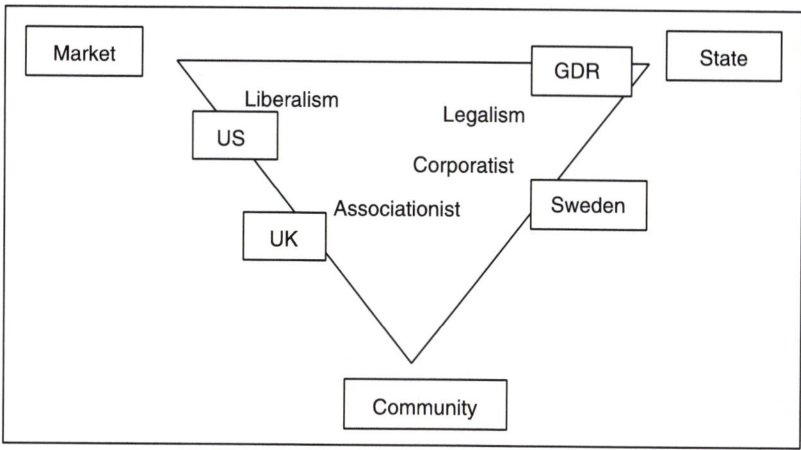

Figure 7.1 Professional body regulation.

Source: Puxty (1997).

groups and incorporates them into its own system of hierarchical control. The implication of Puxty and colleagues' model is quite clear. The status and function of professions within society is political and therefore ethically important.

This point is clearly seen in the post-Enron fallout in the UK, and the many calls for the accounting profession to move towards a corporatist model with the state exercising much more control over the corporate reporting and auditing functions. Yet, from a political economy perspective, many argued that the interests of democracy would be better served by a strong and independent group of professions. A similar issue has arisen in the legal profession, in the UK, over the government's proposed changes to the appointment of judges.

Yet how many of us would be able to provide a defence of the independence of the accounting profession from a political theory perspective, employing the tenets of liberal democracy? We suspect many of you would struggle, not because accountants are not capable of such discussions, but rather because this is not the kind of issue that is routinely explored in professional accounting education.

There are therefore ethical issues associated with the political function that accountants, as a professional group, play within different modes of political organization.

DEFINITIONS OF PROFESSIONALISM: BEING PROFESSIONAL

Professional, like profession, is a much over-used word today. This morning, I ironed my shirt with a professional iron. I guess the manufacturers were trying to convey the idea that it would do a really good job of removing the creases. However, traditionally at least, the idea of professionalism has involved much more than just doing a good job and normally it has been associated with the people who use the equipment,

Box 7.2 Reform of the UK legal profession

Lawyers and many academics have long voiced their concerns over one person, the Lord Chancellor, holding three important and influential roles as head of the judiciary, a Cabinet minister and the speaker of the House of Lords. The Lord Chancellor was responsible, among other duties, for the appointment of judges.

Under the proposed reforms, an independent commission will recommend the appointment of new judges. It is hoped that this will lead to the appointment of younger judges from varying cultures and backgrounds. The commission aims to reflect the population demographic in the selection of new judges, rather than the old breed of judges who are predominantly white, male 'Oxbridge' graduates, and who seem to saturate the current system.

The point of the reforms would appear, in essence, to grant the judiciary greater independence and to bring about the separation of the state from the judiciary. The previous Lord Chancellor's department was heavily criticized for the way in which it appointed its new judges, with cynics claiming that the method was susceptible to political coercion. The purpose of the new system is to commit to eradicating this political anomaly and bringing in fresh young blood from differing backgrounds to preside over matters in court.

Judges were instrumental in demanding this legislation to ensure that every government minister is under a duty to 'safeguard' the judges' independence and to ensure that judges whose court rulings are unpopular with the government cannot be disciplined, moved to other lines of work or denied promotion as a result.

rather than the equipment itself. The idea of a professional iron might be somewhat problematic but is it possible to be a professional executioner? In a fascinating enquiry into some of the normative characteristics that have been associated with the professions and what it means to be professional, Arthur Applbaum (1999) takes a look at how to kill someone, professionally. The remainder of this section explores some of these features, especially as they relate to accountants. We will leave you to decide on the executioners!

While a definitive set of 'professional characteristics' has proved elusive, most scholars agree that professions are supposed to be groups of individuals who come together because they ascribe to a common set of values and have a general consensus about how to promote those values within society. Professions are characterized by a knowledge base, a commitment to public service, independence and education as opposed to training. These characteristics will be expressed both through attitudinal dispositions and structural configurations (Walker 1991; Downie 1990; Mayer 1988; Norris and Niebuhr 1983; Hauptman and Hill 1991; Likierman 1989). Frankel (1989) sums up the strongly ethical nature of professions, commenting that they 'develop social and moral ties among their members who enter into a community of common

Box 7.3 The ethics of being an executioner

Applbaum studied the case of Charles-Henri Sanson, the Executioner of Paris in the eighteenth century, who served under both kings and revolutionaries, and led both to the guillotine. Thousands lost their heads, and the executioner was perhaps the only one guaranteed to keep living. Applbaum asks how Sanson justifies serving several different masters with apparently equal enthusiasm.

Applbaum raises several questions in connection with the case. He asks whether someone can be moral by serving the *process* (the faithful administration of laws), even if the person is immoral by serving the individual *acts* (executing people)? If Sanson objected to executing certain people, would he have undermined the proper enforcement of laws by failing to execute them? Would that failure be worse than faithful execution? Apart from the morality of the death penalty, is it ever just for a man to carry out the orders of two leaders (here the king and the revolutionaries) when clearly you must disagree with at least one of them, since both cannot be on the side of right?

purpose'. He says, a profession can be conceived as: 'a moral community whose members are distinguished as individuals and as a group by widely shared goals and beliefs about the values of those goals . . . about the appropriate means of achieving them, and about the kinds of relations which in general should prevail among themselves'. We wonder how many accountants would be able to identify the reasons behind their choice of accounting as a career in Frankel's quote. Hall (1968) defines professionalism as: 'the extent to which a person possesses attitudes such as belief in public service and a sense of calling to the field'. To be honest, we can't say that we felt a calling to become an accountant. Yet having appreciated the potential that accounting has to contribute towards broader democratic and civic gaols, we certainly feel some compulsion to remain one.

The remainder of this section picks up on three of the more obviously ethical characteristics normally associated with being professional and explores them a little further within the context of accounting. These are: public interest, independence and codes of professional conduct.

THE PUBLIC INTEREST AND SELF-INTEREST

The accounting profession does claim to be operating in the interests of the public. In the UK, public interest claims were at the heart of the profession's efforts to secure a Royal Charter (Sikka *et al.* 1989). In its submission to attain a supplemental Royal Charter (1948) the Institute of Chartered Accountants of England and Wales stated: 'the furtherance of the aforesaid objects would be facilitated and the public interest served'. Similarly, the Supplemental Royal Charter of the Institute of Chartered Accountants of Scotland makes reference to the organization, 'being desirous of

Box 7.4 Characteristics of a profession

Various different writers have come up with several key traits that they see as characteristics of a profession. The most commonly accepted of these are described below. When reading them, think about whether or not they could be applied not just to accountants, but to other occupations whether traditionally recognized as professions (such as medicine or law) or not (such as hairdressing or plumbing).

- *Skill based on theoretical knowledge*: professionals are assumed to have extensive theoretical knowledge, to possess skills based on that knowledge and to be able to apply those skills in practice to further the interests of their clients.
- *An extensive period of education and training*: to acquire skills, a profession requires a period of formal education, as well as a period of training, or 'apprenticeship'.
- *Testing ability*: people wishing to join the profession must submit to and pass a prescribed examination based on their theoretical knowledge.
- *Licence to practice*: an individual must be registered or licensed, thus securing recognition that the individual has achieved membership in the profession.
- *Work independence and autonomy*: professionals retain control over their own work which gives the professional certain independence.
- *Professional associations*: professions have professional societies, one of the purposes of which is to enhance the status of members.
- *Code of professional conduct*: professional bodies usually have codes of conduct or ethics for their members and disciplinary procedures for those who infringe the rules.
- *Self-regulation*: professional bodies tend to insist that they should be self-regulating and independent from government.
- *Public service and altruism*: the earning of fees for services rendered can be defended because they are provided in the public interest.
- *High status and rewards*: the most successful professions achieve high status, public prestige and rewards for their members.

furthering . . . and serving the public interest'. It's a claim that continues to be reiterated. The American Institute of CPA's code of professional ethics (1989b, cited in Claypool *et al.* 1990), for example, states that CPAs should 'act in a way that will serve the public interest, honour the public trust and demonstrate commitment to professionalism'.

The accounting profession therefore claims that what it does is good, not for a specific group of investors or companies, but for society in general. But in what sense? In terms of the normative and analytical ethical theories discussed in earlier chapters, how is the accounting profession good for society? Not surprisingly, there has been a considerable amount of discussion first on what the profession meant when it said that it would facilitate the public interest, and second on whether the assumptions on which the claim was made stand up to critical scrutiny.

So what did the accounting fraternity mean when they said that the public interest would be served if they were granted professional status? Sikka, Willmott and Lowe (1989) suggest that public interest was principally construed as the obligation to produce impartial accounting and auditing knowledge for economic decision-making and the efficient allocation of scarce resources. This primary claim was subsequently construed in terms of ensuring both the *competence* and *character* of those entering the profession.

When the Edinburgh accountants petitioned Queen Victoria in the mid 1800s in order to form the Society of Accountants in Edinburgh, public interest was construed in terms of ensuring that accountants were properly qualified (Lee 1995; Kedslie 1990). One of the initial moves by the group, for example, was to establish entry qualifications in the form of a mandatory period of work experience, the idea being that this period of apprenticeship would ensure that accountants were competent. The development of the accounting profession in the US in the early 1900s similarly reveals a focus on competence, this time, however, through developing university degrees (Carey 1970; Previts and Merino 1979).

So much for competence, what about character? Early in the history of the accounting profession, character seems to have been loosely associated with an individual's class status within society. Many contend that the early development of the profession and the idea of professionalism was bound up in class consciousness. Macdonald (1984; see also Walker 1988, cited in Lee 1995), for example, suggests that applicants were more likely to be accepted into the profession if they were made

Box 7.5 Public interest or personal gain?

While the early accountants argued that the formation of a Society would benefit the public interest, some researchers have suggested that the process was initiated in part by a concern over changes in bankruptcy laws that would have threatened a lucrative business for practising accountants. The effect of these changes would have placed the administration of bankruptcies in the hands of the Sheriff Clerk, a legal officer. At that time accountants dealt with over 80 per cent of bankruptcy cases in Scotland. The accountants were successful in challenging this aspect of the law (Kedslie 1990). As a result of extensive lobbying, the Bankruptcy Act of 1831 did allow accountants to be appointed as official assignees in bankruptcy cases.

One of the most prominent assignees appointed by the Lord Chancellor was a man called Peter Abbott.* Unfortunately, Abbott turned out to be a crook, and perpetrated one of the profession's earliest recorded frauds.

(*Note*: *Edwards (2001) provides an account of the Abbott scandal, along with the profession's response.)

by 'men of acceptable middle class characteristics'. Entrance to the profession depended on the members' 'suitability' for admission and, in many ways, the ability to pay for an indentureship was an important sign of character.

As well as its middle-class orientation, some authors contend that the historical development of the professions also reflected gender divisions. Kirkham and Loft (1993), for example, contend that 'the process of demarcation of accounting tasks not only reflected gender relations ... but helped give meaning to professional accountants'.

Early conceptions of public interest therefore seem to have been articulated in terms of ensuring that those entering the profession were of an appropriate character. Historically, it would seem that professionalism was seen as something that was internal to the individual, not written down, not explicit. It seems that only later, when faced with crisis, that the profession attempted to codify professionalism in the form of professional codes of ethics. As Neu and T'Aerien (2000) suggest, this focus on individual morality, rather than the collective function of the body of professional accountants within broader society, appears to represent a very narrow view of the public interest.

Neu and T'Aerien (2000) sum up the lessons of the historical development of the profession from a critical perspective when they say, 'Accountants, like the rest of us, appear to have just made it up as they went along'. While this conclusion is perhaps a little purposive in its tone, it does seem first that concepts of professionalism were more assumed in the early stages of the professionalization of accountants and second that it is only more recently that terms like professionalism, professional ethics and public interest have been opened up to critical, academic scrutiny. Neu and T'Aerien (2000; Mitchell and Sikka 1993) contend that,

> it looks like ... the profession saw professional ethics as a simple extension of personal, individual morals – transposing codes of individual moral conduct

Box 7.6 Gender inequality in the accounting profession

Even today, women's progress in the accounting profession has been limited. While women have been graduating with accountancy degrees in numbers equal to men since 1998, they comprise only a small percentage of partners in the major accountancy firms, and are underrepresented on the ruling bodies of all the professional accountancy institutes. This is supported by studies which suggest that the structure and ethos of an organization forms an unconscious discriminatory barrier to female career progression.

Even women who do make it to the top of the accounting profession face difficulties. Primrose McCabe, the first woman president of ICAS, stated that she felt her gender 'made it more important to do the job well'. In line with most occupations, female accountants are also still paid less than their male counterparts, despite long-standing equal wage legislation.

('moral rectitude', 'honesty') to the collectivity without examining the behaviour of the body of accountants as a whole in the context of the larger society and the effects of its function on the well-being of society in general.

(Neu and T'Aerien 2000)

Let's leave aside the function of accounting practice for a moment; we discussed the ethical issues associated with this function in the previous chapter and we will pick this theme up again in the following section. There are a number of ethical issues associated with the accounting profession's supplementary, and in some ways implicit, claim that it promotes the public interest by ensuring that accountants are competent to perform this task. There are a number of issues here. First, how should we construe competence and what kind of education would be necessary to ensure that accountants are competent? Within the academic literature there is some considerable criticism of the profession's narrow view of competence, which seems to be viewed almost exclusively in terms of technical proficiency. The concern can be boiled down to a worry that while accountants might be able to engage with accounting at a practical level and while they might be skilled at developing technical solutions to accounting problems, they lack the capacity to critically engage with accounting at a civic and political level. In other words they lack the skills and knowledge base in order to develop the civic and democratic, as well as economic, potential of accounting. Second, how should we construe character, or moral rectitude? Surely not in terms of class status, however measured, or worse, in terms of their ethnic status. And what responsibility does the profession have to ensure not only that people of appropriate character enter the profession, but also that their moral character is developed through membership of the profession? Again the issue of maintaining appropriate ethical standards in the public interest has been narrowly and perhaps negatively construed in terms of disciplinary broads and codes of conduct (we will consider these shortly) rather than more proactively, in terms of moral development. Indeed, it is only relatively recently that a serious discussion of ethics education has emerged within the accounting profession.

Regardless of the traditional public interest rhetoric of the profession, there can be little doubt that the practice of accounting has taken on a distinctly commercial orientation (Carmichael and Swieringa 1968). Roberts (2001), for example, comments on the contrast between the traditional role of a professional and 'the profession's decision to compete in a commercial marketplace in a wide variety of professional services'. Fraser (1997), for example, quotes Stanly Nasberg, an American CA, who says, 'we have arrived because we no longer think of ourselves as merely a profession, we are a business, we are entrepreneurs'. Roberts states that the US practitioner literature is replete with evidence that commercialism is of primary importance to CPA firms[1] (see Craig 1994; Nassuti 1994) and he contends that this commercial re-orientation is primarily driven by declining profit margins (Fraser 1997). He concludes that accounting more generally has become de-professionalized[2] (see Zeff 1987; Briloff 1990, cited in Roberts 2001). Mitchel and Sikka (1993) even claim that audits are now used as loss leaders in order to attract other more lucrative business and there is some concern that this profit orientation has had a detrimental impact on the quality of audit services. In his 1987 study, for example, Larson refers to a number of surveys which indicated that 30–40 per cent of all audits undertaken in the US were substandard[3] (see also Armstrong 1987; Hooks 1991).

However, it would be wrong to suggest that these views are ubiquitous across the profession. There are hints that this new commercialism does not sit well with more established traditional views. This tension can be seen in the following quote from Bruce (1996: 56), who says, 'there were worries that some of the new generation of partners were young marketeers more concerned with profit, less loyal to colleges, than senior partners and more likely to use others instrumentally for their own ambitions'. Bruce (1996) also suggests that a purely commercial view of the accounting profession is too simplistic. He comments on a study by Goodwin that argued that, 'The accountancy firm . . . presents an interesting hybrid of contemporary commercialism and a more traditional professionalism with an emphasis on high standards'. Bruce contends that the large accounting firms, 'have to wrestle with two sides to their central identity. They are businesses, but they are also aloof, dispassionate, independent professionals'.

This conflict creates a serious problem for the profession because these identities are orientated towards two quite fundamentally different sets of interests. Dyckman (1974, cited in Lee 1995), for example, contends that accountants have become business executives rather than professionals and as a consequence self-interest takes precedence over public interest. Radcliffe and colleagues (1994; see also Willmott and Sikka 1997) argue that commercialism and professionalism are incompatible.[4] They specifically argue that the process of commercialization contradicts the idea of professionalism because it represents the pursuit of self-interest over the public interest. While it is possible to reconcile public and private interest within a free-market, utilitarian ethical model, this prevailing worldview cannot accommodate the potential conflict of interest that the provision of both audit and management services creates (Schulte 1966). Roberts (2001) concludes that increasing commercialism detracts from the accountant's fiduciary responsibilities and ultimately brings their claim to professionalism into question (although see Downie 1990).

INDEPENDENCE

The characteristic of independence is closely related to the idea of public interest. Independence is the first rule in the AICPA's (1989) code of practice and Claypool and colleagues (1990) contend that it is 'the key ethical concept'. Yet when the profession talks about professional independence, the discussion is generally restricted to things like single client dependency, non-audit services and the separation of business and professional relationships (Likierman 1989). This narrow conception of independence, although an important ethical issue, has often lacked substance (Bruce 1996). Sikka and Willmott (1995) explore the tactics the UK profession has employed in order to defend its 'aura' of independence. They suggest that these tactics have included, among other things, modifying its ethical guidelines and its disciplinary proceedings. They suggest that these changes are primarily motivated by a concern to ward off any threat to self-regulation. Zeff (1989) conceded that significant structural changes have been proposed both in the US and particularly in

Box 7.7 Fair competition

We saw earlier an extract from the code of conduct of a large accountancy firm. This is what the code says in relation to fair competition:

> Antitrust, as a concept, stands for strict laws that protect free trade and competition. In many jurisdictions these very complex laws prohibit agreements and practices that reduce marketplace competition.
>
> Under no circumstances should you enter into agreements or informal discussions with the firm's competitors regarding any of the following topics:
>
> - Pricing, profitability, or billing terms and conditions of the work you perform
> - Sales and marketing plans
> - A bid or intent to bid on a contract
> - Agreements to divide clients by geography, industry, or type of work
> - Supplier terms and contracts
>
> You should avoid creating even the appearance of impropriety, and use care when having discussions with the firm's competitors. Also, certain restrictions may exist on reciprocal (quid pro quo) business dealings with clients and suppliers. Because antitrust laws are complex and apply to a number of situations, it is essential that you seek advice if you are ever unsure of the appropriateness of any interactions with competitors, clients, or suppliers.

relation to the composition of the board of trustees of the Financial Accounting Foundation (see Zeff 1989); however, he drew on Arthur Andersen and colleagues (1991) *The Public Accounting Profession: Meeting the Needs of a Changing World* to argue that the profession, in the US, tactically attempted to narrow the scope of independence. The demise of Enron and Andersen's indicates both that auditor independence is a crucial issue and that much of the pre-Enron discourse surrounding independence may have lacked substance. The provisions of the Sarbanes-Oxley Act, implemented partly in response to the Enron debacle (Cullinan 2004), similarly construes audit independence as a structural issue.

Yet while the enforced rotation of audit partners and restrictions in certain non-audit services may be important, they do little to develop the profession's capacity to identify intellectually and engage critically with the idea of independence, nor do they help individual accountants ethically manage often subtle and complex conflicts of interest in specific circumstances. This is because the notion of independence is vastly wider and more ethically challenging than maintaining an arm's-length relationship with clients. It is broader than client independence. The discussion in Chapter 4 indicated that accounting is not rights independent. The chapter

Box 7.8 Sarbanes-Oxley and auditor independence

The Sarbanes-Oxley Act came into force in the US in July 2002 and introduced major changes to the regulation of corporate governance and financial practice. It is named after Senator Paul Sarbanes and Representative Michael Oxley, who were its main architects.

The new rules impose more rigorous standards of independence for the external auditors of SEC reporting companies (including foreign private issuers) than under existing SEC rules by:

- Expanding the list of prohibited non-audit services;
- Requiring more frequent partner rotation off an audit engagement team and expanding the scope of partners subject to rotation;
- Disqualifying an accounting firm if any member of the company's management having a 'financial reporting oversight role' was a member of the firm's 'audit engagement team' within the one-year period preceding commencement of the audit procedures;
- Requiring that a company's audit committee pre-approve all audit and non-audit services;
- Disqualifying an accounting firm if an audit partner is compensated for selling non-audit services to the audit client;
- Mandating that, before an audit report is included in a filing with the SEC, auditors must report to a company's audit committee on critical accounting policies and practices, alternative accounting treatments and material written communications between the auditor and management; and
- Expanding a company's disclosure obligations regarding fees paid to, and services provided by, its auditor.

highlighted that because the financial reporting function is based on property rights, it therefore serves the interests of capital providers within a free-market model. Accounting is therefore not independent in its present form, but is biased towards a particular set of values. Regardless of whether these are good or bad values, given its current function, it makes sense to talk of the independence of accounting only in a bounded sense.

Also, given the discussion of the nature of the professions at the beginning of this chapter, it might be important to extend the discussion of independence to incorporate a consideration of political independence.

PROFESSIONAL CODES OF CONDUCT

According to Abbott (1988) you can't be a profession without a code of professional ethics. Claypool and colleagues (1990) likewise contend that a key characteristic of a profession is its self-regulation by a code of ethics. While these codes are generally associated with a complaint-based enforcement system where members are encouraged to report misdemeanours, the evidence suggests that professionals are generally reluctant to report breeches by their fellow practitioners (Bayles 1987, in Beets and Killough 1990).

Some research would suggest that, rather than serving the public interest, codes of professional ethics have tended to serve the interests of the profession (Preston *et al.* 1995; Jamal and Bowie 1995). Huff and Kelly (1989) suggest that the American Accounting Association's 1988 revised code of practice and its associated 'practice-monitoring program' represented a specific attempt to address growing public concerns over substandard audit work. Parker (1994), however, concludes that codes have a dual function and serve both public and private interests. He says, 'while encouraging a sense of social responsibility in the professional member, they also provide justification for professional self-interest'.

Research has identified different types of codes. Frankel (1989) helpfully identifies three different kinds of professional codes: aspirational, educational and regulatory. Claypool and colleagues (1990) also distinguish between 'broad principles' and, 'enforceable rules'. Most of the professional accounting institutes' ethical guidelines find expression in both principles and rules. Some examples of broader aspirational principles include CIMA's by-laws, which warn members against 'dishonourable or unprofessional conduct'. Its ethical guidelines require accountants to 'refrain from any conduct which might bring discredit to the profession'. Similarly, the ACCA requires accountants to 'refrain from . . . misconduct which . . . [is] likely to bring

Box 7.9 Whistle-blowing on other members of the profession

Although most professions encourage their members to report wrongdoing on the part of colleagues, in practice there is often a reluctance to do so. For example, medicine has traditionally centred around a culture of loyalty, one in which you shouldn't 'let the side down'. Dr Stephen Bolsin was a consultant anaesthetist at the Bristol Royal Infirmary who blew the whistle on high mortality rates among babies having heart operations. After initially receiving a 'dismissive' telephone call, he was 'called to the office of James Wisheart', the medical director and a senior heart surgeon. According to Stephen Bolsin, 'He made it quite clear to me this was not the way I should carry on. This was not the way to progress my career in Bristol' (Dyre 1999).

In 2007, accountancy bodies in the UK introduced a new rule which required all members to report to the relevant institute any matters indicating that another member may be liable for disciplinary action. It even goes on to say that failure to do so constitutes professional misconduct. Anecdotal evidence suggests that so far there has been no great rush on the part of accountants to report fellow members – indeed there is some doubt about how many members are aware of this new rule.

discredit to themselves, the association or the accountancy profession' (cited in Fleming 1996). Ruland and Lindblom (1992) convey a related distinction when they discuss the difference between implicit and explicit expectations. They define explicit rules as those outlined in professional codes of conduct. Implicit rules, by comparison, are derived societal expectations in relation to the professional's role in society.

While one would imagine that the enforceable rules-based elements of the codes are reflections of the broader aspirational principles, it is obvious that these principles represent an expectation of something more, something beyond mere rule following. Yet despite the fact that professional accounting codes may contain aspirational elements, Likierman (1989) contends that there are a number of 'accepted professional dilemmas' and that these are generally 'routine' and 'deal with the way in which the profession seeks to maintain its good name'. Claypool and colleagues (1990), in their American study, contend that CPA members' reactions to ethical dilemmas are primarily governed by deference to their professional code of ethics, rather than an ideal notion of professionalism. Brooks (1989) similarly contends that the main source of guidance for accountants is found in the code of conduct. Bruce (1996) comments that 'what was natural, understood and unwritten in partnerships a generation ago now has to be codified and explained'. Velayutham (2003) contends that the 'accounting profession's code of ethics has moved from a focus on moral responsibility for a public good to that of technical specification for a product or service'. He contends that this reflects a change in public values. Technique, he argues, has replaced character as an important virtue.[5]

This is not to imply, of course, that a particular set of aspirational notions, prevalent a few decades ago, in themselves are any better or worse than a codified set of

Box 7.10 Bringing the profession into disrepute

The Institute of Chartered Accountants of Scotland has only two grounds for disciplinary action against its members: professional incompetence and professional misconduct. Punishment depends on the severity of the matter, and ranges from a written warning, to a reprimand, a fine, and in the most serious cases, surrender of membership.

While it is not hard to realize that an accountant who has failed to carry out their work competently should be disciplined, it is important to remember that even behaviour which has no direct bearing on someone's work as an accountant may cause them to be disciplined.

A recent press release issued by the Institute concerns the case of a member whose son was the driver of a vehicle which was involved in a car crash. He collected his son from the scene of the accident and arranged for the uplift and removal of the damaged vehicle, all without informing the police. He was convicted by the criminal courts of attempting to pervert the course of justice. He was also found guilty of professional misconduct by the Institute, who reprimanded him and ordered him to pay a financial penalty.

principles. The issue here is the *way* in which ethical dilemmas are negotiated, not the specific values themselves. Harris and Brown (1990) explain that relying on codified rules and the deference to some external authority represent a relatively low level of ethical awareness. Bebbington and Helliar's (2004) study suggests that many ICAS members appear to adopt more of a rule-based as opposed to a principles-based approach to decision-making, despite the Institute's promotion of a principles-based approach. There is quite a significant discussion of the detrimental impact of a dependence on rule-based approaches to ethics within the literature. Dillard and Yuthus (2002) contend that 'resolutions of ethical dilemmas has become an exercise in rule following'. It is generally considered that such rule-based approaches impede ethical development because they remove the requirement, first to choose between competing alternative courses of actions and second to accept responsibility for those actions. The combination of technical education and ethical rule following is of particular concern for many commentators as they suggest that these characteristics combine to work against the kind of independent, analytical thinking and analysis that is crucial for ethical decision-making.

While a considerable amount of time and effort has been expanded on discussing and developing codes of ethics, other empirical evidence seems to suggest that they often have little practical impact on professionals anyway. Bebbington and Helliar (2004), for example, comment that ICAS's code of professional conduct did 'not appear to actively or self consciously form part of the daily decision making of accountants'. McCarthy's (1997) US study, for example, found that ethical orientation did not significantly improve through exposure to the AICPA code of professional conduct. Jensen and Wygant (1990) make the rather obvious point that a code of ethics is not enough. Professionals need to deal with circumstances when the rules either do not or should not apply. In other words they need to act out of a *sense* of what is right or wrong. Some studies suggest that members may not be aware of the codes to which they are obliged to adhere (see for example Baldick 1980; Davis 1984; Hughson and Kohn 1980, in Beets and Killough 1990). Cooper and Frank (1997), in a study that related to accountants working in business, suggest that accountants drew more on factors in their business environment to help with ethical decision-making rather than resources offered by their profession. By business environment they were referring to the impact of informal organizational climate, for example immediate boss, company culture, and so on.

It is also interesting to note the way codes of professional conduct have changed over time (Arlow 1991). The American Association of Accountants developed a code of professional ethics in 1907, approximately twenty years after its establishment. Among the rules adopted in 1917 was the prohibition of the solicitation of a client of another member (in other words you could not approach another firm's clients) and also a rule requiring a minimum standard of work. It was stated that work which contained an important misstatement or omission would result in disciplinary action (Backof and Martin, 1991). It was not until later that concepts of independence entered the codes of conduct and concepts of integrity and objectivity did not appear in the AICPA code until 1973. Backof and Martin (1991) contend that changes in the code of ethics of the AICPA are a result of three factors: socio-economic change; governmental influence; and change within the professions.

Box 7.11 Principles or rules for accounting standards

In 2006, the Institute of Chartered Accountants of Scotland (ICAS) published a report, *Principles-based or rules-based accounting standards – a question of judgement.* The report argues that global convergence of accounting standards cannot be achieved by a rules-driven approach. The argument for principles, not rules, is that rules-based accounting adds complexity, encourages financial engineering and does not necessarily lead to a 'true and fair view' or a 'fair presentation'.

According to the report, a rules-based approach also hinders accounting standards being translated into different languages and cultures. To achieve the goal of principles-based standard setting would require a radical change in the global profession in order that preparers and auditors of accounts assume more responsibility for making judgements and seek less detailed guidance from standard setters and regulators. This requires the willingness of regulators to accept a broader range of judgement-based outcomes.

Standard setters have responded to the ICAS report by pointing out that they are criticized because they produce rules-based standards, but claim they do so only because they are asked to answer so many specific, detailed questions from accounting experts within the big firms or large corporations.

Over the decades, the willingness and ability of auditors to hold their clients in check through the exercise of good professional judgement is, at best, unclear. There is a view that directors will challenge auditors by asking: 'Where is the rule that says such a proposed action is prohibited?' Auditors may well prefer a situation where, if a client challenges their views, other audit firms will give the same answer because all are applying the same rule, so reducing the risk of losing clients to alternative opinions.

The report points out that it has been suggested that the difference between principles and rules is that rules must be argued against, but principles must be argued for. This requires a different professional attitude and some commentators have questioned whether firms possess such an attitude.

SUMMARY

To summarize, the literature suggests that traditionally the idea of professionalism has included, among other things, a commitment to the public interest; a coherent body of knowledge supported by a rigorous system of education; independence and an implied or explicit professional code of conduct. However, within the context of accounting, it would seem that the profession does not always correspond to this ideal type. There is some concern that professional codes of ethics seem geared towards protecting the profession and also that they engender rule following, a rather stilted way of approaching ethical dilemmas. Finally, there is significant concern over the nature of the public interest claims of the profession. Of particular concern is the apparent inability of practising accountants to explain and evaluate the broader political economy within which accounting functions. There are, therefore, important ethical issues in the socio-political function of the professions in general. There are also important and challenging ethical issues to be addressed in relation to the claims by accountants to be professionals.

Professions and professionals are socially constructed notions. Given that there is nothing predetermined about them, then this allows us to ask some quite fundamental questions, such as: what function should they have in society? And how can we justify their existence?

We currently stand at an interesting and exciting period in the history of professionalism. As a society, the way in which we relate to each other is changing. In particular, the way people relate to the professions and professionals is changing quite perceptibly (Unerman and O'Dwyer 2004). When Bruce (1996) commented that 'the age of deference is over', what he meant was that people are not willing to simply accept what those in authority say and this emerging cultural characteristic is manifest in a shift away from a reverence for and deference towards the professions. Professionals are now construed as equal partners in the process of addressing individual and society concerns. Yet there has been something of a renaissance in the ideals of professionalism recently. Enron, WorldCom and Parmalat have caused us to reflect again on the important, informal function that professions play within society and economic systems in particular. Of course, in many ways these ideas were outmoded, but the work is beginning on how it might be possible to translate many of their core ideals into a form that addresses twenty-first-century concerns. And this is where professionals may have a key role in developing their profession.

QUESTIONS

1 Critically discuss whether accounting is a profession.
2 Critically discuss whether it matters if accounting is or is not a profession.
3 Critically discuss the extent to which accounting does or does not contribute towards the public interest.
4 Discuss whether the practice of accountancy should be independently regulated.

NOTES

1 Increased commercialization, combined with greater litigation has resulted in most of the major accounting practices converting to limited liability firms (Lee 1995). Roberts (2001) also suggests that this focus on commercial services has contributed towards the consolidation of accounting firms and the merger of accounting and law firms and he contends that this process has had a profound impact on the mentality of American CPAs.
2 However, it is important to point out that this reorientation is not peculiar to accountancy. Bruneau (1994; see also Grigg 1993), for example, argues the engineering profession has also been handed over to the forces of the free market.
3 Perhaps in response to these problems the American Accounting Association developed

a new code of professional ethics in 1988. The code was accompanied by a 'practice-monitoring program'. This quality review exercise represented an attempt to address growing public concerns over substandard audit work (Huff and Kelly 1989).

4 Downie (1990) contends that the common assumption that professions aim to act in the interest of their clients while those involved in the market are motivated by their own self-interest is contentious. He introduces the distinction between tuism and non-tuism.

5 This work is based on the codes of the Institute of Chartered Accountants in New Zealand (ICANZ) and the Australian Society of Certified Practising Accountants (ASCPA: now CPA Australia).

RESOURCES

iTunes podcasts

'Personal Ethics and Public Decision-Making', Nancy Kassebaum Baker, Alice M. Rivlin and Steve Tobocman, the Ford School's Lecture Series, University of Michigan.

Lectures on Professional Ethics, Mark Vopat, PhD Lectures on Professional Ethics.

'Moral and Civic Learning', Thomas Erlich, Kenan Institute for Ethics, Duke University.

'Moral Courage and Civic Responsibility', Claire Gaudiani Kenan, Institute for Ethics, Duke University.

'Public Service in the Age of Globalization', Madeleine Albright, Yale University.

Websites

KPMG's Code of Conduct:
<https://secure.ethicspoint.com/domain/media/en/gui/11093/KPMG_Code_of_Conduct_5_06.pdf>.

ICAEW, 'Timeline':
<www.icaew.com/index.cfm?route=155687>; for a summarized history of the development of the accountancy profession in the UK.

ICAS (2006) *Principles not rules: A question of judgement*.
<www.icas.org.uk/site/cms/download/rs_Principles_v_Rules.pdf>.

IES (1997) 'Accountants with attitude: A career survey of women and men in the profession', Report 342, Institute for Employment Studies:
<www.employment-studies.co.uk/pubs/summary.php?id=342>.

Judicial Appointments Commission:
<www.judicialappointments.gov.uk/about/partners.htm>.

PricewaterhouseCoopers (PwC), Code of Conduct: The way we do business:
<www.pwc.com/extweb/pwcpublications.nsf/docid/448AF4746FA421398525722100747151/$file/pwc-codeofconduct.pdf>.

Public Concern at Work:
<www.pcaw.co.uk/>, an independent authority set up to help encourage public interest disclosures; website includes case studies.

Professional Conduct Department of ICAEW:
<www.icaew.com/index.cfm?route=150937>, for some of its recent cases, decisions and rulings.

READING

About the professions

Abbott, A. (1988) *System of professions: An essay on the division of expert labour* (University of Chicago Press: Chicago).

Applbaum A.I. (1999) *Ethics for adversaries* (Princeton: Princeton University Press).

Downie, R.S. (1990) 'Professions and professionalism', *Journal of Philosophy of Education*, 24(2): 147–159.

Hall, R.H. (1968) 'Professionalization and bureaucratization', *American Sociological Review*, 33: 92–104.

Macdonald, K.M. (1984) 'Professional formation: The case of Scottish accountants', *The British Journal of Sociology*, 80(2): 174–189.

Mitchell, A. and Sikka, P. (1993) 'Accounting for change: The institutions of accountancy', *Critical Perspectives on Accounting*, 4: 29–52.

Neu, D. and T'Aerien, R. (2000) 'Remembering the past: Ethics and the Canadian chartered accounting profession, 1911–1925', *Critical Perspectives on Accounting*, 11: 193–212.

Preston, A.M., Cooper, D.J., Scarbrough, D.P. and Chilton, R.C. (1995) 'Changes in the code of ethics of the US accounting profession, 1917 and 1988: The continual quest for legitimation', *Accounting, Organizations and Society*, 20(6): 507–546.

Walker, S.P. (1991) 'The defence of professional monopoly: Scottish chartered accountants and "satellites in the accounting firmament" 1854–1914', *Accounting, Organizations and Society*, 16(3): 257–283.

Willmott, H. (1986) 'Organizing the profession: A theoretical and historical examination of the development of the major accountancy bodies in the UK', *Accounting, Organizations and Society*, 22(8): 831–842.

Commercialism

Roberts, R.W. (2001) 'Commercialism and its impact on the integrity of professional tax services in the United States', *Critical Perspectives on Accounting*, 12: 589–605.

Willmott, H. and Sikka, P. (1997) 'On the commercialization of accountancy thesis: A review essay', *Accounting, Organizations and Society*, 22(8): 831–842.

Professional bodies and regulation

Bayles, M.D. (1987) 'Professional power and self-regulation', *Business and Professional Ethics Journal*, 5(2): 26–46.

Edwards, J.R. (2001) 'Accounting regulation and the professionalisation process: An historical essay concerning the significance of P.H. Abbott', *Critical Perspectives on Accounting*, 12: 675–96.

Sikka, P. and Willmott, H. (1995) 'The power of "independence": defending and extending the jurisdiction of accounting in the United Kingdom', *Accounting, Organizations and Society*, 20(6): 547–581.

Public interest and self-interest

Briloff, A.J., (1990) 'Accounting and society: A covenant desecrated', *Critical Perspectives on Accounting*, 1: 5–30.

Hooks, K.L. (1991) 'Professionalism and self interest: A critical view of the expectations gap', *Critical Perspectives on Accounting*, 3: 109–136.

Lee, T. (1995) 'The professionalisation of accountancy: A history of protecting public interest in a self-interested way', *Accounting, Auditing & Accountability Journal*, 8(4): 48–69.

Sikka, P., Willmott, H. and Lowe, A. (1989) 'Guardians of knowledge and public interest: Evidence and issues of accountability in the UK accounting profession', *Accounting, Auditing & Accountability Journal*, 2(2): 47–71.

REFERENCES

Abbott, A. (1988) *System of professions: An essay on the division of expert labour* (Chicago: University of Chicago Press).

American Institute of Certified Public Accountants (1988) *Code of professional conduct* (New York: AICPA).

Arlow, P. (1991) 'Personal characteristics in college students' evaluations of business ethics and corporate social responsibility', *Journal of Business Ethics*, 10: 63–9.

Armstrong, M.B. (1987) 'Moral development and accounting education', *Journal of Accounting Education*, 5: 27–43.

Armstrong, P. (1987) 'The rise of accounting controls in British capitalist enterprises', *Accounting, Organizations and Society*, 415–436.

Arthur Andersen & Co., Coopers & Lybrand, Deloitte & Touche, Ernst & Young, KPMG Peat Marwick and Price Waterhouse (1991) *The public accounting profession: Meeting the needs of a changing world*, January.

Backof, J.F. and Martin, C.L. (1991) 'Historical perspectives: Development of the codes of ethics in the legal, medical and accounting professions', *Journal of Business Ethics*, 10: 99–110.

Baldick, T.L. (1980) 'Ethical discriminatory ability of intern psychologists: A function of training in ethics', *Professional Psychology*, 11(2): 276–282.

Bayles, M.D. (1987) 'Professional power and self-regulation', *Business and Professional Ethics Journal*, 5(2): 26–46.

Bebbington, J. and Helliar, C. (2004) *Taking ethics to heart*, Institute of Chartered Accountants of Scotland.

Beets, S.D. and Killough, L.N. (1990) 'The effectiveness of a complaint-based ethics enforcement system: Evidence from the accounting profession', *Journal of Business Ethics*, 9: 115–126.

Briloff, A.J. (1990) 'Accounting and society: A covenant desecrated', *Critical Perspectives on Accounting*, 1: 5–30.

Brooks, L.J. (1989) 'Ethical codes of conduct: Deficient in guidance for the Canadian accounting profession', *Journal of Business Ethics*, 8: 325–335.

Bruce, R. (1996) 'Whiter than white?', *Accountancy*, 1233, May: 56.
Carey, J.L. (1970) *The rise of the accountancy profession: To responsibility and authority 1937–1969* (AICPA: New York).
Carmichael, D.R. and Swieringa, R.J. (1968) 'The compatibility of audit independence and management services: An identification of issues', *The Accounting Review*, Oct: 697–705.
Carr-Saunders, A.M. and Wilson, P.A. (1933) *The professions* (Oxford: Oxford University Press).
Claypool, G.A., Fetyko, D.F. and Pearson, M.A. (1990) 'Reactions to ethical dilemmas: A study pertaining to certified public accountants', *Journal of Business Ethics*, 9: 699–706.
Cooper, R.W. and Frank, G.L. (1997) 'Helping professionals in business behave ethically: Why business cannot abdicate its responsibility to the profession', *Journal of Business Ethics*, 16: 1495–1466.
Craig, J.L. (1994) 'The business of public accounting', *CPA Journal*, 64(8): 18–24.
Cullinan, C. (2004) 'Enron as a symptom of audit process breakdown: Can the Sarbanes-Oxley Act cure the disease?', *Critical Perspectives on Accounting*, 15: 853–864.
Davis, R.R. (1984) 'Ethical behavior re-examined', *Critical Perspectives on Accounting*, 54(12): 32–36.
Dillard, J.F. and Yuthas, K. (2002) 'Ethical audit decisions: A structuration perspective', *Journal of Business Ethics*, 36: 49–64.
Downie, R.S. (1990) 'Professions and professionalism', *Journal of Philosophy of Education*, 24(2): 147–159.
Dyckman, T.R. (1974) 'Public accounting: Guild or profession?', in R.R. Sterling (ed.), *Institutional issues in public accounting* (Houston, TX: Scholars Book Co).
Dyre, C. (1999) 'Whistleblower in Bristol case says funding was put before patients', *The British Medical Journal*, 319(27), (November).
Edwards, J.R. (2001) 'Accounting regulation and the professionalisation process: An historical essay concerning the significance of P.H. Abbott', *Critical Perspectives on Accounting*, 12: 675–696.
Fleming, A.I.M. (1996) 'Ethics and accounting education in the UK: A professional approach?', *Accounting Education*, 5(3): 207–217.
Frankel, M.S. (1989) 'Professional codes: Why, how and with what impact?', *Journal of Business Ethics*, 8: 109–15.
Fraser, J.A. (1997) 'How many accountants does it take to change an industry?', *Inc*, 19(5): 63–69.
Grey, C. (1998) 'On being a professional in a Big Six Firm', *Accounting, Organizations and Society*, 23(5/6): 569–587.
Grigg, N.S. (1993) 'Infrastructure and economic development: Role of civil engineers,' *Journal of Professional Issues in Engineering Education and Practice*, 119(1): 51–61
Hall, R.H. (1968) 'Professionalization and bureaucratization', *American Sociological Review*, 33: 92–104.
Harris, C. and Brown, W. (1990) 'Developmental constraints on ethical behaviour in business', *Journal of Business Ethics*, 9: 855–862.
Hauptman, R. and Hill, F. (1991) 'Deride, abide or dissent: On the ethics of professional conduct', *Journal of Business Ethics*, 10: 37–44.
Hooks, K.L. (1991) 'Professionalism and self interest: A critical view of the expectations gap', *Critical Perspectives on Accounting*, 3: 109–136.
Huff, B.N. and Kelly, T.P. (1989) 'Quality review and you', *Journal of Accountancy*, 167: 34–40.
Hughson, R.V. and Kohn, P.M. (1980) 'Ethics', *Chemical Engineering*, 87(10): 132–147.
Jamal, K. and Bowie, N.E. (1995) 'Theoretical considerations for a meaningful code of professional ethics', *Journal of Business Ethics*, 14: 703–714.

Jensen, L.C. and Wygant, S.A. (1990) 'The developmental self-valuing theory: A practical approach for business ethics', *Journal of Business Ethics*, 9: 215–225.

Johnson, T. (1982) 'The state and the professions: Peculiarities of the British', in A. Giddens and G. MacKenzie (eds), *Social class and the division of labour* (Cambridge: Cambridge University Press).

Kedslie, M.J.M. (1990) 'Mutual self interest: A unifying force; the dominance of societal closure over social background in the early professional accounting bodies', *The Accounting Historians Journal*, 17(2): 1–19.

Kirkham, L.M. and Loft, A. (1993) 'Gender and the construction of the professional accountant', *Accounting, Organizations and Society*, 18(6): 507–558.

Lee, T. (1995) 'The professionalisation of accountancy: A history of protecting public interest in a self-interested way', *Accounting, Auditing and Accountability Journal*, 8(4): 48–69.

Likierman, A. (1989) 'Ethical dilemmas for accountants: A United Kingdom perspective', *Journal of Business Ethics*, 8: 617–629.

McCarthy, I.N. (1997) 'Professional ethics code conflict situations: Ethical and value orientation of collegiate accounting students', *Journal of Business Ethics*, 16: 1467–1473.

Macdonald, K.M. (1984) 'Professional formation: The case of Scottish accountants', *The British Journal of Sociology*, 80(2): 174–189.

Mayer, J. (1988) 'Themes of social responsibility: A survey of three professional schools', *Journal of Business Ethics*, 7(4): 313–320.

Mitchell, A. and Sikka, P. (1993) 'Accounting for change: The institutions of accountancy', *Critical Perspectives on Accounting*, 4: 29–52.

Nassuti, C.P. (1994) 'Four case studies in marketing', *Journal of Accountancy*, 178(2): 51–56.

Neu, D. and T'Aerien, R. (2000) 'Remembering the past: Ethics and the Canadian chartered accounting profession, 1911–1925', *Critical Perspectives on Accounting*, 11: 193–212.

Norris, D.R. and Niebuhr, R.E. (1983) 'Professionalism, organisational commitment and job satisfaction in an accounting organisation', *Accounting, Organizations and Society*, 1: 49–59.

Parker, L.D. (1994) 'Professional accounting body ethics: In search of the private interest', *Accounting, Organizations and Society*, 19(6): 507–525.

Parsons, T. (1954) *Essay in sociological theory* (London: Collier-Macmillan).

Power, M. (1992) 'The politics of brand accounting in the United Kingdom', *European Accounting Review*, Summer: 30–68.

Preston, A.M., Cooper, D.J., Scarbrough, D.P. and Chilton, R.C. (1995) 'Changes in the code of ethics of the US accounting profession, 1917 and 1988: The continual quest for legitimation', *Accounting, Organizations and Society*, 20(6): 507–546.

Previts, G.J. and Merino, D.D. (1979) *A history of accounting in America: A historical interpretation of the cultural significance of accounting* (New York: Ronald Press).

Puxty, A.G. (1997) 'Accounting choice and a theory of crisis: The cases of post-privatization British Telecom and British Gas', *Accounting, Organizations and Society*, 22(7): 713–735.

Radcliffe, V., Cooper, D. and Robson, K. (1994) 'The management of professional enterprises and regulatory change: British accountancy and the Financial Services Act 1986', *Accounting, Organizations and Society*, 19(7): 601–628.

Roberts, R.W. (2001) 'Commercialism and its impact on the integrity of professional tax services in the United States', *Critical Perspectives on Accounting*, 12: 589–605.

Ruland, R.G. and Lindblom, C.K. (1992) 'Ethics and disclosure: An analysis of conflicting duties', *Critical Perspectives on Accounting*, 3: 259–272.

Schulte, A.A. (1966) 'Management services: A challenge to audit independence?', *The Accounting Review*, October: 721–728.

Sikka, P. and Willmott, H. (1995) 'The power of "independence": Defending and extending the jurisdiction of accounting in the United Kingdom', *Accounting, Organizations and Society,* 20(6): 547–581.

Sikka, P., Willmott, H. and Lowe, A. (1989) 'Guardians of knowledge and public interest: Evidence and issues of accountability in the UK accounting profession', *Accounting, Auditing & Accountability Journal,* 2(2): 47–71.

Unerman, J. and O'Dwyer, B. (2004) 'Enron, WorldCom, Andersen *et al.*: A challenge to modernity', *Critical Perspectives on Accounting,* 15: 971–993.

Velayutham, S. (2003) 'The accounting profession's code of ethics: Is it a code of ethics or a code of quality assurance?', *Critical Perspectives on Accounting,* 14: 483–503.

Walker, S.P. (1991) 'The defence of professional monopoly: Scottish chartered accountants and "satellites in the accounting firmament" 1854–1914', *Accounting, Organizations and Society,* 16(3): 257–283.

Walker, S.P. (1988) 'The Society of Accountants in Edinburgh 1854–1914', *A Study of Recruitment to a New Profession* (New York: Garland Publishing).

Willmott, H. (1986) 'Organizing the profession: A theoretical and historical examination of the development of the major accountancy bodies in the UK', *Accounting, Organizations and Society,* 22(8): 831–842.

Willmott, H. and Sikka, P. (1997) 'On the commercialization of accountancy thesis: A review essay', *Accounting, Organizations and Society,* 22(8): 831–842.

Zeff, S.A. (1989) 'Recent trends in accounting education and research in the USA: Some implications for UK academics', *The British Accounting Review,* 21(2): 159–176.

Zeff, S.A. (1987) 'Does the CPA belong to a profession?', *Accounting Horizons,* 1(2): 65–68.

8

The ethics of international accounting

Harmonization and terrorism

Learning objectives

By the end of this chapter you should be able to:

- Describe the ways in which accounting systems have historically differed and explain the reasons for these differences;
- Discuss the link between harmonization, globalization and neoliberalism;
- Describe the composition and function of the International Accounting Standards Board;
- Explain and critically appraise the link between accounting harmonization, the World Bank and majority world development;
- Describe the main tenets of Islamic accounting;
- Discuss the link between accounting, harmonization and terrorism.

INTRODUCTION

We are hoping that this book sells well. We were surprised to discover recently that generally accepted accounting practice in Lesotho, a small landlocked country in the middle of South Africa, is the same as that in the UK. It's amazing that people growing up in such a far away and different country are now being taught the same kind of accounting. This similarity, however, is not a consequence of chance; it has happened by design, by a complex and pervasive accounting harmonization agenda that is underpinned by a particular kind of economic theory and a specific set of values.

The harmonization project has resulted in many new accounting developments at an institutional level, for example the International Accounting Standards Board (we will talk about this organization in some detail later in the chapter) and The International Federation of Accountants. This later body in particular is currently in the process of a major ethics project that is designed to address issues of ethics and professionalism across different cultures. Attempts to harmonize accounting practice generate complex descriptive ethical questions relating to, for example, the particular professional values prevalent within different cultural contexts and how these values translate across different cultural systems. These issues are important and interesting, although as we mentioned in the previous chapter, it is questionable whether they can be adequately resolved by simply prescribing an international code of ethics. However, there are bigger issues and more challenging links that need to be drawn between accounting harmonization, development policy and terrorism. Yes, that's not a misprint; I bet you never thought of accounting as a matter of international security! This chapter therefore focuses on the ethical issues associated with the broader political economy of accounting harmonization. The chapter is structured as follows. The first section addresses the issue of international disparity in accounting and considers how the profession has responded to these differences. The second section situates both the accounting problems created by diversity and the profession's response to them within the broader globalization agenda and its underpinning neo-liberal values. The third section links up further with the development literature and focuses on the connection between international accounting standards, the World Bank and development policy. The concluding section of the chapter draws a final link between international accounting harmonization and terrorism.

INTERNATIONAL ACCOUNTING, DIVERSITY AND THE PROFESSION'S RESPONSE

International accounting systems and differences

If you are reading this book in Germany, China or Papua New Guinea, then we'd be prepared to make two assertions with a relative degree of certainty. First, formal reporting requirements for large corporations are ostensibly the same, or at least very similar and second, they used to be quite different.

Accounting systems around the world used to be quite different for some important reasons. A quick scan of the accounting systems employed in different countries will reveal that they differ for structural reasons. The political system impacts on the accounting system, as does the availability of capital and the ownership structures of local enterprises. In continental Europe for example, banks play a particularly important function within the economic system and smaller, family-owned businesses are much more prominent than in the UK. By contrast, in the UK and the US, shareholder equity is more important. In countries like Germany, France and Italy, the banks or the state will nominate directors and thus be able to obtain information and affect decisions within firms. However, by contrast, in countries where there is diverse ownership of companies by shareholders, there will be increased emphasis on the audit function as these shareholders do not have access to internal information.

Over and above these structural factors, cultural characteristics also influence the nature of accounting systems. By cultural factors we mean the extent to which a certain society may be more or less conservative in nature or more or less transparent, for example (Gray 1988).

There is therefore quite a well-developed body of research that has established, explored and classified different international accounting systems. While this work is often used to evaluate both the difficulties and prospects of harmonization, there is an important ethical lesson here that is often missed, a lesson that provides the starting point for understanding some of the broader ethical issues surrounding international accounting. This research reminds us of the essentially socially constructed nature of accounting systems and the fact that these systems reflexively support a set of economic and cultural values. In other words, while accounting is socially constructed, in the sense that it takes different expression within different national contexts, it is also socially constitutive. If a country were to change its accounting system, this would either be associated with a change in values or it would result in a clash of values!

Accounting systems therefore differ across the world. The areas in which they differ are quite important for understanding the financial performance of companies. Some of the main areas of divergence are in the nature of the audit opinion, valuation methods and the level of conservatism. For example, in the UK auditors are still expected to exercise a degree of professional judgement in determining the nature of

Box 8.1 The French general chart of accounts

In contrast to the UK system, the French have traditionally prepared companies' financial statements using a Plan Comptable Générale (PCG). The concept of a general chart of accounts was first developed and adopted in the early twentieth century in Europe by countries which had economies that were highly state controlled, particularly Russia and Nazi Germany. Vichy France adopted its first PCG during the war. It was subsequently developed as a tool for national accounting, as it allowed figures from individual companies to be aggregated to give information on national growth, inflation, exports, and so on.

It did this by allocating a number to each accounting heading, which is the same for every company no matter what its size or industry. The system is highly specific and detailed. For example, account number 4096 represents *Debts receivable for returnable packaging and equipment* – for every company in France. This allows for easy aggregation of all company accounts to arrive at national figures, and also makes the calculation of companies' taxes relatively easy to compute.

Even though France adopted the use of International Financial Reporting Standards (IFRSs) for consolidated accounts in 2005, in common with other EU companies, it still insists on the use of the PCG for the accounts of individual companies.

the financial position of a company. This contrasts with the German approach to audit, which is characteristically more rules-based. There is also a relatively high level of conservatism in Germany, which means that financial analysts usually adjust a German company's profit figures upwards before comparing their performance with UK companies.

It is in this last point that we begin to get some idea of the reason why international accounting harmonization is such a big issue. Diversity in accounting practices causes major problems for investors and companies alike. Regardless of the many deficiencies in financial reporting, and the many different channels through which investors can obtain information about companies, research nevertheless indicates that the audited accounts remain a very important source of information for investors in different countries (Chang *et al.* 1983). However, research also

Box 8.2 International auditing standards

The International Auditing and Assurance Standards Board (IAASB) is an auditing standard-setting body based in New York, which operates under the auspices of the International Federation of Accountants (IFAC). The IAASB's goal is to

> serve the public interest by setting high quality auditing, assurance, quality control and related services standards and by facilitating the convergence of international and national standards, thereby enhancing the quality and uniformity of practice throughout the world and strengthening public confidence in the global auditing and assurance profession.
>
> (International Auditing and Assurance Standards Board (2009) International Federation of Accountants, <www.ifac.org/MediaCenter/files/IAASB_Fact_Sheet.pdf>)

Over one hundred countries are using or are in the process of adopting or incorporating International Standards on Auditing (ISAs), issued by the IAASB, into their national auditing standards or using them as a basis for preparing national auditing standards. ISAs are intended for use in all audits – publicly traded companies, private business of all sizes and government entities at all levels.

Criticisms of the work of the IAASB include its lack of independence – it is mainly auditors setting standards for auditors, with few public members on the Board. In particular, the 'Big Four' accountancy firms are seen to dominate membership. Also, standards are developed at an international level, but enforced at a national level. There are frequently differences between international and national auditing standards as a result of specific national requirements. As the IAASB has no enforcement mechanism, it is reliant on the national regulators to police the standards, which they may do to varying degrees of effectiveness.

suggests that different cultural, institutional and economic characteristics in different countries result in significant differences in many of the ratios that analysts and investors routinely calculate when appraising a company's financial position (Choi *et al.* 1983).

Accounting diversity also causes problems for corporations (Choi and Levich 1991), creating operational problems for both capital market and capital investment decisions. For example, it has major implications for determining the creditworthiness of foreign firms. If you can't establish whether a foreign company will be able to pay its debts, then you may not want to export to it. It also has implications for licensing and franchising agreements. Differences in accounting practices make it difficult to establish the reliability and capability of potential licensees and it also complicates the management information systems required to monitor contract performance. And finally, it also has implications for foreign direct investment (FDI), creating difficulties in assessing the financial position of potential takeover targets, and interpreting the financial statements of foreign competitors.

While investors and companies have developed a series of coping mechanisms for these impediments, including the restatement of foreign financial statements or recourse to information less sensitive to accounting policies, these strategies do not completely remove the problems created by accounting diversity.

The profession's response: the IASC

Ostensibly in response to these problems, the International Accounting Standards Committee was established in 1973 (it is now called the International Accounting Standards Board). This private sector body, which is based in London, attempts to facilitate international consultation on accounting divergence with a view to promoting the convergence of national standards. The IASC state that their object is:

> To formulate and publish in the public interest accounting standards to be observed in the presentation of financial statements and to promote their worldwide acceptance and observance.

This development needs to be viewed in the light of our previous discussions on the nature of the professions and the extent to which they are concerned about the interests of their members. However, beyond its effect of reducing pressure on the accounting profession for alternatives to self-regulation and questions of whether the spread of a Western style of international accounting standards simply expands the market of the large Western accounting firms, the IASC imply that convergence of international accounting standards has obvious benefits for investors, companies and some countries.

Because accounting harmonization allows comparisons to be made between companies, it enables investors to hold shares in companies in many different countries, thus significantly expanding the range of investment opportunities. It reduces costs for companies and increases the pool of potential capital investment opportunities and the ease with which they can be exploited. However, it is claimed that

Box 8.3 International accounting standards

The goal of the International Accounting Standards Board (IASB) is 'to provide the world's integrating capital markets with a common language for financial reporting'.

In order to achieve this goal the IASB aims to have a single set of high-quality accounting standards that are used throughout the world's capital markets. International Financial Reporting Standards (IFRSs) now form the basis of accounting in more than one hundred countries.

In 2005, the countries of the European Union began to use IFRSs, and in Asia, use of IFRSs is expanding. China has just adopted a new set of standards based upon IFRSs, India's prime minister recently called for the adoption of IFRSs, and Korea is considering their adoption by the end of the decade. Canada's Accounting Standards Board has recently announced it will be scrapping its national standards in order to adopt IFRSs.

A convergence project with the US is under way, looking at the move towards convergence with international accounting standards, and it is likely that IFRS statements could be used in the US by 2009.

harmonization also benefits countries because it results in a set of readily available, internationally recognized accounting standards. As there would be no requirement for national standard-setting bodies, these standards would be available at minimum expense.

Thus far we have outlined some of the basic problems surrounding the issue of international accounting harmonization. Hopefully some of the ethical issues associated with this agenda are beginning to become clear. We will explore these ethical issues in more detail in the following sections.

ACCOUNTING HARMONIZATION, GLOBALIZATION AND NEOLIBERALISM

The discussion of the problems caused by accounting diversity and the role of accounting harmonization in addressing these problems, should make one thing clear. Accounting harmonization is not a technical and amoral process. While the technical problems involved in bringing international accounting practice closer together are undoubtedly complex and important, it would be wrong for us to become so preoccupied with finding a technical fix to the problem of diverse valuation methods, for example, that we forget to ask whether harmonization is a good thing, in the traditional moral sense of the word. If we focus exclusively on the technical detail of how to ensure greater comparability, we may miss the fact that the whole endeavour is underpinned by and implicitly supports a specific political and economic agenda. It is inextricably tied up with the global expansion of neoliberal, free-market ideology. The primary assumptions of this worldview are expressed in the following quote from one of its most ardent proponents, Milton Friedman. He said,

> profit-making is the essence of democracy, any government that pursues anti-market policies is being antidemocratic, no matter how much informed popular support they might enjoy. Therefore it is best to restrict governments to the job of protecting private property and enforcing contracts, and to limit political debate to minor issues. The real matters of resource production and distribution and social organisation should be determined by market forces.

The problem is that while accounting practice has contributed towards globalization through facilitating the ability to manage at a distance, different national accounting systems now impede the further development of global capitalism.

Let us remind ourselves of the basic characteristics of the free-market system that we introduced in Chapter 6. The story goes like this: companies produce and sell their services/products. The sovereign consumer decides which product they wish to purchase. Companies that produce products or provide services we want at a price we are willing to pay, in other words the efficient, innovative companies, will prosper and grow. In order to grow and develop, companies require capital. Banks and investors will provide capital only to profitable and efficient companies. Banks and investors require financial information about the company in order to know which companies are profitable and efficient, in other words, in order to make investment and lending decisions. This information is provided by the system of financial reporting. Investors have the right to receive information based on property rights. As we discussed in Chapter 6, it is assumed that this process will bring about the most efficient use of recourses and the most equitable distribution of resources.

A key aspect of globalization therefore involves the removal of all barriers to capital mobility, including international barriers. There are many theoretical justifications proposed for why we might want to support the mobility of capital, for example the creation of trade, the reduction of costs, economies of scale, access to larger markets, competitive advantage, diversification, vertical integration, rationalized production access to production factors, and so on. Yet we should not allow the relatively innocuous language of diversification, integration and rationalization to mask the ethical choices we are making when we, as a profession, help companies to diversify, integrate or rationalize, either literally or by producing international accounting standards that make these things easier. To say that we are only responding to corporate or market requirements may in the end be to expose our claims of professionalism as being unfounded. In what way does this kind of argument sit with our claim to have the public interest at heart?

While this agenda is sufficiently contested at the national level, the globalization agenda proposes this model as the prototype for global, as well as national development. This shift in scale quite obviously adds a new level of ethical complexity, not least because the harmonization of accounting practice enables MNCs to expand across international boundaries. We could discuss many different ethical issues, for example whether the spread of international accounting harmonization allows companies to exploit different levels of legislation in the areas of environmental policy,

Box 8.4 Friedman, corporate social responsibility and Nestlé

Milton Friedman (1912–2006) was a Nobel Prize-winning economist whose views were popular among many politicians in the 1980s and 1990s. According to Friedman, the only social responsibility of companies is to increase their profits, not to indulge in 'good deeds' such as charitable giving, employing disabled people, reducing pollution, and so on. Companies should stick to accounting, finance, marketing and operations, and should not waste time with ethics.

His two main arguments to support this position are, first, that business managers are not qualified to make policy decisions on social and ethical matters. They should therefore concentrate on business matters and leave the rest to politicians, who are elected to make these decisions. Second, business managers are tasked with acting on behalf of the owners of the business (the shareholders) and have no right to give money away to worthy causes, since this reduces shareholder wealth.

One company which seemed to take Friedman's views to heart is the Nestlé Corporation, a Swiss-based multinational. It started marketing its infant formula (baby milk) in parts of Africa and Asia where there are fewer legal restrictions than in the US. The company promoted its powdered baby milk in developing countries by giving free samples to mothers via hospitals and 'health visitors' who were hired by Nestlé. Mothers were persuaded to buy the product, but often ceased to be able to afford it, and even when they could, the water needed to mix the product was often polluted. As a result, many children died of malnutrition and/or water-borne disease.

Nestlé has continued its practice, justifying it on the grounds that its directors had no right to withdraw a profitable and legal product (despite it causing suffering and death according to a recent report (Save the Children 2007)). If we apply Friedman's Theory in its crudest form, as it is often taught in business schools, then the directors' job is to maximize shareholder wealth.

health and safety, or the testing of drugs. However, we would like to focus on one particular issue that is perhaps more obviously related to accounting practice. In Chapter 6, we introduced the concept of distributional justice. This issue is complicated enough when we view it purely within a national context; however, it becomes even more tricky when we start to investigate the way income generated by multinational companies is distributed among the host countries in which it operates, perhaps through taxes and wage bills, the management of the company and its shareholders.

The more radical neo-imperialist critiques of globalization contend that the figures in Box 8.5 represent a fundamental ethical challenge because they are indicative of an asymmetry in power between the dominant West and the dependent South. They suggest that the origins of a country's trade patterns are bound up with the

Box 8.5 Multinationals and distributive justice

Figures in the United Nations' Human Development Report 1997 would suggest that concern over this issue of distributive justice is not just hollow academic postulating. According to the UN, while 37,000 multinational corporations had a collective total of 170,000 overseas subsidiaries, 90 per cent were headquartered in developed, capitalist countries. Other analysis from the UN suggests that the combined wealth of the 225 richest people in the world (a staggering $1.7 trillion) is equivalent to the annual income of almost half the world's population (that's 2.5 billion people). The statistics suggest that the inequality between developed and developing countries is increasing, not decreasing. For example, while the average per capita income of the world's richest countries came in at 38 times that of the world's poorest countries in 1965 this figure had risen to 58 times by 1985. The question is, will accounting harmonization contribute to a global economic system that makes these figures better or worse? And do these figures really represent an ethical challenge anyway?

internationalization of capitalism and they pick out MNCs for major criticism as the primary agents of imperialism. Imperialism has been defined as: 'a network of the means of control exercised by one economy (enterprises and government) over another'. It is generally linked to trade relationships, aid programmes, militarism, and so on.

But it is not only the statistics that provide the basis for questioning the rhetoric of the neoliberal discourse. Many are concerned that both historical and current practice jar with and even contradict the assumptions upon which the supremacy of neoliberalism is based. As we learned from the Milton Friedman quote above, the basic tenets of neoliberalism are: the liberalization of trade and finance, privatization, and allowing markets to operate with little state interference. However, Noam Chomsky, one of the most ardent and erudite critics of neoliberalism, contends:

> in the end, neo-liberals cannot and do not offer an empirical defence for the world we are making. To the contrary, they offer a religious faith in the infallibility of the unregulated market, that draws on nineteenth century theories that have little connection to the actual world.

This is a challenge not only for policy makers and CEOs, but also accountants.

Critics argue that an analysis of the economic policies behind the development of developed countries reveals a litany of protectionism and state intervention. Chomsky, for example, contends that the industrial revolution relied in part on cheap cotton from the US. However, he contends that it was kept cheap by slavery and protectionism rather than market forces. Similarly, he contends that by employing a policy of protectionism, Britain similarly destroyed the Indian textile industry.

Turning his attention to a more contemporary and contentious example, he points out that a significant chunk of the Pentagon's budget is devoted to managing Middle East oil prices. One study suggests that the Pentagon's intervention effectively equates to a 30 per cent subsidy on the real market price of oil, a practice that jars with the rhetoric of neoliberalism. This is not an isolated example either. Ruigrock and Van Tulder (1995) found that almost all of the world's biggest MNCs have benefited from government subsidies and protectionist policies. Indeed many would have gone to the wall if not for government intervention. One report by the Organisation for Economic Co-operation and Development has concluded that oligopolistic competition and mutually supportive relationships between large firms and governments are the real drivers of economic practice rather than the invisible hand of market forces. We could go on and discuss the use of trade restrictions in economic warfare[1] or the appraisal of free trade organizations like the North American Free Trade Agreement (NAFTA);[2] however, we think the point has been well made. The rhetoric of neoliberalism in many cases jars with the reality of business and political practice.

Box 8.6 UK government aid and genetically modified crops

In a statement made to Parliament on 9 March 2004, the Secretary of State for Environment, Food and Rural Affairs set out the government's policy on GM crops as follows:

> The Government has concluded that there is no scientific case for a blanket ban on the cultivation of GM crops in the UK, but that proposed uses need to be assessed for safety on a case-by-case basis. The Government will continue to take a precautionary approach and only agree to the commercial release of a GM crop if the evidence shows that it does not pose an unacceptable risk to human health and the environment. There are currently no GM crops being grown in the UK and no commercial cultivation is expected before 2009 at the earliest.
>
> (<www.defra.gov.uk/environment/gm/crops/index.htm>)

Despite this, the government has actively encouraged the production of GM crops in India, through the giving of development aid to Indian states that are being used to grow these crops commercially. There are widespread objections to the policy among local farmers, many of whom are losing their livelihoods as their land is taken over by large multinational companies, such as Monsanto.

Since the production of GM cotton started several years ago, farmers have reported animal illnesses and deaths after grazing on cotton fields, and allergic reactions of farmers during harvesting. In 2006, a large network of protestors was formed, called the 'Coalition for GM free India', which is currently lobbying against the proposed approval of the commercial production of GM aubergines for human consumption.

Yet as important as these arguments are, it is vital to appreciate that accounting harmonization is linked to more than economic growth. The greater economic interdependence that it supposedly generates is linked to broader agendas. Take the European Union for example. The 1992 Maastricht Treaty on European Union means that goods, services, capital and labour can circulate freely among EU member states. An obvious strategy that the EU has pursued in order to promote this goal is the harmonization of accounting practice. The aim is that all EU countries will use international accounting standards.

But the single market is only part of the broader trilogy of political ideas underpinning the EU: the single market; Common Foreign and Security Policy; and Justice and Home Affairs cooperation. In this particular instance, therefore, accounting is embedded within processes of broader and more fundamental political harmonization. It is not just about markets and economic expediency; it is also about economic interdependence, federalism and peace. It is important to remember that historically the idea of the EU emerged at a time when Europe was trying to come to terms with the aftermath of the Second World War and grappling with the necessity of ensuring that it didn't happen again.

We guess most practising accountants would not see themselves as agents of federalism or imperialism, nor would they view international accounting standards as a useful tool in the exploitation of the oppressed. Yet we need to remember that

Box 8.7 Europe-wide accountancy qualifications

Some of the European accountancy bodies, including the Institute of Chartered Accountants in England and Wales and the Institute of Chartered Accountants of Scotland, as well as professional bodies in France, Germany, Ireland, Italy and the Netherlands, recently published plans for harmonizing qualifications, known as the 'common content project'.

The participating Institutes are considering possible forms of cooperation on global qualifications. They recognize that while the curricula for the acquisition of their national qualification have been developed nationally, there are many similarities among those curricula.

The project has come about as a result of the recognition that there is, increasingly, a single market for professional accountants across the EU. There is an expectation that holders of professional accountancy qualifications can be employed by, or provide certain services to, European and global businesses. Therefore there are market demands for a significant part of the curricula of professional qualifications to be international or 'territory-neutral', and for the mutual recognition of different national qualifications.

If the proposals are adopted, the qualifications of participating institutes will be unified as far as national laws, custom and practice allow. One of the advantages will be to give their members greater freedom of movement across national borders.

accountants and accounting practice, along with a myriad of other professions and professional practice, emerges within and reflexively helps to maintain systems of thought and practice. The problem is that sometimes we end up serving the systems rather than the values that those systems were intended to promote. History is replete with examples of many well-intentioned developments that have ended up oppressing the very individuals they were intended to help. While a more balanced view of global capitalism than that espoused by its more radical critics might conclude that it has produced some major developments as well as some major problems, the question is whether the accounting profession and accountants are capable of engaging with some of the problems it has generated, and whether they have the ability and will to nudge the system towards more socially beneficial outcomes. After all, this ability to engage with the broader societal impact of one's practice has traditionally been a defining characteristic of professionalism.

BACK TO THE IASB

Now that we have gone through some of the ideological issues within which the IASB and accounting harmonization more generally is enmeshed, we might be able to appreciate some of the criticisms levelled at the IASB and the reason why some international bodies have shown a keen interest in its work.

The UN, the African Accounting Council, ASEAN Federation of Accountants, the Confederation of Asian and Pacific Accountants, and governmental bodies such as the EU and the OECD (Organisation for Economic Co-operation and Development) are all involved in the harmonization agenda to differing levels. However, as this list implies, different groups are concerned with different issues. The UN is interested in harmonization because it is concerned about the political, legal, social and economic effects of the activities of MNCs on less-developed countries. The OECD's interest in harmonization, on the other hand, stems from a concern to promote the interests of MNCs and might be viewed, in part, as a counter-move to the UN.

A review of the composition of the IASB and its sources of funding have led many to criticize it for having an Anglo-American influence and consequently focusing too much on the needs of investors. Given the discussion above, it is also easy to see where the claims that IASB also serves the interests of large multinational firms comes from. Both these issues have led to claims that the IASB has tended to be preoccupied primarily with issues specifically related to more advanced economic environments, like intangible assets and accounting for pension contributions. One wonders at the significance of IAS 19, Accounting for Employee Benefits, for example, in a country like Zambia, where the average life expectancy is 30 years, or in Sierra Leone where, on average, you would be lucky to make it to 25.

There are therefore important procedural ethical issues to be addressed in relation to how a powerful body like the IASB should work, for example: whether it should be a private or more democratic body; how it should be funded; and how the consultation procedures surrounding the development of standards should operate. Try and link these questions back to our discussion of Jürgen Habermas in Chapter 5.

Box 8.8 Composition of the IASB

(Note: correct at time of publication.)

Sir David Tweedie, Chairman, former Chairman of the UK Accounting Standards Board.

Thomas E. Jones, Vice-Chairman, former CFO of Citicorp and last Chairman of the IASC.

Professor Mary E. Barth (part-time), Joan E. Horngren Professor of Accounting and Senior Associate Dean for Academic Affairs, Graduate School of Business, Stanford University.

Stephen Cooper (part-time), Managing Director and Head of Valuation and Accounting Research at UBS.

Philippe Danjou, former Director of the accounting division of the Autorité des Marchés Financiers (AMF), the French securities regulator.

Jan Engström, former CFO of Volvo Group and CEO of Volvo Bus Corporation.

Robert P. Garnett, former Executive VP of Finance for Anglo American plc.

Gilbert Gélard, former partner, KPMG France and member of the French Accounting Standards Board.

James J. Leisenring, former Vice-Chairman of the US Financial Accounting Standards Board (FASB).

Warren J. McGregor, former CEO of the Australian Accounting Research Foundation.

John T. Smith, former Partner of Deloitte & Touche, United States.

Tatsumi Yamada, former partner, PricewaterhouseCoopers, Japan.

Zhang Wei-Guo, former Chief Accountant and Director General of the Department of International Affairs at the China Securities Regulatory Commission.

Source: <www.iasb.org/About+Us/About+the+IASB/IASB+Chairman.htm>

ACCOUNTING HARMONIZATION, THE WORLD BANK AND MAJORITY WORLD DEVELOPMENT

Thus far we have considered some of the broader ideological and political agendas with which accounting harmonization is associated. This section of the chapter takes a closer look at the relationship between international accounting standards and development policy and in particular focuses on another major global institution: the World Bank.

The World Bank is one of the most significant players in international development (see Annisette 2004). It is one of the most powerful advocates of the neoliberal agenda and the most influential proponent of International Accounting Standards.

Box 8.9 The World Bank – structure and ownership

The bank is owned by 183 national governments each of which has voting rights based on the amount of equity they have contributed to the bank. As of 2001, the five developed economies of USA, Japan, Germany, the UK and France contributed a total of approximately 36 per cent of the bank's equity base. This contrasts with the 42 sub-Saharan African members of the Bank who collectively contributed less than 5 per cent. The former are part of a group of countries who do not borrow from the bank, the latter from a second group that do.

The International Bank for Reconstruction and Development (IBRD), the World Bank, was set up in 1944 with the official aim of 'reduce[ing] poverty by promoting sustainable economic development' (World Bank Annual Report 2000 available online <www.worldbank.org/html/extpb/annrep2000/index.htm>) and since then it has distributed around $310,000 million in loans. The World Bank effectively determines which countries receive international development money and which countries do not (Anissette 2004). The membership of the bank reflects its underlying capitalist ideology and it is therefore no surprise that the provision of aid is contingent upon the implementation of an onerous programme of economic reforms designed to reduce state control, liberalize trade and generally create an 'Enabling Environment', conducive to economic development. The problem is, however, that these conditions are often enforced with little regard to the local economic context of a particular country. Some of the stipulations include the removal of government subsidies on basic goods and services, removing taxes on exports and imports; the deregulation of capital markets; eliminating barriers to foreign ownership and repatriation of profits; the privatization of public services and other state-owned enterprises and the devaluation of the country's currency. The belief is that the reforms will result in increased productivity and employment, more efficient companies, increased foreign investment and ultimately increased economic growth. In particular, the World Bank justifies privatization by emphasising the positive role it can play in combating the lack of accountability and transparency purportedly associated with state-owned enterprises. The argument is that the discipline of the market improves accounting controls, all of which is essential for attracting foreign investment. These economic and fiscal changes, of course, involve a shift in values and the reformulation of rights.

So what has all this got to do with accounting? There are two important accounting issues here. First, the World Bank requires borrower countries to adopt international accounting standards as their national accounting practice. However, second, there must be some accounting for the moneys given to the developing countries by the World Bank.

However, the evidence on the success of the reforms is weak. Some have expressed concern that the privatization process is corrupt. Larson and Kenny (1995), for example, found no substantive relationship between economic growth and the adoption of IASs, and Narayanaswamy (1996) also found little improvement in the quality of financial reporting in India following sweeping reforms. Others report large instances of non-compliance. Indeed some have argued that the public adoption of IASs might be construed simply as a legitimation exercise.

There are many examples in the literature of instances where the structural readjustments promoted by the World Bank, along with the application of international accounting standards, have had quite negative results. Concern has been expressed over the impact on local jobs. For example, the sacking of workers in Bangladesh who resisted privatization or the approximately 10,000 workers who lost their jobs in the cashew industry alone in Mozambique when the government was forced to remove an export tax designed to protect local employment. In Haiti, the World Bank demanded privatization of profitable public companies that generated revenue for desperately needed services. There is also concern over who benefits from the privatization of national assets. Martin's (1995) study indicates that the privatization of the Mexican telecommunications system resulted in a $12 billion increase in share values to foreign buyers. However, this increase was largely due to planned rises in tariffs. While foreign investors benefited, local customers lost out to a tune of $33 billion. Other studies have found that denationalized industries did not perform any better (Sobhan and Ahsan 1984). The World Bank's own studies of Bangladesh indicated that many jute and textile mills in Bangladesh either went into liquidation or made significant losses after privatization. The Bangladesh Minister of Industries commented: 'out of 520 privatised industries 60% of them closed down'. The World Bank's own research concluded that private investment did not increase as fast as expected in Bangladesh (Uddin and Hopper 2003; Chomsky 1999)

However, others have made accusations of a more sinister and disturbing nature. These allegations specifically relate to 400 Maya people from the village of Rio Negro who were killed in 1982. The village was located on the sight of a hydroelectric dam project. The claim is that when the villagers refused to relocate, the Bank looked away while the army systematically killed those who would not leave their ancestral land (see Chomsky 1999). The bank was forced to address the issue in 1996 under pressure from human rights groups. Others have suggested that the Bank exists purely to serve the interests of private capital. Annisette (2004), for example, points out that despite its claim to be a non-profit organization, the Bank has consistently made a profit exceeding $1 billion for the past fifteen years. The claim is that much of this profit comes from interest charges on loans that cripple already fragile economies. Annisette points out that the Bank made $9.7 billion in 2003; of this sum, 85 per cent came from interest charges and $7.1 billion of it was paid out in the form of interest charges on loans granted to developing nations.

This, of course, is not the only role that accounting could or does play in international development. It is important also to reflect on how accounting might help developing countries in a broader sense. One of the key problems in many of these countries is tackling corruption. Systems of accountability could help to ensure money given to developing countries is used appropriately.

These are hugely contentious issues, but they are issues that fall within the professional jurisdiction of accountants, they are something to do with us. The point

Box 8.10 The World Bank and water privatization in Bolivia

Bolivia's experience with Bank-forced water privatization is a good example of the gap between World Bank theory and how things actually work in the real world.

World Bank officials claim the best intentions when they make the push for water privatization. The Bank has argued that poor governments are often hampered by local corruption and do not have the ability to run public water systems efficiently. Handing water over to foreign corporations opens the door to needed investment and skilled management.

Under pressure from the World Bank, the Bolivian government agreed to privatize its state-owned water industry. In Cochabamba in 2000, the water contract with Bechtel, a private company with headquarters in San Francisco, and the Abengoa Corporation of Spain, resulted in price increases of more than double for poor water users. Those steep price hikes, needed in part to finance the 16 per cent annual profit demanded by the companies, led to citywide protests and eventually to the collapse of the contracts with the two corporations, but only after the Bolivian government declared martial law in an effort to save the companies' contract, leaving one teenage boy dead and more than a hundred people wounded.

Five years later, the citizens of El Alto in Bolivia took to the streets en masse to demand that their water system, privatized in 1997 under World Bank pressure, be returned to public hands. Three days later Bolivia's president cancelled the water concession, led by the French water giant Suez, and an arm of the World Bank itself.

Privatization of the public water system was forced on the people of Bolivia, as it has been in many poor nations around the world, when the World Bank made privatization an explicit condition of aid in the mid 1990s. Poor countries such as Bolivia, which rely heavily on foreign assistance for survival, are rarely in a position to resist such pressures.

here is that international accounting and harmonization is part of a larger project of global development that is underpinned by a specific set of values. The evidence is that this process is not working as well as it could for developing countries. Others would even have us believe that the whole process is quite sinister, and intentionally biased in favour of developed countries. However, whatever story we are convinced by, the point is that accounting plays a massively important role in international development policy. These issues fall within the scope of our professional boundaries and the question again is whether accountants are capable of engaging with them.

ACCOUNTING HARMONIZATION AND TERRORISM

Contentious as these issues are, we need to make one final conceptual link to appreciate fully the ethical importance of the international accounting agenda.

Al-Qa'ida, the CIA, Islamic Jihad, Interpol, Hezbollah, Hamas, the World Bank and the IASB: the IASB isn't an organization you would normally mention in the same sentence as terrorism. However, it is a short step from accountings' relationship to globalization and development policy, and issues of national security.

In order to understand the issues here we are going to look back in time at the historical role that accounting has played, internationally, in the subjugation of indigenous peoples and their cultures. At this stage of the argument, we want to move beyond the purely economic, distributional justice issues of whether an unjust level of resources are being channelled out of some developing countries and into other developed countries under the auspices of global economic development, to cultural issues, and in particular the claim that globalization and harmonization more specifically represent a smokescreen masking the fact that values and tastes are being imported into these countries. The concern is that the importation of the values and rights underpinning Western accounting practice might effectively extinguish other national cultures.

Many writers argue that accounting was involved in different ways in the enslavement of indigenous peoples and indeed continues to play a powerful role in their subjugation. The process of assimilation has taken many forms. In Canada, for example, children were forcefully removed from their parents and sent to boarding school to be re-educated. Neu (2000), however, argues that accounting, broadly defined, was also used in this subjugating process. He comments on two cases in particular. First, he contends that financial incentivization, in the form of payment for scalps, played an important role in the elimination of aboriginal peoples. Neu recounts Lord Cornwallis's proclamation in 1774, 'His Majesty's Council do promise a reward of ten Guineas for every Indian Micmac taken or killed, to be paid upon producing such savage taken or his scalp (as is the custom in America) if killed to the Officer Commanding at Halifax'.

However, second, Neu contends that, commencing around the 1600s, colonial governments developed a policy of giving gifts annually to indigenous people. While initially these gifts consisted of food, clothing and gunpowder, the colonial government adopted a policy of encouraging settler economic dependency on agriculture. He comments: 'The provision of specific presents as opposed to more generic medium of exchange such as money was intended to influence how indigenous peoples used the present'. Neu contends that this policy was part of a process of reproductive genocide, 'that is, a conscious attempt to eliminate a culture through the slow and steady dissimulation of the productive apparatus of that culture'. One of the key developments in this policy was the decision to give aboriginal Canadians 'of appropriate character' land in an attempt to create the idea of private property rights, a key operational characteristic of Western economics and accounting as we have highlighted in previous chapters. Neu (1999) explains, 'the incentive of an individualised, as opposed to a collective, land holding was intended to encourage a different sort of social relationship between indigenous peoples and settler society'.

The story of the indigenous peoples of Canada is not dissimilar to the experiences of the Aboriginal people of Australia. Both cases are also similar in that they are relatively powerless peoples. The final section reflects on the same issue of the perceived cultural threat that the broader harmonization project may represent in relation to Islam.

Box 8.11 Shell in Nigeria

Shell is the second largest oil and gas company in the world. It operates in more than 145 countries. Shell's operations in Nigeria are often held up as an example of how badly companies can affect the communities they operate in.

Shell has been working in the Niger Delta since 1956. In the 1990s tensions arose between the native Ogoni people of the Niger Delta and Shell. There were two concerns of the locals: the very small percentage of the money earned from oil on their land that was getting to the people who live there, and the environmental damages caused by Shell's practices.

In 1993 local people organized a large protest against Shell and the government. Shell withdrew its operations from the Ogoni areas but the Nigerian government raided their villages and arrested the protest leaders, some of whom were later executed.

Shell continues to operate in the region despite widespread local and international opposition to its practices, including calls to boycott Shell petrol stations. According to Shell's own *Sustainability Report*:

> We are committed to helping the country achieve its ambitious goals for increasing energy production, meeting domestic energy demand and diversifying the economy. We need to do this in ways that keep the people who work for us safe and make business sense for our shareholders. We make concerted efforts to use local contractors and suppliers in ways that spread economic wealth without increasing conflict. We are providing logistical support to government security forces in the Delta as they seek to re-establish law and order, as well as providing training to help them avoid human rights violations.
>
> (2007: 24)

The protests continue, however, and have become more violent. There has been an increase in the number of attacks by the volatile Niger Delta militant groups, the Movement for the Emancipation of the Niger Delta (MEND) in particular. These recent attacks on its oil facilities, the taking of expatriate oil workers hostage, and crude oil thefts have resulted in the loss of close to 30,000 barrels of crude oil per day for the company. This is reportedly costing the company more than €2 million in revenue loss per day.

ISLAMIC ACCOUNTING

This concluding section attempts to connect accounting harmonization and religio-cultural issues to the current climate of terrorism and political instability. Of course we are not contending that all terrorism would end if the Taliban or Islamic Jihad were given a seat on the International Accounting Standards Board; we are sure that members of both organizations are completely oblivious to its existence. These are hugely complex issues and the connections between accounting and terrorism are also complex, but the IASB, due to its connection to globalization and the broader neoliberal ideology, is an important factor in understanding these issues.

The question here is the extent to which Islamic ideology, particularly in relation to finance and economics, is or is not compatible with the assumptions underpinning conventional market-based finance (see Gambling and Karim 1991).

The characteristics of an Islamic financial system are based on *Shari'ah* law and can be summarized as follows. First, it is characterized by the absence of interest(riba)-based financial institutions and transactions. Second, surplus funds are supposed to be allocated based on whether the project is worthwhile rather than on financial return per se. Third, it is characterized by a system of undisclosed giving. Loqman (1999) points out that

> There are two types of financing which are necessary in both conventional and Islamic systems. In the contemporary conventional system, equity financing takes place throughout the issuance of shares on which dividends are earned while debt financing takes place by way of loans and borrowings on which interests are given or taken. The Islamic financial system has its own unique norms and regulations as regards both equity and debt financing. In equity financing, the Islamic system is based on profit sharing contracts. . . . In the case of debt financing Islam permits the contract of exchange which involves deferred payments.

These later types of contracts are:

- *Bai Muajjal*: in which an individual can buy goods and pay for them by instalments later;
- *Ijarah*: which allows the individual to pay a lease on the goods required;
- *Murabahah*: where the individual is allowed to purchase raw materials and pay later on sale of the finished goods.

Despite the fact that we have only very briefly outlined some of the differences between the Islamic ideology and that underpinning the IASB's harmonization project, we nevertheless have enough information to be able to envisage some potential problems between the two. First, the IASB bases the development of its standards on the concept of substance over form. In what sense then do accounting standards translate into an Islamic context and how could substance over form be applied to the above three concepts? How could we account for Murabahah, employing a substance over form approach? Who bears the risks involved? Is it, in substance,

Box 8.12 The principle of multifaceted ownership

Islam differs from both capitalism and socialism in the nature of the principle of ownership which it acknowledges. Capitalism believes in the private individual form of ownership. It allows individuals private ownership of different kinds of wealth according to their activities and circumstances. Public ownership is introduced only when required by social or economic necessity, such as the funding of a national army. Under socialism, common ownership is the general principle, which is applied to every kind of wealth.

Islam does not agree with capitalism that private ownership is the overriding principle or with socialism in its view that common ownership should be the overriding principle. Instead, it acknowledges different forms of ownership at the same time – the principle of multifaceted ownership. From an Islamic viewpoint, ownership is accepted in a variety of forms instead of the principle of only one kind of ownership.

Islam is not capitalist, although it allows private ownership of a number of kinds of property and means of production, neither is it socialist. It has adopted public ownership and state ownership for some kinds of wealth and property.

Individual ownership, state ownership, and public ownership are three parallel forms in Islamic law. Real ownership belongs to Allah, and man holds property in trust for which he is accountable to Him in accordance with rules clearly laid down by Islamic Teaching. Absolute ownership by man is a concept alien to Islam, as everything belongs to Allah alone.

the same as an interest-charging arrangement? And does it restrict borrowing to within the Islamic community? Also, at a more general level, apart from the technical complexities of pulling Islamic concepts into IASB standards, how would the accounts be used within an Islamic context? Of course, in our discussion of the practical and conceptual jarring that may exist between the two systems we also need to engage in the critical appraisal of both systems; as we appraised the neoliberal system of market economics critically, so it is equally important for us to appraise the equity of the Islamic system critically. We appraised the neoliberal system by assessing its rhetoric against the reality. How does the rhetoric of financial systems under Shari'ah law compare with the reality of those systems? A growing number of academic studies conclude that there is little substantive difference between Islamic and mainstream banking and that Islamic financing is really about providing a veneer of legitimacy to normal capital investments rather than social justice (see Kuran 2004). It is contended that the main beneficiaries are large Western banks who have exploited a niche market, and their wealthy, Gulf-State clients who can generate a return on their capital with a clear conscience (Henry and Wilson 2005).

Hopefully now we can begin to understand some of the political tensions behind the broader harmonization project. We commented at the beginning of the chapter that the fact that accounting systems differ from one country to another tells us that accounting systems reflect different economic structures and values within different countries. However, the corollary is also true: change the accounting system and you may, in part, change the values of that system. The problem is that accounting harmonization is about imposing a new system of accounting in developing countries and some members of these countries may view this as an attack on their values and part of a broader undermining of their religious beliefs. In one sense it does not really matter whether MNCs are the agents of imperialism or not, or whether globalization really does represent a challenge to indigenous belief systems. Many of the world's poorest believe they are. Many world leaders believe the increasing gap between rich and poor is a potentially destabilizing factor in global politics and international security.

Many aspects of certain indigenous value systems are oppressive and disrespectful of basic human rights, in the same way that many of the outcomes of the neoliberal value system may also be ethically indefensible. A particular value system should not be seen as sacrosanct just because it is the value system of indigenous or oppressed peoples. By the same token, however, no part of the prevailing grand narrative should be exempt from critical reflection just because it invokes the language of democracy or has the appearance of development. The point of the chapter has not been to evaluate any particular culture. The purpose has not been to determine whether globalization is good or bad. Rather it has been to show that international accounting harmonization is, in its present form, a facilitator of globalization. Of course, there is no theoretical reason at least why the international system of accounting could not take a different form. If it did, then it might result in a different kind of globalization. These are big ethical questions, but they are issues that accountants and accounting students rarely discuss, at least as accountants. We don't seem to appreciate just how important accounting really is.

SUMMARY

In this chapter we have introduced some of the broader ethical issues associated with accounting harmonization. We introduced some of the ways in which accounting systems have historically differed and discussed the link between harmonization, globalization and neoliberalism. We thought a little about distributional justice from an international perspective and critically discussed the composition of the International Accounting Standards Board and the way this body operates. We explained the link between accounting harmonization and international development policy and towards the end of the chapter suggested that an apparent failure within the prevailing system to distribute the outcome of the global economic system justly, combined with a belief that globalization represents a cultural threat, may be connected to global terrorism.

QUESTIONS

1 Explain and critically appraise the link between the IASB and globalization.
2 Explain and critically appraise the link between the IASB and the World Bank.
3 Critically discuss the extent to which you think there is a link between accounting harmonization and global terrorism.
4 Discuss whether a private body like the IASB is the best institutional structure for setting international accounting standards.

NOTES

1 For example, the Helms-Burton Act compels the US to impose sanctions against foreign companies that do business in Cuba. See what you can find out about the role of trade barriers in US policy in relation to Nicaragua, Haiti and also the Zapatista uprising in Mexico.
2 One of the main research bodies of Congress, for example, contended that while NAFTA would benefit a relatively small group of investment and finance companies, it would have a detrimental impact on most of the population of North America.

RESOURCES

Film

The Corporation (2004), directors Mark Archbar, Jennifer Abbott and Joel Bakan. This cinema, full-screen documentary looks at the growing prominence of large global businesses, and the way that their decisions are impacting the world. The film shows how corporations have ballooned in size and power since the industrial revolution, and explains the laws and loopholes that allow them to remain nearly unaccountable for their actions. For information see <www.thecorporation.com/index.cfm ?page_id=2>.

iTunes podcasts

'The Politics and Psychology of a New World Order', Jonathan Glover, Kenan Institute for Ethics, Duke University.

'Conversations with History: Globalization and Islam', with Olivier Roy UCTV: UC Berkeley, Conversations with History.

'How Arab Countries Are Coping with Globalization', Knowledge@Wharton Podcasts, University of Pennsylvania.

'Conversations with History: Globalization and the Conservative Movement in the United States', with John Micklethwait, UCTV: UC Berkeley Conversations with History.

'Conversations with History: Reflections on Empire Nationalism and Globalization', with Kenneth D. Kaunda UCTV: UC Berkeley.

'Conversations with History: Business Government and Ethics in an Era of Globalization', with David Vogel UCTV: UC Berkeley.

'Globalization and its Effects', Frederic Mishkin, Governor of the Federal Reserve Board Department of Economics, Duke University.

'Globalization and the US Economy', Judith Goldstein, Stanford.
'Globalization: Is there a Role for Developing Nations?', Supachai Panitchpakdi, Stanford.
'Liberation, Globalization and Neoliberalism', Nathan Sayre Geog, UC Berkeley.

Websites

Accounting

Accounting and Auditing Organization for Islamic Institutions:
<www.aaoifi.com/>.

BBC Radio 4, *In business*, Peter Day, interview with Sir David Tweedie, Chairman of the IASB, at:
<www.bbc.co.uk/radio4/news/inbusiness/inbusiness_20080605.shtml>. (The BBC 'blurb' related to this interview is: 'Sir David Tweedie is the most powerful accountant in the world. Don't yawn: as chairman of the International Accounting Standards Board, he is the man who tries to keep global capitalism honest in the face of bubbles, corporate lies, corruption, and huge changes in what companies do and the way they value their businesses. Peter Day hears from Sir David about his ceaseless quest for clarity in a world of often baffling facts and figures'.)

European Commission, Directorate General XV, Internal Market and Financial Services, Company Law, Accounting and Auditing:
<http://ec.europa.eu/internal_market/index_en.htm>.

French national accounting code (PCG), at:
<www.minefe.gouv.fr/fonds_documentaire/reglementation/avis/avisCNCompta/pcganglais/pcganglais1.htm>.

International Accounting Standards Board (IASB):
<www.iasb.org/Home.htm>.

International Auditing and Assurance Standards Board (IAASB):
<www.ifac.org/IAASB/>.

International Federation of Accountants:
<www.ifac.org/>.

International Forum for Accountancy Development (IFAD):
<www.iasplus.com/resource/ifad.htm>.

GM crops

Department for Environment, Food and Rural Affairs (DEFRA):
<www.defra.gov.uk/environment/gm/crops/index.htm>; the UK government's position on GM crops outlined.

Institute of Science in Society, 'Mass Protests against GM Crops in India', press release, 30/04/08, online:
<www.i-sis.org.uk/gmProtestsIndia.php>.

Nestlé

The two sides of the infant formula argument and Nestlé can be found at:
Baby Milk Action:
<www.babymilkaction.org/>.

Nestlé:
<www.nestle.co.uk/Nutrition/InfantAndChildNutrition/ProductInformation/>.

Nestlé:
<www.nestle.co.uk/Nutrition/InfantAndChildNutrition/Baby/AlternativeFeeding.htm>.

Shell

Responsible energy: The Shell sustainability report 2007:
<www.shell.com/static/responsible_energy/downloads/sustainability_reports/shell_sustainability_report_2007.pdf>; includes an account of Shell's operations in Nigeria.

Shell Accountability Coalition (2007) 'Use your profit to clean up your mess':
<www.foei.org/en/publications/pdfs/mdshellh.pdf>; includes a critical view of Shell's activities in Nigeria.

UNDP

United Nations Human Development Report (2007/2008) *Fighting climate change: Human solidarity in a divided world*:
<http://hdr.undp.org/en/media/hdr_20072008_en_complete.pdf>.

World Bank

Barlow, M. and Clarke, T. (2004) 'Water privatization: The World Bank's latest market fantasy', article at Global Policy Forum:
<www.globalpolicy.org/socecon/bwi-wto/wbank/2004/01waterpriv.htm>.

Independent Evaluation Group:
<www.worldbank.org/ieg/.

The World Bank:
<www.worldbank.org/>.

World Bank Annual Report 2000 available online:
<www.worldbank.org/html/extpb/annrep2000/index.htm>.

READING

Accounting harmonization, culture and impact on capital markets

Bhushan, R. and Lessard, D.R. (1992) 'Coping with international accounting diversity: Fund managers' views on disclosure, reconciliation, and harmonization', *Journal of International Financial Management and Accounting*, (2): 149–164.

Cañibano, L. and Mora, A. (2000) 'Evaluating the statistical signficance of *de facto* harmonisation: A study of European global players', *The European Accounting Review*, 9(3): 349–369.

Choi, F.D.S., Hino, H., Min, S.K., Nam, S.O., Ujiie, J. and Stonehill, A.I. (1983) 'Analysing foreign financial statements: The use and misuse of international ratio analysis', *Journal of International Business Studies*, Spring/Summer: 113–131.

Fogarty, T.J., Hussein, M.E.A. and Ketz, J.E. (1994) 'Political aspects of financial standard setting in the USA', *Accounting, Auditing & Accountability Journal* 7(4): 24–46.

Gray, S. (1988) 'Towards a theory of cultural influence on the development of accounting systems internationally', *Abacus*, 21(1): 1–15.

Hoarau, C. (1995) 'International accounting harmonization: American hegemony or mutual recognition with benchmarks', in L.G. van der Tas, C. Nobes and A. Haller (eds), *European Accounting Review*, 4(2): 217–261. (You may find it helpful to consult two responses by Chris Nobes and Axel Haller to this article in the same issue of *European Accounting Review*.)

Hofstede, G. (1984) 'Cultural dimensions in management and planning', *Asia Pacific Journal of Management*, 1(2): 81–99.

Hopwood, A.G. (1994) 'Some reflections on the harmonisation of accounting within the EU: Problems, perspectives and strategies', *European Accounting Review*, 3(2): 241–253.

Nobes, C.W. (1998) 'Towards a general model of the reasons for international differences in financial reporting', *Abacus*, 34(2): 162–187.

Nobes, C. and Parker, R.B. (2008) *Comparative international accounting* (Harlow: Pearson Education).

O'Connor, N.G., Chow, C.W. and Wu, A. (2004) 'The adoption of Western management accounting controls in China's state-owned enterprises during economic transition', *Accounting, Organizations and Society*, 29(3–4): 349–375.

Puxty, A.G., Willmott, H.C., Cooper, D.J. and Lowe, A.E. (1987) 'Modes of regulation in advanced capitalism: Locating accountancy in four countries', *Accounting, Organizations and Society*, 12(3): 273–291.

Saudagaran, S.M. and Biddle, G.C. (1992) 'Financial disclosure levels and foreign stock exchange listing decisions', *Journal of International Financial Management and Accounting*, 4(2): 106–147.

Accounting and indigenous cultures

Gallhofer, S. and Chew, A. (2000) 'Introduction: Accounting and indigenous peoples', *Accounting, Auditing & Accountability Journal*, 13(3): 256–267.

Gibson, K. (2000) 'Accounting as a tool for Aboriginal dispossession: then and now', *Accounting, Auditing & Accountability Journal*, 13(3): 289–306.

Greer, S. and Paterl, C. (2000) 'The issue of Australian indigenous world-views and accounting', *Accounting, Auditing & Accountability Journal*, 13(3): 307–329.

Ivanitz, M. and McPhail, K. (2003) 'ATSIC: Autonomy or accountability', in I. Holland and J. Fleming (eds), *Government reformed: Values and new political institutions* (Aldershot: Ashgate, 185–202).

Neu, D. (2000) 'Accounting and accountability relations: Colonization, genocide and Canada's first nations', *Accounting, Auditing & Accountability Journal*, 13(3): 268–288.

Accounting and less developed countries

Abu-Nassar, M. and Rutherford, B.A. (1996) 'External users of financial reports in less-developed countries: The case of Jordan', *British Accounting Review*, 28(1): 73–88.

Briston, R.J. (1978) 'The evolution of accounting in developing countries', *International Journal of Accounting Education and Research*, Fall: 105–120.

Hertz, N.I.O.U. (2004) *The debt threat and why we must defuse it* (London: Fourth Estate).

Hove, R.M. (1986) 'Accounting practices in developing countries: Colonialism's legacy of inappropriate technologies', *International Journal of Accounting*, Fall: 81–100.

Le Veness, F.P. and Fleckenstein, M. (2003) 'Globalization and the nations of the south: Plan for development or path to marginalization', *Journal of Business Ethics*, 47: 365–380.

Perera, H. (1989) 'Accounting in developing countries: A case for localised uniformity', *British Accounting Review*, 21(2): 141–157.

Reed, D. (2002) 'Resource extraction industries in developing countries', *Journal of Business Ethics*, 39: 199–226.

Violet, W.J. (1983) 'The development of international accounting standards: An anthropological perspective', *International Journal of Accounting, Education and Research*, 18(2): 1–12.

Wallace, R.S.O. (1990) 'Accounting in developing countries: A review of the literature', *Research in Third World Accounting*, 1: 1–22.

Globalization

Barber, B. (1995) *Jihad vs. McWorld: How globalism and tribalism are reshaping the world* (New York: Ballantine Books).

Chomsky, N. (1999) *Profit over people, neoliberalism and global order* (New York: Seven Stories Press).

Preston, A.M. and Young, J.J. (2000) 'Constructing the global corporation and corporate constructions of the global: A picture essay', *Accounting, Organizations and Society*, 25(4/5), May/July: 427–449.

Ruigrok, W. and van Tulder, R. (1995) *The logic of international restructuring* (London: Routledge).

Singer, P. (2002) *One world, the ethics of globalization* (New Haven, CT: Yale University Press).

Sørensen, A. (2002) 'Value, business and globalisation: Sketching a critical conceptual framework', *Journal of Business Ethics*, 39: 161–167.

Stiglitz, J. (2002) *Globalization and its discontents* (London: Allen Lane/The Penguin Press).

Islam and accounting

Gambling, T. and Karim, R.A. (1991) *Business and accounting ethics in Islam* (London: Mansell Publishing Ltd).

Henry, C. and Wilson, R. (2005) *The politics of Islamic finance* (Edinburgh: Edinburgh University Press).

Kuran, T. (2004) *Islam and mammon: The economic predicaments of Islam* (Princeton: Princeton University Press).

Tinker, T. (2004) 'The enlightenment and its discontents: Antinomies of Christianity, Islam and the calculative sciences', *Accounting, Auditing & Accountability Journal*, 17(3): 442–475.

Wardi, I. (2005) 'Global politics, Islamic finance and Islamist politics before and after 11 September 2001', in C. M. Henry and R. Wilson (eds), *The politics of Islamic finance* (Edinburgh: Edinburgh University Press), 37–62.

Regulation, de-regulation and accountancy

Bailey, D., Harte, G. and Sugden, R. (2000) 'Corporate disclosure and the deregulation of international investment', *Accounting, Auditing & Accountability Journal*, 3(2): 197–218.

Briston, R.J. (1984) 'Accounting standards and host country control of multinationals', *British Accounting Review*, 16(1): 12–26.

Jaruga, A.A. (1990) 'Accounting functions in socialist countries', *British Accounting Review*, 22(1): 51–78.

Puxty, A.G., Willmott, H.C., Cooper, D.J. and Lowe, A.E. (1987) 'Modes of regulation in advanced capitalism: Locating accountancy in four countries', *Accounting, Organizations and Society*, 12(3): 273–291.

The World Bank

Annisette, M. (2004) 'The true nature of the World Bank', *Critical Perspectives on Accounting*, 15(3): 303–323.

Danaher, K. (2004) *10 reasons to abolish the IMF and World Bank* (New York: Seven Stories Press).

Lehman, G. (2005) 'A critical perspective on the harmonisation of accounting in a globalising world', *Critical Perspectives on Accounting*, 16(7): 975–992.

Uddin, S. and Hopper, T. (2003) 'Accounting for privatisation in Bangladesh: Testing World Bank claims', *Critical Perspectives on Accounting*, 14(7): 739–774.

REFERENCES

Annisette, M. (2004) 'The true nature of the World Bank', *Critical Perspectives on Accounting*, 15(3): 303–323.

Chang, L.S., Most, K.S. and Brain, C.W. (1983) 'The utility of annual reports: An international study', *Journal of International Business Studies*, 14(1): 63–84.

Choi, F.D.S., Hino, H., Min, S. K., Nam, S.O., Ujiie, J. and Stonehill, A.I. (1983) 'Analysing foreign financial statements: The use and misuse of international ratio analysis', *Journal of International Business Studies*, Spring/Summer: 113–131.

Choi, F.D.S. and Levich, R.M. (1991) 'Behavioural effects of international accounting diversity', *Accounting Horizons*, 5(2): 1–13.

Chomsky, N. (1999) *Profit over people, neoliberalism and global order* (New York: Seven Stories Press).

Gambling, T. and Karim, R.A. (1991) *Business and accounting ethics in Islam* (London: Mansell Publishing Ltd).

Gray, S.J. (1988) 'Towards a theory of cultural influence on the development of accounting systems internationally', *Abacus*, 24(1): 1–15.

Kuran, T. (2004) *Islam and mammon: The economic predicaments of Islam* (Princeton: Princeton University Press).

Larson, R.K. and Kenny, S.Y. (1995) 'An empirical analysis of international accounting standards, equity markets, and economic growth in developing countries', *Journal of International Financial Management & Accounting*, 6(2): 130–157.

Loqman, M. (1999) 'A brief note on the Islamic financial system', *Managerial Economics*, 25(5): 56–7.

Martin, B. (1995) 'A plan for legalised mugging', *Weekly Mail and Guardian*, South Africa, 12 December.

Narayanaswamy, R. (1996) 'Voluntary US GAAP disclosure in India: The case of Infosys Technologies Limited', *Journal of International Financial Management and Accounting*, 7(2): 137–166.

Neu, D. (2000) 'Accounting and accountability relations: Colonization, genocide and Canada's first nations', *Accounting, Auditing & Accountability Journal*, 13(3): 268–288.

Save the Children (2007) 'A generation on: Baby milk marketing still putting children's lives at risk', <www.savethechildren.org.uk/en/54_2514.htm>.

The Shell Sustainability Report (2007) <http://sustainabilityreport.shell.com/2007/servicepages/welcome.html>.

Sobhan, R. and Ahsan, A. (1984) 'Disinvestment and denationalisation: Profile and performance', Bangladesh Institute of Development Studies Research Report.

Uddin, S. and Hopper, T. (2003) 'Accounting for privatisation in Bangladesh: Testing World Bank claims', *Critical Perspectives on Accounting*, 14(7): 739–774.

9

Ethics, intellectual capital and accounting reporting

Learning objectives

By the end of this chapter you will be able to:

- Introduce the ethical challenges related to the knowledge economy;
- Introduce the broader civic and democratic ideals associated with the knowledge economy;
- Critically appraise the way in which ethics is emerging as a component of intellectual capital reporting within the knowledge economy.

INTRODUCTION

When I was born there was no Internet. My first computer was a Sinclair ZX81, with 16K RAM pack. I'm also not that old! There have been massive developments in telecommunications in the past two decades. So much so that they define the age we live in. I, we, live in the Information Age. It's quite obvious from all the gadgets we carry around with us that information is important to us as individuals. We value both the information with which these devices provide us, and the networks of personal relationships they help to sustain. It should be quite obvious to we accountants that information, or knowledge, and networks are also valuable to corporations. To use accounting speak, knowledge is quite obviously a corporate asset, it's part of the intellectual assets or *intellectual capital* of the firm. However, the extent to which ethical knowledge is, or should be, construed as being an important element in a firm's intellectual capital may be less obvious to us. The problem for many accountants is that ethics is neither construed as intellectual nor capital! Yet many corporations are now bringing ethics into their management and reporting structures.

This chapter explores the emergence of intellectual capital within corporate reporting, and more specifically, introduces an example of one corporation's attempts to measure and report on a category of intellectual capital that we might call *ethical knowledge*. We want to get you thinking about whether ethical capital plays a role in the function of an organization, how this asset could be construed, and the dangers of thinking about ethics as a corporate asset. To put it succinctly, in this chapter we want to explore the link between financial reporting, ethics and your iPod!

INTRODUCTION

Such is the significance of information within our economy that many commentators now talk in terms of 'knowledge capitalism' (Peters 2001). However, it's important to appreciate right at the start of the discussion that knowledge and technology are not only seen as the key to global economic success. They are also presented as the key to reinvigorating democracy. Benjamin Barber (1997: 208), for example, comments,

> Telecommunications technologies are everywhere celebrated: celebrated as the key to the new global economy – this was Bill Gates' theme at the 1997 World Economic Forum in Davos, for example; celebrated as the secret of America's new global economic recovery; . . . and celebrated as the beginning of a 'new era in American Politics' and of a new stage in the evolution of global democracy.

The proliferation of information and communication technologies provides the opportunity for greater surveillance and the erosion of human rights. But they have also allowed anti-hegemonic, grassroots and NGO networks to monitor, mobilize and coordinate resistance (Van Benschoten 2000; Chopak 2001). They have also been used to facilitate more deliberative forms of democracy, like the CIVITAS project, mySociety, and TheyWorkforYou. They allow citizens to organize, engage and monitor as well as be monitored. Barber (1998–1990: 582) concludes that 'despite the potential of the telecommunications market for inequality and of the technology it supports for abuse, the new technologies, in themselves, can also offer powerful assistance to the life of democracy'. The prolific social geographer, Nigel Thrift (2005), concludes that there is in knowledge capitalism, perhaps more than in previous forms, the possibility for empowerment and a strengthening of the 'democratic public sphere'. Try to link this kind of perspective back to our discussion of Jürgen Habermas in Chapter 5. Think about how and whether new technological forms contribute towards the kind of communicative processes that Habermas promotes.

Hopefully you can begin to see where we would like to go with this chapter. We want to think about how some companies are beginning to construe and report ethics as a category of intellectual capital and the implications of this development for the possibility of greater participative democracy. Let's start by making the link between the knowledge economy and accounting.

Within the conventional accounting literature, the link between the knowledge economy and accounting is often associated with the discrepancy between book and market values. It is suggested that traditional accounting concepts and methods fail to capture the intangible nature of key sources of corporate competitive advantage

Box 9.1 Democratic civic initiatives and the Internet

CIVITAS – the Institute for the Study of Civic Society
The stated purpose of CIVITAS is to deepen public understanding of the legal, institutional and moral framework that makes a free and democratic society possible. In particular, the goal of its studies is a better division of responsibilities between government and civil society. Their current focus is on issues such as education, health, crime, social security and immigration. Their online reports on these and other issues are widely distributed via their website, and in 2007 over 600,000 documents were downloaded.

mySociety
mySociety has two stated missions. The first is to be a charitable project for building websites that give people simple, tangible benefits in the civic and community aspects of their lives. The second is to teach the public and voluntary sectors, through demonstration, how to use the Internet most efficiently to improve lives. Unlike CIVITAS, which is a right-wing organization, mySociety is not party political, but tries to build useful digital tools for anyone who wants to use them.

TheyWorkForYou
TheyWorkForYou is one of the websites run by mySociety. It aims to make it easy for people to keep tabs on their elected and unelected representatives in Parliament and other assemblies. It does this by aggregating content from the records of Parliament, along with other publicly available data such as the MPs' Register of Members' Interests, election results and Wikipedia entries. Users can also be alerted via email about speeches made by their MP. The site won the Community and Innovation award in the 2005 New Statesman New Media Awards, with the judges saying that TheyWorkForYou was the nomination that has done most to contribute to civic society in the UK.

FixMyStreet
This is another initiative from mySociety, which helps people report, as well as view or discuss, local problems they've found to their local council by simply locating them on a map. Graffiti, unlit lampposts, abandoned beds, broken glass on a cycle path; anything like that can be easily reported to people's local council to be fixed. After entering a postcode or location, you are presented with a map of that area. You can view problems already reported in that area, or report ones of your own simply by clicking on the map at the location of the problem.

and that this explains the discrepancy between the value of the corporation reflected in the accounts and the value of the corporation as reflected in the market.

Guthrie and colleagues (2003) identify a number of emerging discussions of the impact of the knowledge economy on accounting. These include the relationship between intellectual capital and performance, the practice of reporting intellectual capital, the impact of these new types of corporate assets on management accounting and control systems, identification and classification of intangibles, capital market use of intellectual capital information and the interface between companies and financial analysis on the issue of intellectual capital. As you can see, the discussion has been fairly mainstream to date and has not really engaged with the broader discussion about democracy that we introduced above.

It might be helpful at this point in the discussion to note that this kind of disclosure is quite different from more established forms of corporate social reporting (CSR) responsibility. Pedrini (2007), for example, argues that while there is a 'strong shared interest', there are important conceptual differences between ICR and CSR. He says,

> Intellectual capital reports demonstrate the different kind of attention paid to issues relating to human capital and the orientation of intellectual capital compared to that which is described in the Global Reporting Initiative. The Intellectual Capital Reports consider human capital as an asset of the company and therefore, examine how it can be best developed according to management strategy. Corporate Responsibility collates the consideration of human resources within the

Box 9.2 Knowledge management and the accounting profession

A report from the Chartered Institute of Management Accountants (CIMA) pointed out that 'the move to a knowledge-based economy has had a direct effect on the accountancy profession. Information once represented power and accountants had access to data that few others understood or knew how to get hold of. Advances in technology mean that information is more widely available and accessible, and much of routine processing and analysis can now be left to IT. There are also more people, such as those with MBAs, who are trained to understand and use financial information. The importance of non-financial information has also increased.'

The report goes on to conclude that if accountants are to add value they will have to 'combine the knowledge and understanding of 'traditional' financial information within their control with more sophisticated interpretation techniques. This means ensuring they develop greater commercial awareness, including fostering better links with other departments and appreciating how their role contributes to the strategic direction of their companies. Accountants in business will increasingly have to position themselves not as number crunchers but as strategic advisers who can help companies to understand and evaluate their financial and competitive position'.

> fabric of the company, it responds to the expectations of the workforce and, by demonstrating ethical behaviour and respect for its value and social issues, aims to develop and maintain a social justification for the company.
>
> (Pedrini 2007: 360)

Vuontisjarvi (2006: 335), drawing on the work of Rob Gray (see, for example, Gray *et al.* 1988), suggests that while 'corporate social reporting was born largely to be a response to the widespread societal questioning of the propriety of measuring things solely in terms of their market value', intellectual capital reporting is perhaps more intent on communicating previously undisclosed assets in terms of their market value. Yet, despite these different orientations there does seem to be a connection between ICR and CSR, not least given the broader contextual discussion of the knowledge economy above and in particular the suggestion that it represents substantive opportunities for enhancing deliberative democracy.

Ok, so maybe we can now begin to make the link between accounting and intellectual capital, but where does ethics come in? Well, there is a range of ethical issues associated with the knowledge economy. We will mention these in passing later in the chapter; however, we are more interested in the specific links between intellectual capital and the potential of construing ethical knowledge as a corporate asset. Consider the following observation by the Nobel Prize-winning economist, Amartya Sen (1997: 5). He says,

> There is an interesting asymmetry between the treatments of business principles and moral sentiments in standard economic analysis. Business principles are taken to be very rudimentary (essentially restricted, directly or indirectly, to profit maximisation, but with a very wide reach in economic matters covering effectively all economic transactions). In contrast, moral sentiments are seen to be quite complex (involving different types of ethical systems), but it is assumed that, at least in economic matters, they have very narrow reach (indeed, it is often presumed that sentiments have no real influence on economic behaviour).

Sen (1997: 8) comments that moral sentiments 'exist, they are important, they are productive, and we can ignore them only by impoverishing economic analysis and by demeaning the sophistication and breadth of human conduct'. Sen is telling us that we are both naïve and wrong to assume that business and ethics are somehow two unrelated principles. Hugh Willmott (1998: 81) similarly contends that 'supporting business practice is a raft of moral norms which keeps economic activity afloat'. It does not seem wholly unreasonable to wonder whether at some point companies might just try to construe this raft of moral norms that sustains their business in terms of a corporate asset. One link between intellectual capital reporting and ethics therefore relates to the extent to which ethical knowledge is emerging as a category of intellectual capital as companies become more aware of previously unrecognized sources of corporate advantage.

Hopefully these comments by Amartya Sen help us to make the link between ethics and intellectual capital. As we progress through the remainder of the chapter we want to explore how intellectual capital is being construed and whether ethical

Box 9.3 Corporate social reporting

Corporate social reporting (CSR) is the process whereby companies account for the impact of their activities not just on shareholders, but on the wider community of employees, customers, suppliers, local communities and other stakeholders, including the environment. CSR started to become popular in the 1990s, with a few pioneering companies leading the way. The initial focus of such reports tended to be on the environment, and was often merely a public relations exercise for the businesses involved – lots of glossy photographs of fish-filled lakes, lush forests and pollution-free beaches, without much substance or many facts to back up their claims.

Now, the focus has broadened out to include wider social impacts, and many companies are producing detailed and lengthy reports, some of which are independently audited. As an example, the introduction to the latest Corporate Social Responsibility Report from H.J. Heinz shows the range and type of information companies are providing:

> The H. J. Heinz Company measures success by the value we deliver to our different stakeholders, including shareholders, consumers, customers, employees, and communities. A critical area that encompasses many of these stakeholders is corporate social responsibility.
>
> In this, our second Corporate Social Responsibility Report, we provide a snapshot of our principles, goals and activities in key areas such as health and wellness, nutrition, product quality, safety, labor and social concerns, environmental practices, business ethics, and corporate governance.
>
> This report focuses on the activities of the H. J. Heinz Company and its affiliates (excluding joint ventures) over the last two fiscal years, ending May 2, 2007. We strive to include the most comprehensive data available in our reports and have applied our own high standards in collecting clear and accurate information, while building capacity to extract and compile global information for certain areas of our corporate social responsibility performance.
>
> As such, we did not seek external assurance for this report. We are working to address data collection challenges through enhancing global information reporting capabilities.
>
> (http://heinz.com/CSR_2007/index.html)

Critics of CSR argue that it is a still being used by many companies as a PR tool, with voluntary disclosures being used to disguise bad practice, particularly by large multinationals in developing countries. A recent report by the charity Christian Aid claims that CSR is in some cases counter-productive, worsening relations between business and local communities. Christian Aid highlights Shell, British American Tobacco and Coca-Cola as firms that – it alleges – preach CSR but fail to deliver on the ground.

knowledge should also be construed in such terms. In contrast to the broader discussion of power and global democracy associated with the knowledge economy, the accounting literature seems to have narrowly focused on the inability of traditional accounting concepts and methods to deal with the intangible nature of contemporary capitalism. There is little exploration of the new threats and opportunities it presents for greater corporate accountability and democratic progress. In this chapter, we hope to get you thinking more about these broader questions. The following section introduces some of the concepts of intellectual capital; this is followed by a discussion of the ethical challenges peculiar to the knowledge economy. The penultimate section provides a case study of one company's attempts to incorporate ethics into their intellectual capital statements and the final section tries to get you thinking more broadly about how we could alternatively construe ethical knowledge as an asset.

INTELLECTUAL CAPITAL: CONTEXT, CHARACTERISTICS AND CONCEPTS

This section of the chapter elaborates a little further on the structure of intellectual capital. While you will find the idea of human capital and its contribution towards economic growth and development discussed in the work of Adam Smith ([1776]/1976), the current prominence of the knowledge economy as an idea can be attributed to developments at the Organisation for Economic Co-operation and Development (OECD) and World Bank during the 1980s and 90s.

The composition of intellectual capital

You will find lots of different attempts to identify the key components of intellectual capital within the accounting literature. The OECD (1996), for example, has defined intellectual capital as the economic value of two key elements: structural capital and human capital. However, most taxonomies are a little broader. Some identify three different types of intellectual capital: human, structural and relational, and others present a four-component model consisting of market assets, human-centred assets, intellectual property and infrastructure assets. Some models make the distinction between internal and external elements. Sveiby (1997), for example, contends that intellectual capital includes employee competence, internal structure and external structure. Whereas internal structure covers things like patents, models and computer systems, external structure includes things like the company's relationship with its customers, trademarks and brands.

Other taxonomies begin to unpick what human capital in particular might involve. Seminal work by Jan Mouritsen (see, for example, Mouritsen *et al.* 2001) suggests that human capital incorporates employee knowledge, customer confidence, company infrastructure and information technology. Mouritsen and colleagues (2001) explain that the intellectual capital statements of companies tend to include aspects related to 'employee knowledge and expertise, customer confidence in the company and its

Box 9.4 Intellectual capital in traditional financial accounting

Some intellectual capital is already included in traditional financial statements in the form of intangible assets. The accounting rules for reporting intangible assets have been evolving over the past twenty years or so, and the current rules are laid down in IAS 38 Intangible assets. An intangible asset is defined as 'an identifiable non-monetary asset without physical substance'.

IAS 38 specifies that a company can recognize an asset only if:

- it is identifiable;
- it is controlled;
- it is probable that future benefits specifically attributable to the asset will flow to the enterprise;
- its cost can be reliably measured.

If the item does not meet the above criteria, IAS 38 requires the expenditure on it to be recognized as expense when it is incurred. Much of what is commonly regarded as intellectual capital would not pass the recognition test. The main reason for this is that many intangibles cannot be controlled, one of the central tests for the definition of an asset. Control must be through custody, or legal rights. Portfolios of customers or a team of skilled staff could not be recognized as assets under IAS 38, as there is insufficient control to stop customers deciding to buy elsewhere, or employees moving to alternative employers.

products, company infrastructure, the efficiency of the business process, and the sophistication of information technology'.

Finally, other classifications break human capital down into psychological character traits and values, as well as knowledge (Sveiby 1997; Brennan and Connell 2000; Mouritsen *et al.* 2001). Guthrie and Petty (2000: 166), for example, suggest that employee competence and human capital include things like know-how, education, vocational qualifications, work-related knowledge, work-related competencies, entrepreneurial spirit, innovativeness and changeability.

This is by no means an exhaustive list of taxonomies of intellectual capital. However, they do help identify recurring themes in both the different categories and composition of intellectual capital. Corporate value and advantage are seen to reside in things like organizational structures, technological systems and human capital, in the form of competencies and even particular psychological traits. It is within these broader conceptualizations of sources of corporate value that there would seem to be scope for greater discussion of the kind of important and productive function of ethics within business that Amartya Sen, Hugh Willmott and many others discuss. These expanded taxonomies may hint towards the different kinds of ethics-based human, structural and relational assets that the intellectual capital discourse might bring into being: from individual employees' knowledge of ethical codes, to more tacit ethical competencies, to information technology systems perceived to enhance these skills, and so on.

Knowledge

It should come as no surprise that a lot of the discussion about knowledge capitalism addresses the issue of different types of knowledge and ways of knowing. Pause for a moment and try to reflect on the different types of knowledge involved in buying and playing a new Wii game. For a start we need to know where to buy the game, how to load the game and the rules of the game. We need to know how to operate the control unit (which may by now be so deeply embedded that it is second nature). We may also know specific friends that are experts in that particular game that we can contact for advice, and so we could go on. The point is that it's actually surprising how many different types of knowledge we use everyday without being fully aware of the value of this knowledge to us. The same is true when we are working and more generally within the economic sphere. In their promotion of the knowledge economy, the World Bank (1999) suggests that two different kinds of knowledge are important for developing countries: knowledge about technology, or know-how, and knowledge

Box 9.5 Intellectual capital reporting

We have seen that traditional financial reporting is not capable of adequately recording and reporting intellectual capital, other than in the limited circumstances allowed by IAS 38.

There is currently no common international framework for the identification, measurement and disclosure of information on intellectual capital, but several European research projects have investigated ways of allowing companies to report more broadly on intellectual capital. The best known of these is an EU-funded project 'Measuring Intangibles to Understand and Improve Innovation Management', known as MERITUM. Based on best practice observed in more than eighty European companies, the MERITUM Guidelines suggest that companies should start publishing a supplement to the annual report – an intellectual capital statement.

The Guidelines provide a conceptual framework (which defines and classifies intangibles), and describe the process firms must follow to manage their intangibles and report externally. The intellectual capital statement should be composed of three elements: First, a vision of the firm, comprising a statement of the management team on the corporate strategic goals and their related intangibles; second, a summary of the intangible resources the company has and of the intangible activities carried out to develop, maintain or increase them; and third, a system of indicators to measure resources owned and activities executed.

about attributes (in other words how you know when something is good quality). Michael Peters (2001) makes the distinction between 'know-what' or propositional knowledge, 'know-how' and 'know-who'.[1] The last two types are more tacit in nature. Nahapiet and Ghoshal (1998) similarly distinguish between practical, experience-based, know-how and theoretical, know-what or know-that knowledge. In 1998, the UK Department for Trade and Industry published a white paper entitled, *Our Competitive Future: Building the Knowledge-Driven Economy*, in which they differentiated between codified and tacit knowledge. Whereas codified knowledge can be converted into electronic formats quite easily and is therefore quite portable, tacit knowledge is more difficult to isolate and translate into a form easily accessible to others. Much of the discussion, then, relates to the distinction between tacit and explicit knowledge but the problem with tacit knowledge is that it is characteristically incommunicable and difficult to manage.

Knowledge and the nature of knowledge are therefore key themes in the intellectual capital discourse. Yet the question is whether and how organizations are attempting to recognize, create, organize and sustain any categories of intellectual capital that could be construed as ethical knowledge. If ethical knowledge should be regarded as an important category of intellectual capital, how might we conceptualize this category of *asset*. Is it something that resides within individual employees like moral sentiment (Sen 1995) or emotional intelligence (McPhail 2004) or is it a characteristic of particular kinds of practice or networks (Nahapiet and Ghoshal 1998; Krackhardt and Hanson 2000)? If your employees have the ability to utilize some of the theoretical perspective that we discussed in Part I, for example, if they can put themselves behind Rawl's veil of ignorance, or if they can argue the categorical imperative, is this an organizational asset?

Managing and measuring knowledge

After the different categories of intellectual capital have been identified, the next stage is to get knowledge into a form in which it can be packaged, presented and transported electronically, in other words to make it useable and manageable. Jan Mouritsen and his co-authors (2001) suggest that this process involves taking knowledge that is implicit and making it amenable to codification, storage, transportation and sharing. It involves the conversion of tacit knowledge into an explicit form. Some of the management literature even proposes the use of social network analysis techniques in order to map informal networks of employee relationships (Krackhardt and Hanson 1993). These relationships are often mapped in relation to themes like 'advice networks' and 'trust networks'.

Finally, let's consider how we could go about measuring these new assets. Brennan and Connell (2000) provide some examples of measures that have been used to indicate levels of human capital in particular. These include the number of employees with a university degree as a measure of education; annual training costs or the number of training days per employee as a measure of education cost; and questionnaires on job satisfaction to measure motivation. Based on a review of the literature, they suggest that leadership skills, employee satisfaction, employee

Box 9.6 Ethics as a corporate asset

High ethical standards are recognized as an asset for many companies, and unethical behaviour is a liability. A 'clean' image attracts both customers and investors and there is a direct correlation between ethical conduct and job satisfaction.

Texas Instruments (TI), a US electronics corporation, is one company which places great emphasis on encouraging ethical behaviour among its employees. The company's corporate social responsibility statement includes the following explanation of why:

> It's the right thing to do and has always been a part of TI's culture – to know what's right and do what's right. It also gives us a competitive advantage as our customers know our reputation and trust us to be responsible corporate citizens. Our employees know our reputation and have a loyalty to TI because of that. Our turnover rates remain low in our peer group, which keeps our recruiting costs low. And, in the long run, we believe we avoid huge expenses that other companies may incur when they cut corners and adversely affect consumers or the environment.
>
> (www.ti.com/corp/docs/csr/faq/)

The company promotes ethical behaviour by providing advice and guidance to employees (known as TIers) through articles in the company's in-house magazine. On the subject of mismanagement of time, for example, the advice includes:

> Employees who are treated with dignity and respect, who take pride in their organization and its ethics, tend to respect the assets of that organization. One of the most evident indicators of the employees' opinion of their organization is their conduct at work. Employees who have respect for their organization and co-workers will avoid such practices as
>
> - Padding of labor charges and expense accounts
> - Personal long distance phone calls on company accounts
> - Untidy work areas, break areas and rest rooms
> - Taking office supplies home
> - Excessive breaks or sick days
> - Improper use of copy machines and computer equipment.
>
> There are many forms of theft. In addition to lost supplies and equipment, an employee with little self- or organizational pride can subject that organization to losses in time, production, overhead charges, initiative, professionalism, customer respect, reputation, attitude, spirit and drive. Every TIer can play an important role in creating an environment where people are valued as individuals and treated with respect and dignity, fairness and equality, where people perform with unquestionable ethics and integrity. In such an environment, employee pride blossoms and theft losses disappear.

Box 9.7 Relational networks

You may wish to have a go at modelling some of your own relational networks within your group of friends, including Facebook friends! Try and map out trust relationships. Are there any key individuals in the network (we might call these people nodes) that act as conduits of information or mediation? Think about the way in which that network is sustained.

motivation and the number of years of experience are perceived to be the most useful indicators in relation to human capital. It is therefore possible to think of measures that could be used to record human capital. However, we shouldn't uncritically accept these measures. Roslender and Fincham (2001), for example, point out that conflating human capital into these types of measures is a reflection of both an accounting calculative mentality and a managerialist mindset that reduces sentient human beings to a set of numbers.

We have now gone through some of the concepts and categories that are common within the discussion of intellectual capital. The issue we would like you to consider at this point is how it might be possible to develop measures of ethical capital or individual competence in order to code, store, share and manage something that could be construed as ethical capital? But also think about whether this process of identifying and managing ethics ultimately removes the challenge that the whole idea of ethics represents.

The following sections explore the new kinds of ethical challenges associated with the knowledge economy.

ETHICS AND THE KNOWLEDGE ECONOMY

There are many new ethical challenges associated with the knowledge economy. Some of these issues are quite specific and relate to things like the ethics of information collection and protection, for example the types of information that should be held on databases. However, at a broader level they relate to access to information and transparency, particularly in relation to knowledge about institutions and what they do. Nobel Prize-winning economist Joseph Stiglitz (2002), for example, comments on 'the necessity for increased transparency, improving the information that citizens have about what . . . institutions do, allowing those who are affected by the policies to have a greater say in their formation'.

Another significant part of the discussion seems to focus on the implicit ethics of the knowledge economy that is, the ethical capital required for the knowledge economy to work properly. For example, there are new kinds of risks associated with the knowledge economy and therefore trust is essential. This is particularly the case in relation to knowledge sharing, the issue of property rights and the codification of tacit knowledge. Trust, solidarity and a common set of values are considered to

Box 9.8 Workplace monitoring

Employers in the UK have the right to monitor the activities of their employees in many situations at work. Monitoring in the workplace can include recording on CCTV cameras, opening mail or email, checking phone logs or recording of phone calls, checking logs of websites visited, and drug and alcohol testing.

All of these forms of monitoring are covered by data protection law. They are allowed as long as the employer has taken reasonable steps to let employees know that the monitoring is happening, what is being monitored and why it is necessary.

Critics have argued that these forms of surveillance have an adverse effect on the morale of the workforce. A recent study carried out on behalf of the Economic and Social Research Council found that 'the spread of ICT surveillance has led to a sharp increase in work strain, reflected by feelings of exhaustion, anxiety and work-related worry. There is an overall 7.5 per cent rise in strain among employees whose work is checked by ICT systems compared with those in similar jobs which are controlled by more traditional methods. Evidence of work strain is particularly strong among administrative and white-collar staff in places such as call centres, where it rises by 10 per cent among employees whose work is continually checked by ICT systems' (Economic & Social Research Council 2007, <www.esrcsocietytoday.ac.uk/ESRCInfoCentre/PO/releases/2007/december/workplace.aspx?ComponentId=24944&SourcePageId=17700>).

Many companies are also alleged to have abused their rights to monitor employees. The German discount supermarket chain Lidl has been accused of excessive spying on its employees, including recording how many times they went to the toilet as well as details about their love lives, personal finances and menstrual cycles. Union representatives have alleged that a second large German chain Schlecker has been watching its employees through spyholes. Workers at the discount drugstore have reported that store detectives and security staff peered into stores through spyholes in walls for hours at a time. Although the snooping was allegedly to cut down on theft, many employees thought they were the real targets.

be particularly important for new organizational models associated with the knowledge economy. In this case, ethics is viewed as an important network facilitator. Certain types of ethical values are therefore seen to be important assets within the knowledge economy. The knowledge economy requires certain values and ethics for it to function adequately and this seems to resonate with Amartya Sen's (1997) advice not to denigrate ethics in economic analysis. If anything, ethics has become more functionally important within this new form of capitalism.

There are also ethical challenges and dilemmas arising from the new organizational forms characteristic of the knowledge economy (Chatzkel 2003). These problems

Box 9.9 NHS data and privacy

The National Health Service (NHS) in the UK is introducing web-based personal health records (PHR). According to the government,

> this hails an emerging era in healthcare that promises to revolutionise communication between patients and their clinicians. PHR is an internet-based set of tools that allows people to access and coordinate their lifelong health information and make appropriate parts of it available to those who need it – in essence, a 'communications hub' controlled by the patient. Offering patient-empowering features such as online appointment calendars, patient-provider messaging, and the capability for patients to view and annotate their health records, the PHR has the potential of leveraging information to provide new avenues for measuring health and service outcomes over time. Conceivably, PHRs will also help to forge the important link between the provision of information and improved health. As the PHR gains momentum and the patient role evolves, survey findings corroborate consumer interest in maintaining their own health records.
>
> (www.connectingforhealth.nhs.uk/newsroom/worldview/protti7)

However, this move has not been universally welcomed. Recently, a series of massive data losses from government data systems has exposed a serious lack of even the most basic security to protect personal data. There have been more than a dozen major lapses in major government IT projects in the last two years, including a security lapse which allowed the personal details of junior doctors to be accessed online by the general public. Phone numbers, addresses, previous convictions and sexual orientation were among details available. More recently, two CDs containing the government's entire database of child benefit claimants, including the bank details of over 7 million families, were sent from HM Revenue and Customs to the National Audit Office. They never arrived.

Civil liberty groups as well as some members of the medical profession are united in expressing concerns about the proposed PHR project. Approximately 300,000 people will have access to the NHS database. It's not impossible to foresee a situation where a doctor, administrator or other healthcare professional accidentally leaves a laptop on a train, which includes the health records of the entire nation.

might be described in terms of space, speed and time. In terms of spatial orientation, the fragmentary nature of knowledge networks may result in a lack of control and a corresponding 'disaggregation of ethical and legal responsibility' (Daboub and Calton 2002, 85). However, there are also ethical and organizational issues caused by the speeding up of time (Argandona 2003). As organizations grow quickly, they may not have the time to acquire and develop the appropriate organizational cultural context. Nahapiet and Ghoshal (1998) elaborate that this particular argument relates to relationships that develop over time. These relationships often provide the source of trust that is required for the networks to operate (Stiglitz 1999). Chatzkel (2003) speculates that this may have been a factor in the demise of Enron.

It is within this context that values and ethics are considered to be of increased importance to the continued viability of a company. Consider this quote from Hubert Saint-Onge (cited in Chatzkel 2003: 129):

> We are dealing here with the increased importance of values, the increased importance of the moral fabric, the increased importance of the behavioural element, and the stewardship that needs to be exercised when you move to more intangible assets, because the checks and balances have to be inserted explicitly in the management processes.

Chatzkel (2003) comments that the nature of the organizational changes associated with the shift towards the new knowledge economy requires a significant amount of 'values work' by management, comments which again would seem to affirm Sen's views on the importance of ethics in business practice. Values continue to be important, perhaps more so in knowledge capitalism.

While there is an appreciation of the 'increased importance of the moral fabric' in facilitating knowledge networks and securing economic growth, this type of knowledge has yet to be explored within the discipline of accounting in any detail. Also, while there is some recognition of the 'values work' required by management in this new knowledge era, there is little theoretical engagement with how we might conceptualize this work and little analysis of the kinds of work that is going on within organizational contexts in order to generate, sustain and manage 'values'.

Because there isn't much in the accounting literature at present, the following section explores an early example of intellectual capital reporting.

CASE STUDY: ETHICAL KNOWLEDGE IN CARL BRO'S INTELLECTUAL CAPITAL STATEMENTS

This section provides a case study of an example of the emergence of ethics in the intellectual capital reports of an early innovator in this form of disclosure: the Danish company, Carl Bro.[2] We will look at the historical emergence and evolution of the concept of ethics from Carl Bro's first ICR in 1999. This case study will provide us with the basis for exploring some important questions in relation to the possibilities for thinking about ethics as an intangible asset and element of intellectual capital. We will consider examples from its 1999, 2000, 2003 and 2005 accounts.

Enumerating and managing ethics as a purpose of the firm, 1999

In its 1999 intellectual capital accounts, Carl Bro presents ethics as one of the firm's defining characteristics. It says, 'Customer orientation, added value, multi-disciplinary technology and ethics are fundamental values that ensure intelligent solutions'. 'Ethical correctness' is presented as a key factor of intelligent solutions. It says, 'We strive to supply socially and ethically correct integrated solutions'. The company clearly attempts to convey that it views ethics as a key part of its intellectual capital and indeed, ethical knowledge seems to be linked to an understanding of why the company exists. This is an important point, because it challenges some notions that you will find in many finance textbooks and which you may have been taught in your finance courses: the assumption that corporations exit purely to maximize profit. They don't. Nonaka and Toyama (2005: 420) explain this point well when they say,

> Profits are not necessarily the sole purpose of a firm. If we ask managers why their firms exist, their answer would probably differ from 'to maximise profit'. 'Making a good car' is certainly a way to maximise a profit, but it is also the goal itself – the reason to exist – for Honda. Put simply, firms differ because they want to strive to differ. They evolve differently because they envision different futures which are based on their own dreams and ideals.

If Honda exists to make a good car then, according to its 1999 intellectual capital statement, Carl Bro believes that it exists to produce ethically correct intelligent solutions. Nonaka and Toyama's (2005) explanation of why companies differ is important because, as they say, 'we have to deal with the subjective elements of management such as management vision [and] the firm's value system'. They, like Amartya Sen, challenge the misconception that moral sentiments have no real influence on economic behaviour. Carl Bro's 1999 intellectual capital accounts seem to represent an attempt to sustain a subjective vision of the purpose of the collective action constituting the firm and part of this subjective vision is ethics.

Box 9.10 Carl Bro's seven core values

- 'Our Employees are Carl Bro's Strongest Values'
- 'Focus on Quality'
- 'Professionalism'
- 'Career Opportunity Employer'
- 'Commitment and Dedication'
- 'A Sound Business'
- 'Business Ethics'.

As the narrative of the 1999 intellectual capital accounts unravels, the nomenclature shifts from ethics and ethical correctness to 'Business Ethics'. Business ethics is presented as the last of seven core 'values' (see Box 9.10). The firm comments, 'We believe in defining and following common guidelines for ethical behaviour in all our business activities'. However, exactly what these guidelines are is not clearly articulated. There are a few points that we would like to make here in relation to the constructs discussed in the first section of the chapter. First, ethics seems to be construed as both a structural asset and a human-centred asset. On the one hand value is seen to reside in the guidelines and policies that the company has developed and on the other, it is construed as a tacit employee competency. Secondly, it would seem that this aptitude is, in part, construed in terms of a predisposition to follow a certain set of predetermined guidelines.

As the second section above suggested, a key function of the intellectual capital statement is the bringing of assets into being and rendering them manageable. It is therefore not surprising to note Carl Bro's efforts to render ethical knowledge manageable. For example, Carl Bro's 1999 report includes reference to an 'Employee Satisfaction Survey', in which employees were obliged to comment on their immediate supervisors' abilities in various areas. The company reports that 92 per cent felt that their immediate supervisor would comply with the company's common guidelines for ethical conduct and 91 per cent of the business management would comply with the guidelines, although it is difficult to establish the basis on which such judgements were made. Epistemologically, ethical knowledge is construed not simply in terms of the individual's knowledge of the guidelines, but in some more tacit ability to enact them.

This assessment and enumeration are clearly part of the process of making what started as 'ethics' both a demonstrable competency and a manageable one. The company states, 'The internal survey illustrates that Carl Bro is good at defining and observing common guidelines for ethical behaviour in all its business activities'. The Employee Satisfaction Survey is a managerial technology that works to transform ethical knowledge (in this instance perceptions about another's ability to enact ethical codes) from something that is tacit and internal to the individual to something that is amenable to intervention and management. As Mouritsen and colleagues (2001) comment, management 'are on the look out for a black box they can mobilise and that is constructed to fit their moves in business organisations' and the Employee Satisfaction Survey clearly serves these ends.

So in its first ICR, Carl Bro clearly attempts to present ethical knowledge as a key way of understanding why the firm exists and it also attempts to make it manageable. Let's see how things evolve in their 2000 Intellectual Capital Report.

Community engagement and management policy, 2000

While the 1999 accounts contained some ill-defined reference to 'common guidelines for ethical behaviour', the 2000 accounts elaborate slightly on what these guidelines entail. Under the subheading of 'Ethical Behaviour', Carl Bro comments,

> Supplying ethically correct solutions that take into consideration individual welfare and the surrounding community, including the environment, is an important element in intelligent solutions. This being the case, the Management has prepared a policy on ethical behaviour. For instance, the company has adopted the World Banks Fraud and Corruption Policy, which requires the highest ethical standard in the selection and undertaking of tasks. All employees holding managerial responsibility or employees working worldwide are required to *sign a statement* that they observe these common ethical guidelines.
>
> (Annual Report 2000: 11; emphasis added)

The narrative implies that some skilful (human) ability to reflect on 'the local community', 'individual welfare' and 'the environment' is required for solutions to be 'ethically correct' and in an attempt to engender these types of insights, and perhaps also to convey the intent to manage ethics, we are told, 'management has prepared a policy on ethical behaviour'.

Under the heading of 'The Community' they comment, 'Finally, the Carl Bro Group intends to play an active role in the public debate through the media and it's website on subjects of interest such as, a determination to participate in public debate, social responsibility, ethics and interaction between the corporate and public sectors'. While these comments seem to reflect the broader and more democratic possibilities inherent in the emergence of the knowledge society we mentioned in the introduction, there seems to be a disjuncture between the types of ethical skills, knowledge, education and technology that one would imagine should be required in order to effectively promote such debates and the types of ethical knowledge promoted through the companies codes and internal narrative. What skills do you think Carl Bro's employees would require in order to be able to participate in such debates, and what kind of management policy do you think would be needed in order to build up these skills?

Budgeting for ethics and responsibility, 2003

From 2003, Carl Bro's disclosure on intellectual capital is incorporated into the company's annual accounting reports. Under the heading of 'Values', the reports from 2003[3] till 2005, all contain the following commitment: 'we are responsible in our daily actions and through ethical, environmental and social practice'. In 2003, the company reports a table of 'Values', 'Action areas' and 'Indicators' along with a series of ethical 'Targets'. Have a look at Figure 9.1. You can see that the 'Implementation of uniform Carl Bro Code of Conduct' is presented as an appropriate action in response to the value 'We are responsible'. This in turn is connected to a measurable indicator, 'The business unit's ability to act according to ethical practices', as recorded via the Employee Satisfaction Survey. These indicators suggest that Sweden, the UK and Ireland, and Denmark are 69 per cent, 97 per cent and 95 per cent respectively 'able to act in accordance to ethical practices', and a minimum target of 95 per cent was set for 2005 for all locations. This setting of targets for ethical compliance seems

Value	Action areas	Indicators	Sweden	UK/Ireland	Denmark	Target 2005 (Min.)
We enjoy creating value	1. Creation of closer relations to the clients	Customer loyalty (Would you like to engage Carl Bro Group again?) (CS)	-	97%	97%	97%
		Customer satisfaction (average index) (CS)	-	93	95	95
		Ten largest customers' share of production	54%	59%	26%	SW+UK/IR: Maintain, DK: Increase
	2. Optimisation of project management	The Carl Bro Group's ability to manage the projects (CS)	-	94%	94%	95%
		The Carl Bro Group's ability to provide quality service (CS)	-	94%	95%	95%
		The Carl Bro Group's ability to keep the agreed deadlines (CS)	-	91%	91%	93%
		The Carl Bro Group's ability to keep within the financial framework (CS)	-	91%	91%	93%
	3. Development of managerial competencies (line management)	Average satisfaction with the line manager (Min. 0, Max. 4) (ES)	2.9	3.1	3.1	3,2
We insist on growth	4. Systematic development of professional and personal qualifications	Appraisal interviews (percentage held by deadline) (ES)	75%	57%	77%	85%
		Further training (DKK per employee)	4,700	11,700	14,301	SW: 5,000, UK/IR: 12,500, DK: 19,000
		The line manger's ability to create opportunities for professional and personal development (ES)	68%	71%	80%	85%
	5. Creation of a stronger brand and image	Average number of homepage hits per month	-	22,000	66,000	UK/IR: 25,000, DK: 100,000
		Are you proud of working at Carl Bro Group? (ES)	69%	93%	79%	SW: 85%, DK + UK/IR: 90%
		Berlingske Tidendes Nyhedsmagasin's image survey (total ranking)	-	-	149	DK: Top 100
We create opportunities	6. Promotion of innovation and creativity	R&D investments (DKK per employee)	7,200 [b]	-	4,200	7,500
		The business unit's ability to promote innovation (ES)		78%	56%	80%
We are responsible	7. Implementation of uniform Carl Bro Code of Conduct	The business unit's ability to act according to ethical practices (ES) [a]	69%	69%	95%	95%
		The business unit's ability to be responsible towards the environment (ES) [a]	82%	97%	96%	95%
		The business unit's ability to be socially responsible (ES) [a]	56%	98%	86%	90%
	8. Focus on health and safety	Number of industrial accidents/injuries	-	10	10	Decrease
		Average number of sickdays per employee	7.20	3.96	6.35	Maintain
We are a colourful community	9. Promote knowledge sharing across professions and borders	The business unit's ability to promote knowledge sharing across the organisation (ES) [a]	32%	70%	56%	75%
		Multidisciplinary work (as % of the production)	-	16%	16%	Increase
		Multidisciplinary projects with fees in excess of DKK 50.000	-	29%	45%	Increase
	10. Promotion of a culture based on commitment, cooperation and willingness to change	The line manager's ability to promote commitment and dedication to the work (ES)	65%	91%	78%	SW: 85%, DK + UK/IR: 90%
		The department's ability to cooperate in daily actions (ES)	80%	94%	91%	90%
		The business unit's ability to open to change (ES) [a]	49%	89%	85%	90%

CS = Customer satisfaction, ES = Employee satisfaction
a. In Sweden this question covers "The company's ability to".
b. This figure covers Carl Bro Energikonsult, which is approximately 1/3 of the employees in Carl Bro Sweden.

The employee satisfaction survey should be interpreted in light of the fact that Swedish employees in general are less satisfied than, e.g., the Danish employees (cf. European Employee Index 2003), and that the possible answer categories in Sweden varied slightly from the Danish and British survey. This possible source of error will be adjusted in next year's employee satisfaction survey.

Figure 9.1 Intellectual capital 2003.

to represent a further development in the process of making 'ethics' a manageable component of intellectual capital.

From ethics to risk and compliance, 2005

In the 2005 accounts, the issue of 'Business Ethics' is discussed under the heading of 'Risks', a linguistic change that may reflect the influence of the 2002 Sarbanes-Oxley Act, although there is no explicit reference to the Act in the accounts.

The company states,

> To ensure that the company's employees act in compliance with the business ethics to which Carl Bro Group is committed; the Group took steps in 2005 to specify and highlight the company's guidelines for good business ethics and has for instance incorporated these guidelines into its project management system in Denmark. Moreover the company in Denmark is close to completing the implementation of a Business Integrity Management System (BIMS) in accordance with the intentions of FIDIC's [The International Federation of Consulting Engineers] code of ethics as an integral part of the company's management system.
>
> (Annual report 2006: 10)

Risk, compliance and integrity enter the lexicon as part of Carl Bro's narration of ethical capital. This change in narrative seems to indicate a shift away from earlier softer notions of ethically correct intelligent solutions and an associated commitment to contribute towards public debate, the community, individual welfare and the environment.

Another significant development in the 2005 report is the discussion of the implementation of a Business Integrity Management System (BIMS), which is presented as an important piece of structural capital. This represents quite a significant development in the transformation of 'ethical knowledge' from a rather nebulous concept to a manageable and managerial technology. Ethical knowledge is represented by changing sets of processes and procedures, implemented by managers 'in the name of knowledge' (Mouritsen *et al.* 2001).

These three example reports provide some insights into the efforts of Carl Bro to identify and communicate ethics as a productive category of both human and structural capital, or in other words, to present ethics as an asset of the company.

Let's pause at this point and consider what may be going on in these intellectual capital accounts. You may recollect from our discussion of ethical theory in Part I that some postmodern perspectives try to get us thinking about how notions of ethics are constructed and sustained. How do you think the postmodern perspective might help us understand what is going on in Carl Bro's accounts? Try to reflect on the relationships between the terms used in the ICRs: phrases like 'ethics', 'ethical correctness' and 'integrity', the new sets of processes and actions that these terms represent, and the impact of both the language and the behaviour on Carl Bro employees. There does seem to be an obvious tension between Carl Bro's aspiration to 'play an active role in the public debate through the media and its website on subjects of interest such as a determination to participate in public debate, social responsibility, ethics and interaction between the corporate and public sectors' and the constituent databases of staff numbers, survey results, signatures, module completion dates, and test results[4] that operate in different powerful ways. At one level power operates quite overtly. For example, some companies are now withholding individuals' pay until they have completed online ethics compliance modules. However, at another level, we might be able to see traces of Foucault's notion of disciplinary power that we discussed in Chapter 6, with the technologies of peer and self enumerations that Carl Bro implements in the name of ethical knowledge, for example assessments of the ability to comply with company ethical guidelines.

So while it might be interesting at one level to explore the ways in which corporations may be recognizing how important an asset ethics is, we need to remain critical in our appraisal of whether or not the way in which ethics is construed and managed will ultimately help to promote a more democratic and accountable business sphere. While the narrative in the early reports seemed committed to public debate, community, interaction and participating in ethics, the new technologies, practices and forms of ethical knowledge that subsequently emerge seem to mitigate against these broad civic aspirations and the kind of relationships and trust that this type of interaction and participation may involve. The final section of the chapter picks up on this discussion of the broader civic possibilities within the knowledge economy.

Box 9.11 Ethical conduct and employee performance appraisal

In a recent US survey, only 43 per cent of human resources (HR) professionals said their organizations include ethical conduct as part of employees' performance appraisals. In the study released jointly by the Society for Human Resource Management (SHRM), Virginia and the Ethics Resource Center (ERC), Washington, DC, human resource professionals said they are their organizations' primary resource for ethics-related issues, and they help create ethics policies. But most don't feel that they are truly part of the ethics infrastructure. Instead, they are just asked to 'clean up' the situations caused by ethics violations.

According to the study, only 23 per cent of HR professionals say that their organizations have a comprehensive ethics and compliance programme in place, and 7 per cent report that their employer has no programme at all.

Box 9.12 Ethics and supplier audits

Supplier audits and codes of conduct allow the purchaser of goods or services to make informed judgements about the ethics of the companies from whom they are buying. The idea is that the suppliers should meet the same ethical standards applied within that organization.

KPMG has recently launched a new code of conduct for its suppliers. The accountancy firm is the first in the UK to implement such a code. It has written to its contract suppliers to request they agree to the code of conduct, which covers ethical and environmental principles.

Other areas of employee fairness and environmental impact are also included in the code, which is designed to be part of the firm's 'sustainable procurement programme'. As well as requiring suppliers to adhere to all applicable laws and regulations, the Supplier Code of Conduct also expects KPMG to treat employees fairly and not to discriminate against candidates on the basis of differences, and for suppliers to reduce their environmental impact by developing and using environmentally friendly technologies across their business.

DEMOCRATIC POTENTIAL AT THE MARGINS?

The purpose of the case study has been to provide a concrete example of one company's attempts to begin to think about ethics as an asset, a piece of intellectual capital that needs to be managed and reported on. However, to conclude this chapter we want to go back to the contention that the knowledge economy holds out the prospect of reinvigorating democracy. We saw traces of this aspiration in Carl Bro's early reports. We want to get you thinking about the distinction between ethical capital as a practice that might serve exclusively business ends and the kind of ethical capital that might serve broader civic and democratic purposes.

In this last section we want to discuss some other concepts and technologies that you may routinely use within other spheres of your life and begin to explore potential links to alternative ways in which ethics could be construed as an asset, as a piece of intellectual capital. For example, you may at some time have used Wikipedia to do some research for course projects. Wikipedia is an 'open source' project. You may also use Facebook or Bebo. Both these sites are examples of the increasing awareness of the importance and value of networks. We will start with a brief look at some emerging research on social network analysis.

Ethics Facebook and Network Science

Much of the kind of ethical knowledge being discussed and captured within Carl Bro's statements seemed to construe ethical behaviour as an individual achievement,

Box 9.13 Ethics as a means of improving profits

Behaving ethically is often perceived as what companies should do simply because it is the right thing to do. But does it also pay in terms of profitability?

The Institute of Business Ethics (IBE), London carried out a survey to investigate some indicative measures of ethical commitment and corporate responsibility and then to compare them against financial performance measures over a period of four years. In this way, the research set out to investigate whether it can be shown that a commitment to business ethics does pay.

The sample consisted of between 41 and 86 companies taken from the FTSE 350 for which full and comparable company data was available for the years 1997–2001. It was divided into two cohorts: those who have had codes of ethics/conduct/principles for five years or more and those who explicitly said they did not. Having an accessible ethical code was then used to investigate the relationship between ethical commitment and financial performance over the four-year period.

The general conclusion from the study was that there is strong evidence to indicate larger UK companies with codes of ethics, e.g. those who are explicit about business ethics, outperform in financial and other indicators those companies who say they do not have a code. The authors conclude that having a code of business ethics might, therefore, be said to be one hallmark of a well-managed company.

rather than a network achievement. However, some new thinking in the field of Network Science (see Barabasi 2003) may provide the basis for a shift away from viewing ethics as the outcome of a process of rational dialogue, or ethics as an individual achievement, to ethics as a network achievement. Recasting accounting and business ethics in these terms might be helpful for beginning to explore both the kinds of networks and the type of network characteristics conducive to broader civic goals. Try to think of this point as an expansion of Habermas' notion of communicative rationality that we discussed in Chapter 6.

Appling a networked perspective to ethics may similarly lead us to explore the kinds of networked forms of organization, corporate and otherwise, required for a particular normative ethic to *work*, or which might allow moral sense to function.[5] For example, we discussed Rawls' *veil of ignorance* and *original position* in Chapter 3. However, both these ideas may work only within a particular kind of networked configuration of relationships, a network that provides us with connections into other people's lives. This is just one ill-defined example of the ways in which networked configurations may be seen to be significant, in the same way, for example, that particular social conditions might be seen to follow from Rawls' position. See if you can think of any other links between networks and ethics.

Open source ethics

Similarly, open source methodology[6] may also provide an interesting counterpoint to the forms of governmental technology identified at Carl Bro. Open source software provides new economic and project-based examples of new kinds of economic networks: networks that are self-organizing and collaborative.[7] The open source approach has been proposed as a more general methodology for solving complex problems. Indeed, Schweik and Semenov (2003) postulate that open source might provide a model for addressing complex management and public policy problems. They specifically discuss how this model might be adapted to their International Forestry Resources and Institutions (IFRI) study of forestry management. They comment,

> Imagine applying an 'Open Content' approach to this endeavour. It would involve an 'Open Publication License' . . . which follows generally the same principles as the Open Source Definition described earlier, but applies them to information content (e.g., documents, databases, etc.) rather than computer programs.
>
> (Schweik and Semenov 2003: n.p.)

In a similar manner, it might be possible to at least begin to 'imagine' how an open source approach might be applied to ethical codes, ethical dilemmas within a corporate setting and constructing ethical knowledge databases around particular dilemmas, for example.

Blogs, pods and ethics

A final example of a potentially more democratizing form of knowledge technology might be found in the networking technologies of activist groups and independent

Box 9.14 Sharing ethical knowledge

There is just the beginning of some awareness of the need for linked and cross-company ethical knowledge management systems within the International Federation of Accountants' (IFAC) work on ethics and professionalism. For example, one of the objectives of a recent forum was to 'consider the proposal from the Professional Oversight Board that the Consultative Committee of Accountancy Bodies (CCAB) should facilitate the establishment of arrangements by which selected experience of the accountancy firms in dealing with ethical issues and fraud can be shared with other firms and, as appropriate, with the wider profession for use in CPD'. Again, it is at least possible to envisage how an open source methodology might be applied to this particular proposal.

media developments on the Web. Examples of networked models of ethics can be found in, for example, the type of podcasts[8] and blogs[9] emerging on activist networks and corporations. These types of innovation might be used as prototypes for capturing tacit and other forms of ethical knowledge and developing ethical knowledge networks more generally either within corporations or including corporations.[10]

Of course, all of these new technologies could result in more surveillance, colonization and governmentality (try to link these ideas back to our discussion of Foucault in Chapter 6), but they do mitigate against an overly simplistic and overly oppressive and negative view of the potential of knowledge economy ideas and developments.

SUMMARY

In this chapter we introduced the links between the knowledge economy, ethics and intellectual capital reporting. The first section introduced some of the concepts of intellectual capital; this was followed by a discussion of the ethical challenges peculiar to the knowledge economy. The third section presented a case study of Carl Bro's intellectual capital accounting in 1999, 2000, 2003 and 2005 and the concluding section tried to get you thinking more broadly about how we could alternatively construe ethical knowledge as an asset.

QUESTIONS

1 Critically discuss whether corporations exist just to make a profit.
2 Discuss whether ethics should be construed as a corporate asset.
3 Develop a measure of ethical capital for inclusion in an intellectual capital report.
4 Discuss the extent to which the way that Carl Bro tried to incorporate ethics into its intellectual capital statements may or may not contribute towards more ethical forms of business practice?
5 In what sense might it be possible to capture, measure and manage networked forms of corporate and other organizations?

NOTES

1 Some managerial technologies now employ social network analysis tools to map employees' knowhow (Krackhardt and Hanson 1993).
2 Carl Bro merged with Grontmij in 2006.
3 The report also includes Carl Bro's position in an image survey. We are told that Carl Bro's image for responsibility, among Danish executives, slipped from 16th in 2002 to 48th in 2003.
4 In terms of the number of attempts and time spent on the module.
5 This is relevant for what one might construct as part of intellectual capital, and in particular the structural capital component of intellectual capital.
6 Open source is not only a methodology, it is also a community, a social network (Madey *et al.* 2002). At its core, open source methodology changes the way content is generated.

The content is not so much generated about participants, as is the case in some of the technologies discussed above, but rather it is generated by participants (although the system can collate information about who contributed what and who has looked at which pieces of information!). Of course, there are certain ethical preconditions associated with open content programming and a similar set of ethical guides governing the sharing of information about ethics, ethical dilemmas, ethical conflicts, trust, rights, and so on would need to be developed in order to facilitate this type of approach.

7 This form of programming, where source code is freely available for others to modify, emerged as an attempt to counter the dominance of established software megaliths. The Linux operating system and the Apache Web server are both products of open source programming.

8 A comprehensive definition and examples can be found at <http://en.wikipedia.org/wiki/Pod_cast>.

9 A comprehensive definition and examples can be found at <http://en.wikipedia.org/wiki/Blog>.

10 Blogging is beginning to make its way into the professional context. For example, the Law Society has recently encouraged legal firms to consider using blogs as a way of engaging with the broader public.

RESOURCES

iTunes podcasts

'Panel 1: Knowledge and society', Phil Costanzo, Richard Brodhead, Ruth Grant, Sam Wells, Robert Cook-Deegan, Kenan Institute for Ethics, Duke University.

'High performance organizational communities: Are ethics and performance in conflict?', Fuqua/Coach K Leadership Conference, Fuqua School of Business, Duke University.

Websites

Background information

IASB, summary of IAS 38 *Intangible assets*, can be downloaded from the IASB website: </www.iasb.co.uk/>. Select IFRSs from the left-hand menu, then IFRS summaries, then IAS 38.

Business ethics

Macalister, T. (2004) 'Social responsibility is just a PR tool for businesses, says report', *Guardian*, 21 January, available online at:
<www.guardian.co.uk/business/2004/jan/21/voluntarysector.society>; an article outlining the Christian Aid Report criticizing CSR.

Webley, S. and More, E. (2003) *Does business ethics pay?*, available online at:
<www.ibe.org.uk/DBEPsumm.htm>; Institute of Business Ethics survey.

Case study

Carl Bro:
<www.grontmij-carlbro.com/en/Frontpage.htm>.

Civic initiatives

FixMyStreet:
<www.fixmystreet.com/>.

Institute for the Study of Civil Society (CIVITAS):
<www.civitas.org.uk/>.

mySociety:
<www.mysociety.org/>.

TheyWorkForYou:
<www.theyworkforyou.com/>.

Corporate initiatives

CIMA (2003) *Understanding corporate value: Managing and reporting intellectual capital*, available at:
<www.valuebasedmanagement.net/articles_cima_understanding.pdf>.

H.J. Heinz Company (2007) *Corporate responsibility report*, available at:
<www.heinz.com/CSR_2007/index.html>.

KPMG supplier codes of conduct and audits:
<www.kpmg.co.uk/news/detail.cfm?pr=3105>.

MERITUM Guidelines, available at:
<www.pnbukh.com/site/files/pdf_filer/MERITUM_Guidelines.pdf>.

Texas Instruments (2007) *Corporate citizenship*, report available at:
<www.ti.com/corp/docs/csr/index.shtml>.

Employee monitoring

Citizens Advice Bureau, Advice Guide on 'Employment in England: Monitoring at work', available at:
<www.adviceguide.org.uk/index/life/employment/monitoring_at_work.htm>; with links for other regions.

Economic and Social Research Council, report on employee monitoring, available at:
<www.esrcsocietytoday.ac.uk/ESRCInfoCentre/PO/releases/2007/december/workplace.aspx>. (The whole report is published in a book; see McGovern *et al.* 2007 in 'Books' under 'Reading'.)

For details of the Ethics Resource Centre's survey of ethics and employee performance appraisal, 'The ethics landscape in American business', see <http://ethics.org/about-erc/press-releases.asp?aid=1150>. Information on how to obtain a copy is provided at the bottom of the webpage.

Spiegel Online International, 'Discount chain accused of spying on workers': <www.spiegel.de/international/germany/0,1518,544372,00.html>.

Spiegel Online International, 'Second retail chain accused of spying on staff': <www.spiegel.de/international/business/0,1518,543485,00.html>.

Personal data protection

NHS Connecting for Health, 'Personal health records and sharing personal information', available at: <www.connectingforhealth.nhs.uk/newsroom/worldview/protti7>; the UK government's position on web-based personal health records.

Social network sites

Bebo: <www.bebo.com/>.

Facebook: <www.facebook.com/>.

READING

Articles

Barber, B.R. (1997) 'The new telecommunications technology: Endless frontier of the end of democracy?', *Constellations*, 4(2): 208–228.

Barber, B.R. (1989–1990) 'Three scenarios for the future of technology and strong democracy', *Political Science Quarterly*, 113(4): 573–589.

Edvinsson, L. (2000) 'Some perspectives on intangibles and intellectual capital', *Journal of Intellectual Capital*, 1(1): 12–16.

Guthrie, J., Johanson, U., Bukh, P.N. and Sanchez, P. (2003) 'Intangibles and the transparent enterprise: New strands of knowledge', *Journal of Intellectual Capital*, 4(4): 429–40.

Mouritsen, J., Larsen, H.T. and Bukh, P.N.D. (2001) 'Intellectual capital and the "capable firm": Narrating, visualising and numbering for managing knowledge', *Accounting, Organizations and Society*, 26: 735–762.

Nahapiet, J. and Ghoshal, S. (1998) 'Social capital, intellectual capital and the organizational advantage', *Academy of Management Review*, 23(2): 242–266.

Nonaka, I. (1994) 'A dynamic theory of organisational knowledge creation', *Organization Science*, 5(1): 14–37.

Prusak, L. and Cohen, D. (2001) 'How to invest in social capital', *Harvard Business Review*, 79 (June): 86–93.

Roslender, R. and Fincham, R. (2001) 'Thinking critically about intellectual capital accounting', *Accounting, Auditing & Accountability Journal*, 4: 383–398.

Sen, A. (1997) 'Economics, business principles and moral sentiments', *Business Ethics Quarterly*, 6(3): 5–15.

Books

Barabasi, A. (2003) *Linked: How everything is connected to everything else and what it means for business science and everyday life* (New York: Penguin Group).

Lessig, L. (2002) *The future of ideas: The fate of the commons in a connected world* (New York: Vintage Books).

McGovern, P., Hill, S., Mills C. and White, M. (2007) *Market, class, and employment* (New York: Oxford University Press).

Stiglitz, J. (2002) *Globalization and its discontents* (London: Allen Lane).

Sveiby, K.E. (1997) *The new organisational wealth: Managing and measuring knowledge based assets* (San Francisco: Berrett Koehler).

Thrift, N. (2005) *Knowing capitalism* (London: Sage).

REFERENCES

Argandona, A. (2003) 'The new economy: Ethical issues', *Journal of Business Ethics*, 44: 3–22.

Barabasi, A. (2003) *Linked: How everything is connected to everything else and what it means for business science and everyday life* (New York: Penguin Group).

Barber, B.R. (1997) 'The new telecommunications technology: Endless frontier of the end of democracy?', *Constellations*, 4(2): 208–228.

Barber, B.R. (1989–1990) 'Three scenarios for the future of technology and strong democracy', *Political Science Quarterly*, 113(4): 573–589.

Brennan, N. and Connell, B. (2000) 'Intellectual capital: Current issues and policy implications', *Journal of Intellectual Capital*, 1(3): 206–240.

Chatzkel, J. (2003) 'The collapse of Enron and the role of intellectual capital', *Journal of Intellectual Capital*, 4(2): 127–143.

Chopak, J. (2001) 'Citizen participation and democracy: Examples in science and technology', *National Civic Review*, 90(4): 375–383.

Daboub, A.J. and Calton, J.M. (2002) 'Stakeholder learning dialogues: How to preserve ethical responsibility in networks', *Journal of Business Ethics*, 41: 85–98.

Gray, R.H., Owen, D. and Maunders, K. (1987) *Corporate social reporting, accounting and accountability* (London: Prentice Hall).

Guthrie, J., Johanson, U., Bukh, P.N. and Sanchez, P. (2003) 'Intangibles and the transparent enterprise: New strands of knowledge', *Journal of Intellectual Capital*, 4(4): 429–440.

Guthrie, J. and Petty, R. (2000) 'Intellectual capital: Australian annual reporting practices', *Journal of Intellectual Capital*, 1(3): 241–251.

Krackhardt, D. and Hanson, R.R. (1993) 'Informal networks: The company behind the chart', *Harvard Business Review* (July–August): 104–111.

McPhail, K.J. (2004) 'An emotional response to the state of accounting education: Developing accounting students' emotional intelligence', *Critical Perspectives on Accounting*, 15(4–5): 629–648.

Madey, G., Freeh, V. and Tynan, R. (2002) 'The open source software development phenomenon: An analysis based on social network theory'. Paper presented at the Eighth Americas Conference on Information Systems.

Mouritsen, J., Larsen, H.T. and Bukh, P.N.D. (2001) 'Intellectual capital and the "capable firm": Narrating, visualising and numbering for managing knowledge', *Accounting, Organizations and Society*, 26: 735–762.

Nahapiet, J. and Ghoshal, S. (1998) 'Social capital, intellectual capital and the organizational advantage', *Academy of Management Review*, 23(2): 242–266.

Nonaka, I. and Toyama, R. (2005) 'The theory of the knowledge creating firm: Subjectivity, objectivity and synthesis', *Industrial and Corporate Change*, 14(3): 419–436.

OECD (1996) *The knowledge-based economy* (Paris: The Organisation for Economic Co-operation and Development).

Pedrini, M. (2007) 'Human capital convergences in intellectual capital reporting and sustainability reports', *Journal of Intellectual Capital*, 8(2): 346–366.

Peters, M.A. (2001) *Poststructuralism, marxism and neoliberalism: Between theory and politics* (Oxford: Rowman & Littlefield).

Roslender, R. and Fincham, R. (2001) 'Thinking critically about intellectual capital accounting', *Accounting, Auditing & Accountability Journal*, 4: 383–398.

Schweik, C.M. and Semenov, A. (2003) 'The institutional design of open source programming: Implications for addressing complex public policy and management problems', *First Monday*, 8(1), available online at: <http://firstmonday.org/issues/issue8_1/schweik/index.html>.

Sen, A. (1997) 'Economics, business principles and moral sentiments', *Business Ethics Quarterly*, 6(3): 5–15.

Smith, A. ([1776]/1976) *The theory of moral sentiments* (Oxford: Oxford University Press).

Stiglitz, J. (2002) *Globalization and its discontents* (London: Allen Lane).

Stiglitz, J. (1999) 'Public policy for a knowledge economy', lecture at the Department for Trade and Industry and Centre for Economic Policy Research, London, 27 January, available online at: <www.worldbank.org/html/extdr/extme/jssp012799a.htm>.

Sveiby, K.E. (1997) *The new organisational wealth: Managing and measuring knowledge based assets* (San Francisco: Berrett Koehler).

Thrift, N. (2005) *Knowing capitalism* (London: Sage).

Van Benschoten, E. (2000) 'Technology, democracy, and the creation of community', *The National Civic Review*, 89(3): 185–192.

Vuontisjarvi, T. (2006) 'Corporate social reporting in the European context and human resource disclosures: An analysis of Finnish companies', *Journal of Business Ethics*, 69: 331–354.

Willmott, H. (1998) 'Towards a new ethics? The contributions of poststructuralism and posthumanism', in M. Parker (ed.), *Ethics and organization* (London: Sage), 76–121.

World Bank (1999) *World development report, 1998/99, knowledge for development* (Washington, DC: International Bank for Reconstruction and Development).

Index